T0062225

How Language Creates and Sustains Religion

How differences between language-mediated
thought processing and evolved preconscious
thought processing gives rise to religion

Published by Conatus Publishing
Royal Oak Michigan USA
Cover Photo: Magritte's window
By David Johnson
Reprinted by Permission

Order this book online at www.trafford.com
or email orders@trafford.com

Most Trafford titles are also available at major online book retailers.

Printed in the United States of America.

ISBN: 978-1-4269-2470-5 (sc)

ISBN: 978-1-4269-2471-2 (hc)

Library of Congress Control Number: 2010910224

*Our mission is to efficiently provide the world's finest, most comprehensive book publishing
service, enabling every author to experience success. To find out how to publish your book,
your way, and have it available worldwide, visit us online at www.trafford.com*

Trafford rev. 9/16/2010

 www.trafford.com

North America & international
toll-free: 1 888 232 4444 (USA & Canada)
phone: 250 383 6864 ♦ fax: 812 355 4082

TABLE OF CONTENTS

Chapter One

A Quest For The Source Of Religion

The Universality of Religion

In his book *The Descent of Man*, Charles Darwin wrote, "A belief in all-pervading spiritual agencies seems to be pervasive." Artifacts such as cave drawings and grave goods attest to the presence and the importance of some form of religion among Neanderthals and Cro-Magnon *Homo sapiens* as early as forty thousand years ago. Such artifacts indicate that religion has been a major force in human groups since well before the end of the Stone Age. Some scholars give major credit to religion for the rapid ascent of the human species to its dominance over all of the creatures on Earth today. Whether this is so or not, unquestionably religion has been an important personal and cultural/societal phenomenon among all human groups in every age and in every location since long before recorded human history.

Unfortunately, there can only be speculation about the origin of religious rituals and beliefs in the Paleolithic era, a time long before the invention of writing. From its very beginnings the importance of religion within society has waxed and waned but it has never completely vanished.

The practical value of the time and effort that individuals spend observing religious ritual has often been questioned. Still, some form of religious ritual is widely practiced in all societies, from the most primitive tribes in remote regions of Africa, and South America to the most sophisticated of North American, European, and Asian societies.

Over the years various societies have seen resurgences of fervent fundamentalist religion after quiescent periods. The United States was founded in the seventeenth century by a number of groups that lived in devoutly religious colonies. By the middle of the eighteenth century, about the time of the American Revolution, deism and the moderation of religious fundamentalism held sway among the American elite, including many of the framers of the Declaration of Independence. Unitarianism became popular in this era. By the middle of the nineteenth century, the trend returned to a more orthodox form of religious belief and practice. This more intense religiosity prevailed until the middle of the twentieth century, when secularism became popular. In the second half of the twentieth century, there was, once again, a revival of fundamentalist religion. Religious fundamentalism has become a major social and political force in the United States today.

Vestiges of beliefs that were central to ancient religions, such as astrology, shamanism, pantheism, animism, and paganism, remain popular and potent to this day. Aspects of these ancient religions survive as incidental features of mainstream religions of today. Customs such as decorating Christmas trees; praying to saints; lighting candles; faith healing; celebrations around the times of the winter solstice or the vernal equinox; tea leaf reading; attaching predictive symbolism to various events; and many superstitions, can be traced back to much earlier religions or religious practices.

Many who disdain established religions or claim to be atheists can still be highly spiritual and superstitious with regard to their behavior. Some of those who eschew traditional religions, with their pompous ceremonies, demands for normative behavior, and anachronistic beliefs, nonetheless subscribe to new-age religious notions that embrace the energy output of vortices the mystical power of pyramids. Wicca and homeopathy are both being practiced among a minority of people. Some people reject traditional religions but yet subscribe to occultism, alternative medicine, or cosmic humanism.

What is the explanation for religion? What is its source? Are specific beliefs or the varieties of modes of worship and rites determined and demanded by God? Did religion simply begin and continue because it is, in many ways, a useful aspect of human culture? Or has some evolutionary development resulted in a predisposition for human religion? How did religion arise in the first place, and what accounts for its extraordinary staying power? Such are the questions that this book will explore and seek to answer.

The Mystery of Religion

Well-argued criticism by skeptics such as Christopher Hitchens, Sam Harris and Richard Dawkins, has drawn the public's attention to contradictions, anomalies and clear evidence of self-serving human intent in the origination and redaction of scripture. This has sparked doubt as to whether there is any divine input whatsoever in scripture. Such criticisms are borne out by carefully documented textual analyses of the revered scriptures themselves.[1] In addition, there is considerable unassailable evidence of evolutionary and genetic processes as well as discoveries in archaeology and paleontology that cannot be reconciled with scripture or religious dogma. Critics point to cruel practices that have been carried out in the name of every religion at various times in the past. Such criticism, however, has had little impact on believers. The practices and beliefs of religions continue to thrive in all parts of the globe and in all sectors of society.

Evolutionary psychologists and biologists generally hold that a behavioral trait that is enduring and nearly universal among all members of a species is innate in the sense of it being a direct or an indirect consequence of some evolved genotype. Flinching in response to a sudden unexpected movement, an aversion to snakes, a tendency to panic in the presence of a predator—these are not learned behaviors. Some theorists hypothesize that religion could be latent behavior that in some indirect way has been genetically coded to spontaneously develop when circumstances warrant.

A problem with this thesis is that religion and religious behavior are vague and ill-defined terms. Religion can encompass belief in god or gods that are either anthropomorphic or ineffable, reincarnation, astrological influences, a variety of superstitions, the powers of pyramids and vortices, and many more. Religious devotion is described by a wide range of behaviors that vary from group to group, and even within a group, as well as from situation to situation and over time. What is the religious equivalency among one who believes and acts as a result of tarot card or tea leaf readings, a practitioner of Wicca, and a committed Baptist church elder who, as an insurance salesman, profits indirectly from his religiosity? Any scientific inquiry with regard to religion's innateness is problematic because of the lack of operationally defined terms.

Religion remains not only by its very nature but also by the intent and design of its sages, leaders, and practitioners to be both mysterious and amorphous. Neither natural science nor social science has been able to satisfactorily explain the entire gamut of religion as a phenomenon.[2] Numerous theories and definitions of religion can be found, but none of them is accepted as universally authoritative. Tomes have been written on theories of religion. Some of them offer conflicting notions, and many of them co-opt the field of religion as a subset of some other discipline, such as psychology, anthropology, or sociology.

Functional and Pragmatic Theories

For Karl Marx, religion was a means for the elites to suppress and control the common people. Peter Berger in his book, ' *The Sacred Canopy*' has conceived of religion as a natural part of every person's worldview, which he calls their "nomos."[3] Everyone, according to Berger, projects their own subjective notions onto the external world. They consider their subjective projection to be objective reality. Through a process of mental recursion, they reify and internalize this subjective reality. Rodney Stark has proposed a quasi-economic exchange theory in which individuals benefit socially, economically, and psychologically in return for the costs of adhering to religious strictures (this includes nonmonetary costs, such as time, effort, and commitment). For Sigmund Freud religion was simply an inability to cope with the vicissitudes of life, particularly those arising from problems and difficulties in dealing with family members and the opposite sex.

For the most part, such psychological and sociological theories are functional theories that explain religion based on its uses in serving the needs, or of ameliorating the frailties and failings, of individuals. Religion is a potent means of stabilizing social order and maintaining cohesion in large groups.

A conceptual problem with these functional explanations of religion is that they deal with the uses of religion as its origin or source. Admittedly, in circular fashion, uses can indeed become sources as people seek advantage or comfort through the use and promotion of religion. But does this imply that some of religion's uses are a predicate to its sources? There is no particular use that I can discern that is the sine qua non of religion. By its nature, it is conceivable that religion could exist and be devoutly practiced without any overt psychological, sociological, or pragmatic benefit at all. In fact, almost all religions promote the notion that religion is to be practiced for its own sake alone.

The problem is that the circular explanation of the "use as source" approach tends to cloud the search for a pure basis for religion. Unquestionably religion, as Karl Marx opined, can be used to control a population and render the masses docile while they are being exploited by those in power. However, this presupposes the invention of religion, out of whole cloth, for the explicit purpose of controlling a population. But if religion was created to serve one of the functional uses as claimed, how can this be reconciled with other functional uses, such as the Freudian explanation of religion as a coping mechanism with respect to neurosis or mental illness?

A comparison of other functional uses, as well as a cursory review of the history of religion, does not account for religion's origins in the distant past, its continued existence, and its cultural power. It does not support the notion that any of the function explanations are the seminal explanation of the origins of religion.

Theories Based on Innateness

As early as 1902, William James proclaimed, in his book *The Varieties of Religious Experience*, that "all of our raptures ... our questions and beliefs... are equally organically founded." Following James, some of the more recent theories of religion are based on evolution and neuroscience.

Three streams of such theories can be delineated. Theorists such as Matthew Alper and D. S. Wilson suggest that, in a clear-cut manner of evolutionary adaptation, individuals belonging to religious groups tended to survive and procreate while nonreligious groups dwindled and died off. This concept is based on what has been termed "kin selection," where there is a tendency for an individual to sacrifice himself for his kin in order to benefit a group of his relatives. It also relies on the concept of genetic drift, where traits that are useful but not critical for individual survival are gradually inherited by the majority of a population after many generations. Thus, over eons, the human brain adapted to support kin selection, which, after language developed, was embedded in culture and expressed more formally by means of religion.

Those individuals who did not inherit this kin selection/religious, genetically-based proclivity tended to be loners, rebels, and social misfits. They left, were driven from the safety of the clan, or could not find mates. Most of them had few offspring or perished before they had a chance to breed. Over many generations, due to genetic drift, a majority of humans came to possess an innate God or worship function somehow embedded as part of their genetic makeup. As Matthew Alper characterizes it in his book, it is the God part of the brain.

Inference Theories

Anthropologist Pascal Boyer, in his book *Religion Explained,* introduced an "inference theory," suggesting that religion is an indirect consequence of brain architecture that developed to serve other survival purposes. He suggests that the brain has become hardwired by nature to infer patterns or general characteristics that it assigns to important classes of creatures and objects. Thus one need not have had direct experience with tigers or snakes to be afraid of them. Our brains are hardwired to fear creatures with similar, potentially dangerous characteristics. By this process we also infer that unseen agents are directing the forces of nature that act upon us. Such inference has enabled humans to make sense of nature, and to ascribe meaning to events.

A similar theory, informally labeled a "gaps theory," posits that survival in the long-ago past depended on forming provisional patterns of association in order to attempt to make sense of baffling aspects of the environment. Humans have evolved to being innate pattern-sensing and pattern-making creatures. We instinctively try to make sense of our environment and to create meaning. With respect to significant or important matters where no natural patterns emerge or none are discernable, people tend to concoct trial patterns, often adding reasonable speculation. Proximal events and objects that are deemed to be salient are used in creating patterns in the hope that later events will corroborate and justify them. With regard to the ultimate mysteries of life, such as the nature of death, people create stories to explain them so as to reduce the anxiety that is produced by uncertainty.

Tentative pattern formation and the concoction of explanatory stories are attempts to satisfy the need for explaining unknown forces in nature that affect our fate.

Balancing Selection and Genetic Drift

A related category of explanation is based on a theory in the field of behavioral genetics called "balancing selection." Behavioral geneticists assert that there are genetic components that probabilistically affect individual traits and behaviors, and in turn affect the rate of survival. Such variation is a necessary condition for evolution. The effects may be large or small, depending on the nature of the genes involved, experiences encountered, and many other intervening factors, but they exist. Many traits are useful for the survival of individuals but are not critical for the survival of the entire species or in all locations. Genes supporting such traits drift slowly throughout the entire population of a species over many generations. They survive in the population because they are not harmful in that they do not reduce the chances of procreation and under some conditions may improve them.

For example, if the majority of a population is passive and risk averse, the more aggressive risk-taking individuals among them may thrive under certain conditions. The aggressive individuals will succeed in acquiring more food, selecting better mates for breeding, having more offspring, and protecting more of their offspring to maturity. In doing so, they pass their genes on to a large number of progeny, and gradually, over generations, more and more of the population inherits the genes that support aggressiveness and risk taking.

However, as a result of this genetic drift, when many or most of a population has become overly aggressive risk takers, they will viciously fight among themselves. Out of desperation they will push risky behavior to the limit, often with disastrous results. Consequently their rate of survival and procreation will fall, and their specific genes will gradually fade in the population as a result of genetic drift.

As this transpires, the nonaggressive, or risk-averse, individuals will have greater success in surviving and passing their genes to progeny. According to the theory, there are many genetically supported behavior traits that are continually waxing and waning within a population. These traits tend to move toward a dynamic homeostasis, which is disrupted when there is a permanent change in the environment. Such a change can either favor or impede a genetically supported behavioral trait. According to the theory of balancing selection, genes that foster a tendency to religion are selectively balanced in human populations.[4]

Religion and Brain Research

Recently, neuroscientists Joseph Giovannoli and Andrew Newberg have offered theories based on empirical studies of the operation of the brain itself. Newberg, a radiologist, has used fMRI equipment to observe Buddhists in the act of meditating, Franciscan nuns praying, and Pentecostals speaking in tongues. In this "from the bottom up" approach, the specific brain activity generated by such religious activities was found to correspond with subjective religious experiences as described by the subjects.

Once again, I must try to finesse a thorny issue. Details of the relationships between the psychology of the mind and the neurobiological processes of the brain remain largely unknown. Obviously, a theory such as that presented in this book, which ascribes the conception and perpetuation of religion to effects that stem from discrepancies between mental and neurological processes, would benefit greatly from a comprehensive understanding of how the mind-brain connection works. Unfortunately this knowledge is beyond the state of neuroscience or psychology at this time. There is no doubt however that a disjunction in thinking does exist, and it has significant effects, as shall be illustrated in later chapters. I am content, and I hope the reader will be as well, after reading this book, that the existence of effects of this disjunction, when coupled with the effects of language, can give rise to certain beliefs and behaviors that are unique to language-enabled humans.

Religion Derived from Neurological Adaptation

A more general top-down approach to religion has been proposed by philosopher Daniel C. Dennett. Dennett is a foremost exponent of what has been dubbed "neural Darwinism." Neural Darwinism explains religion as a natural phenomenon that is generated by the evolved human brain. It adds a neural twist to the gaps theory. Religion in this view is a normal outcome of the neural processing of sensory information acting on the human brain. It is a consequence of brain function adaptations that are designed to increase the probability of survival.

Learning, which is required for survival, is facilitated by the dopamine system in the human brain. When a beneficial event occurs, certain neurons in the brain release the neurotransmitter dopamine. This has the effect of creating an emotion or feeling of pleasure. As discovered by Wolfram Schultz in the early 1970s, dopamine is released in the brain as soon as there is a glimmer of recognition that prevailing conditions may be similar to those that have, in the past, led to a reward. That is, dopamine production anticipates the overt conditions or even the subtle cues that precede or lead to reward. For example, if a light is always turned on shortly before a monkey is given a treat, the production of dopamine in the monkey's brain will begin when the light is turned on. A dopamine rush may start even before the light if there is some indication that the light will soon be turned on and the treat forthcoming. In this way a creature learns about beneficial or harmful patterns in nature that are required for maximizing chances of survival. This dopamine effect induces the creature to act as a result of certain indirect or "second order" signals so as to induce actions that might obtain a similar reward as before.

If the experimenter withholds the treat several times after the light is turned on, an error-related negativity signal is generated, and the dopamine will not be produced when the light is turned on. So powerful can the dopamine reward system be that creatures, including humans, will lose interest in sex, starve themselves, or commit all sorts of crimes in order to obtain a dopamine rush. This neural mechanism is involved in compulsions and addictions.

For humans many serendipitous beneficial events or rewarding experiences occur randomly in nature. The deemed salient predictive factors that precede or accompany such beneficial events later trigger dopamine rushes in the brain whenever they are perceived. A surprising or unanticipated reward triggers a dopamine rush that is two to three times as great as an anticipated reward, and, consequently, the deemed proximal or predictive causes also create major dopamine rushes when they are later perceived. Where there is no obvious cause for such brain events, they may be attributed to an unseen power, such as God. Rituals, which are held to precede God's beneficence, also trigger dopamine production and release in anticipation of God's rewards. Rituals become pleasurable activities in their own right whether or not they succeed as requests for God's beneficence.

Since individuals have control over their rituals, they tend to be repeated in an autostimulative manner in order to make the person feel good. The more the rituals are repeated, the stronger neural connections become. It is by means of a form of functional displacement that the more a ritual is practiced, the greater and more consistent the dopamine rush it generates in anticipation of God's rewards, even though the occurrence of those presumed rewards may objectively be random in their occurrence. Rewards may be subjectively interpreted or vague in their practical benefits when they do occur. In my estimation this neural theory of religion provides the best explanation for why some people are much more devout than others and why there are often resurgences of ardent religiosity after periods of relative dormancy. There will be more on this topic after the topic of language has been introduced.

The Pious Theory

Perhaps the most common theory of religion, although it is not usually couched in terms of theory, is what I have dubbed "the pious theory." It is an explanation, based on theology, inferred by people who are passionately committed to various conventional religions, especially the revealed religions of Christianity, Islam, and Judaism. Other, nonrevealed religions also universally recognize supernatural forces. Religious belief and behavior are based on faith in God or some sort of supernatural power. According to Lewis Wolpert, "religion is almost always regarded by its believers as a way of obtaining help from supernatural powers."[5] Paul Tillich has said that "faith is belief in the unbelievable." Religion is a form of self-protective reason that is beyond ordinary standards of rationality.

The pious theory of religion asserts that God (i.e., a supernatural force or entity) commands the universe and demands particular behaviors and certain beliefs of all humans, but particularly those belonging to certain groups of people. He will reward compliance to these requisites in some way. The nature of such beliefs and behaviors has been specially revealed or communicated to certain men and a few women in one or more ways. Communication can come directly, as the voice of God, through the appearance of angels to pious men and women, through the inspiration of sages, through inspired interpretations of holy scripture by sages, by means of reason in interpreting nature, through various unexplainable experiences, or by an interpretation of the occurrence and the sequence of historical and natural events. All of these are taken to be clear evidence and signs of God's existence, influence, and desires.

Once it is conceded that there is an omnipotent force and omniscient intelligence that created the world, and that governs events in the unfolding of the universe—be it called God or some synonym, such as Allah, Elohim, Yahweh, or Vishnu—then it is reasonable that God's omnipotent management of the unfolding of the universe must affect all creatures, although differentially, according to His omniscient and omnipotent whim and will.

The evidence for the existence of God has been explored and debated over the centuries. Thomas Aquinas, borrowing from Aristotle, proposed five "proofs," which are, in brief, as follows: cosmological, that the complex universe exists and therefore some power must have created it; moral, that we instinctively know right from wrong, sacred from profane; experiential, that millions of people over the centuries and even today have authentic mystical or religious experiences that cannot be explained in any other way; teleological, that there must be a purpose to life; and ontological or the intuitive argument proposed by Avicenna and Anselm. They reasoned that if we can conceive of God, He must exist. Thus, the postulated creator must have created man to worship Him or why else would we exist?

The pious theory holds that public and private human conduct and even personal beliefs do make a difference to God. God is basically beneficent but can turn nasty when defied. We owe our very lives to God. Each of us has a nonphysical essence, or soul, that is present at conception and remains intact after death. If we humans do not conform or obey heavenly edicts, it will go very hard for us and for our families, our nations, and our eternal souls. For Hindus and Buddhists, bad karma results in being reincarnated as some vile creature that seems to us to endure a miserable life. We must please God and do what God commands. The spirit and the faithfulness with which we please God will affect our fate. Not only does our own and our kin's welfare hang in the balance but also that of all humanity and the world.

The Role of God in the Present Study

It is not my intention in this book to attempt to either establish the existence and the influence of God or to reject the concept of God. Similarly, religion, its believers, and its practices are not regarded as foolish or necessarily malevolent. The major thrust of this analysis is to delve into the primary source of religion as a natural phenomenon. The thesis rejects the notion that an analysis of the evidence or the logic for either the existence or the nonexistence of God is the only reasonable starting point.

Although the text may contain some unflattering illustrations regarding the ideology and practices of various religions, this is done strictly in service of exploring the general nature of the phenomenon of religion, and is not intended to offer either proof of or a rejection of the concept of God or to favor any one religion over others.

With or without God, I believe that humans would still contemplate supernatural causes for mysterious phenomena, and would continue to formulate religious concepts and engage in religious activities. In exploring the possible scientific bases for religion, questions about the existence of God and Her role with respect to religion have been held in abeyance to the extent possible.[6] In my view arguments about the existence and the nature of God tend to obfuscate productive lines of inquiry about the fundamental nature of the phenomenon of religion.

In this analysis religious practices and beliefs are regarded as outcomes of natural processes that are amenable to systematic and systemic inquiry. Such a course would be unfeasible if the only explanation permitted was that religious belief and behavior are exclusively due to the will of God. Regarding religion as a natural phenomenon that arises because of evolutionary adaptation will be seen as a terminal error by those readers who insist that any discussion of religion must begin (and end) with a discussion of God and Her role as the progenitor and enforcer of religion. I maintain, however, that religion and religious belief can productively be studied as phenomenon independent of any discussion of God.

The challenge is to relate religion, as a personal and social phenomenon, to natural and biological processes, and by doing so, to comprehend the devotion that religion commands and gain insight about its genesis. The goal is to arrive at an understanding of the conscious and subconscious drives that induce modern, highly intelligent individuals to spend a large portion of their lives, energies, and fortunes engaging in what are arguably nonfunctional pursuits in the service of religion.

Many have argued that religion arose in order to foster internal unity in groups, by brokering peaceful internal relations, as well as to provide for coordination in clashes with other groups and to cultivate cooperation in the exploitation of nature. Although such pragmatic uses of religion are undeniable, the internalization of socially cohesive practices does not fully explain spirituality, the extensive and gratuitous amount of time spent in unproductive religious rituals, or the influence of religion to induce people to act against personal self-interest. I have tried to rationally explain extreme cases, such as where, under the banner of religion, individuals are encouraged to engage in illegal, cruel, and even suicidal acts, without having to resort to the convenient hackneyed answer that such behavior is a delusion commanded by their particular wrongheaded interpretation of their duty to God in order to obtain Her rewards and blessings or avoid dire punishments.

The Robustness of Religion

In the former Soviet Union, the Communist government took active measures to suppress the overt practice of religion and to propagate the message of the irrationality and fecklessness of all traditional religions. Despite sustained efforts on a national scale for three generations, religion continued to be practiced. When in 1989, after seventy years, the USSR finally dissolved there was a resurgence of religion in the countries that had formerly been part of the Soviet Union. In South Korea, an economically prosperous country with a high level of education and technology, an updated form of shamanism, a religion that was practiced from the Stone Age to modern times among primitive people, has recently had a major resurgence.

There are other indications that religion is capable of spontaneous regeneration. In a Minnesota study of adopted identical twins that were raised separately, the researchers concluded that heritability accounted for 50 percent of a predisposition to either become or not become religious. Generalizing from that study, individuals with a genetic predisposition are susceptible to becoming religious if exposed to others who are religious, from reading about religious doctrines, or simply because of their attempts to rationalize the mysteries of life.

Surveys have recorded a slight negative correlation between level of education and a person's degree of religiosity, but neither intelligence nor education appears to be a determining factor. A minority of past and present prominent scientists was or is devoutly religious.[7] At present, a highly regarded scientist, Francis S. Collins, who led the Human Genome Project and is currently the head of the U.S. National Institute of Health, is unabashedly religious. He not only is a firm believer in God but has also written a book and given numerous speeches in which he professes his faith in the supernatural. According to a recent survey, 2 percent of the scientists polled said that they believe humans have existed in their present form from the beginning of time.

Although poverty seems to exaggerate religious convictions, many of the poor disregard religion or treat it cynically, while many of the wealthy are sincere and dedicated patrons of a variety of religious causes.

Many fundamentalist religions cling fiercely to archaic practices that might have been appropriate centuries ago but are acutely out of place in the modern world. Religiously endorsed practices such as persecuting homosexuals or amputating the hand of a thief are regarded as anachronistic as well as wrongheaded. An extreme case that is tolerated by some religions is the honor killing of young women by their own fathers or brothers if they have lost their virginity before marriage. By tradition, Muslim women in some countries are obliged to wear a garment, such as a burka, that completely covers their bodies in order to protect their modesty. I am told that there is no explicit scriptural requirement in the Koran to do so, yet it is promoted by religious authorities.

The Amish, living in the heartland of the industrialized United States, insist on farming, dressing, and living as did their ancestors of several centuries ago. Many of them shun television, tractors, telephones, automobiles, computers, and other modern conveniences that, presumably, could make their lives much easier. Hasidic Jews living in the heart of New York, a most cosmopolitan city, dress as eighteenth century Polish nobles, wearing long black coats and fur hats even in the hottest weather. They conspicuously sport earlocks and fringes on their religious undergarments, and they converse in Yiddish, a vestigial language spoken by their forebears in Eastern Europe before World War II.

In the Western world, many of the most extreme practices dictated by archaic or dysfunctional religious tradition are not personally observed by the majority of nominal adherents of those religions. In most cases the majority of people who identify as belonging to these religions blend easily with their fellow nationals of other religious persuasions. Still, the extreme practices and views of the ultrareligious are honored, respected, and defended by their much less observant rank-and-file coreligionists.

Cosmopolitan Mormons and Southern Baptists support rejection of homosexuals and oppose gay rights even though many of them warmly accept these people in their personal lives. Catholics practice birth control at the same rate as most other groups despite official church sanctions. Some Catholics even tolerate abortion for members of their own family while at the same time devotedly supporting the church's position on these matters. Islam is defended as a religion of peace, even while some of its adherents justify killing young women who seek to choose their own mates. Many Muslims refuse to unequivocally condemn the perpetrators of the 9/11 mass murder of innocent workers in the World Trade Towers in New York City.

In the United States, while membership in some of the traditional Christian denominations has waned of late, there is burgeoning growth in the more fundamentalist and demanding denominations such as Pentecostal and Evangelical. In Europe, churches of traditional Christian denominations remain largely empty, attracting meager attendance on Sundays. But in many places in Africa, Asia, South America, and the United States, predominantly fundamentalist Christian megachurch congregations, with as many as ten thousand or more active members, are springing up.

Evangelical congregations in the United States have taken over entire sports stadiums and fill them most Sundays. Christian-themed novels, music, movies, and theme parks have become huge and lucrative businesses. Similarly, in parts of the Islamic world, there has been a marked shift toward the more fundamentalist traditions. In some measure this shift is sponsored by the oil-rich Saudis, who actively promote the extreme Wahhabist version of the theology and traditions of Islam. They encourage Islamic fundamentalism throughout the world by doling out lavish grants and paying the salaries of approved clergy. At the same time, it seems that Shi'a clerical leaders of Iran have imposed theocratic rule over their nation of 70 million people, desiring to garner religious as well as political influence in other areas throughout the Middle East and world Islam by encouraging others to follow their example.

Spirituality and Religiosity

To render the phenomenon of religion more amenable to inquiry, it will be convenient at times to examine two major aspects of religion separately even though both are inextricably intertwined with respect to overall religion. These two are religiosity and spirituality. Religion can also be discussed as either a personal phenomenon or a group phenomenon. All forms of religion are generally regarded as having spiritual as well as behavioral dimensions, and as affecting both individuals as well as groups, though in different measures. Various theories of religion tend to emphasize one or the other of each of these dimensions. At the margin, four possibilities arise for analysis with regard to degrees of spirituality and religiosity attributed to an individual or group. These are (1) high spirituality, low religiosity, (2) low spirituality, high religiosity, (3) high spirituality, high religiosity, and (4) low spirituality, low religiosity. People can be found whose religious tendencies can be attributed to each of these four categories. Separating the two concepts at the extremes can provide a useful strategy for analysis.

Spirituality relates to a subset of an individual's beliefs. These mainly concern, but are not restricted to, cognitive inferences about the supernatural and consequent notions about the origin and the meaning of life. Both emotion and cognition are intertwined in spirituality. Religiosity is characterized as particular forms of behavior. It constitutes activities that are not primarily pragmatic or functional in the ordinary sense. Religious activities are overtly and even covertly performed primarily for their religious value, though they may have secondary practical payoffs for the individual. Religiosity often includes public and private rituals and other routine behaviors that are regarded as manifestations of a particular religious doctrine. Behavior that is considered as religious may also be prompted by nonspiritual considerations of a psychological or sociological nature. Pragmatic activities, such as social networking by attending church services and interacting with other congregants, listening to gospel music, and reading religiously themed novels, may also be regarded as religious in nature.

Spirituality offers humans a deductive means of making sense of the many mysteries of their environment. Religiosity provides individuals in groups, with experiential applications of religion, a means of identifying like-minded individuals, detecting and policing the religiosity of their fellows, and influencing and transmitting values and beliefs. Religiosity also provides an empirical, if tautological, means of confirming the effects of spirituality and religiosity. Events, both good and bad, are attributed to the observance or nonobservance of religious practice, or to the widespread acceptance of, or the flaunting of, certain spiritual beliefs. Thus they are construed as evidence confirming the efficacy of religion.

Is Religion a Good or a Bad Thing?

As with the existence of God, I attempt to be neutral with respect to judgment about the existential value of religion. The backdrop to any discussion of religion, however, is its role in the human drama. Even if it is not critical to survival, religion has played a significant role in enabling modern humans to dominate in nature. Religion has comforted individuals in their times of trouble, and it has been instrumental in organizing ancient and modern societies. Adherence to religious practices assists many individuals at most times in living secure lives marked by good nutrition and many creature comforts. Over the past millennia, however, unspeakable acts of heinous cruelty have been perpetrated in the name of each of the world's major religions. In the words of one detractor, Steve Weinberg, "With or without religion you would have good people doing good things and evil people doing evil things. But for good people to do evil things, that takes religion."

The case against religion has been summarized most succinctly by Stanley Fish, of the *New York Times*, in his review of the books *The End of Faith: Religion, Terror, and the Future of Reason,* by Sam Harris, *The God Delusion,* by Richard Dawkins, and *God Is Not Great: How Religion Poisons Everything,* by Christopher Hitchens. Fish presents four propositions on which, he asserts, all three reviewed authors more or less concur:

- "First, religion is man-made: its sacred texts, rather than being the word of God, are the 'manufactured' words of fallible men."
- "Moreover ... these words have been cobbled together from miscellaneous sources, all of which are far removed in time from the events they purport to describe." [That is, they are calculatedly dishonest.]
- "Third, it is in the name of these corrupted, garbled and contradictory texts, that men (and occasionally women) have been moved to do terrible things." [No terrible act in defense of a religion is too extreme to be proscribed by the religion.]
- "Fourth (and this is the big one), the commission of these horrible acts—"trafficking in humans ... ethnic cleansing ... slavery ... indiscriminate massacre (Hitchens)—is justified not by arguments, reasons or evidence, but by something called faith ... "Faith is what credulity becomes when it finally achieves escape velocity from the constraints of terrestrial discourse—constraints like reasonableness, internal coherence, civility and candor." (Harris) "Faith is an evil precisely because it requires no justification and brooks no argument." (Dawkins) "If one must have faith in order to believe something ... then the likelihood of that something having any truth or value is considerably diminished." (Hitchens)[8]

Fundamentalists and Martyrs

Paradoxically, today, just as scholarship and new scientific knowledge seem to be questioning the divine origin of scripture and undercutting the supernatural basis of religion, in many places the theological pendulum seems to be swinging toward the fundamentalist end of its arc. A large and hard-core segment of various populations seems to need fundamental religious belief. There is a growing dichotomy that sometimes erupts into open hostility between those who are attracted to modern, knowledge-based, scientific secularism and those who are inexorably drawn to time-honored spirituality and the fundamentalist religions that are based on devout, inflexible faith in two-thousand-year-old precepts.

Many individuals, from Christian martyrs who were fed to lions in the Roman Coliseum to Muslim and Jewish martyrs, have willingly, and in some cases voluntarily, gone to their deaths for their religious beliefs. On the whole, from stories of martyrdom and a myriad of examples throughout the ages of sacrifice and suffering for religion, it seems that religion must address some fundamental and powerful human need that transcends secular benefits and a need for personal safety. Though undeniably producing horribly tragic outcomes at times, religion must generally be regarded as beneficial for individual humans and for the human condition, or it would not have emerged so early in human history, survived so tenaciously, and become so compelling and omnipresent throughout human history and for all existing human societies.

A Clash of Cultures

In the United States today, there is a running polemical trench warfare being waged between those who are certain of their fundamentalist beliefs in the literal truth of the scriptures and those who are equally confident that eons-long evolutionary processes serve to provide a more valid explanation for the current state of flora and fauna and modern civilization than does the biblical story of creation or the other canonical scriptures. Both sides are deeply entrenched in the particular beliefs of their own camp and often lob verbal grenades that dismiss and denigrate the beliefs of the other group.

- Some U.S. Christian fundamentalists continue to seethe about the forced removal of a large monument listing the Ten Commandments from a courthouse in Montgomery, Alabama, in 2003. Controversies over crèches depicting the birth of Jesus that are placed on public land break out on an annual basis.

- Pious Christians have declared that abortion is tantamount to murder and want it made illegal under any circumstance whatsoever. Some religious fundamentalists maintain that a human blastocyst (i.e., a fertilized ovum that has grown to contain about a dozen cells) used for stem cell research results in the destruction of an unborn human baby. They maintain that killing a human blastocyst is an absolute evil that cannot be mitigated or justified on any grounds, even if it leads to the cure for devastating diseases or the saving of human lives.

- Religious fundamentalists are certain that sex education in schools will promote promiscuity and result in unwanted pregnancies among teenage girls. The secular opposition is equally convinced that sex education is an effective deterrent to teen pregnancy and would obviate many abortions.[9]

- The clash in the United States between fundamentalists and secularists has intensified and spilled over into many areas of life, the most important of these being the political arena. At the present time, there is no sign that hard-core advocates of either position can reach any kind of an amicable modus vivendi.

The significance of religion in current affairs has leapt to greater prominence recently with the rise of geopolitical conflicts in which, despite denials, theology or divergent religious belief is implicated. In Iraq, as this manuscript is being written, Sunni Arabs are pitted against Shi'i Arabs and against Muslim but non-Arab Kurds for control of territory and oil revenues, and control in the government. Sunni Arab Saudi Arabia is engaged in a high-stakes, covert struggle with Shi'i Muslim, non-Arab Iran for domination in the region. Both groups are nonetheless united in their hatred of Israel and especially in what they regard as the corrupting influences of the immoral, secular West that is encroaching on their idealized notions of the past under the Muslim caliphate. All of this is being played out in the context of what Samuel P. Huntington, in 1993, labeled a "clash of civilizations."

This ideological, and sometimes armed, conflict pits the fundamentalist beliefs in the primacy of Islam together with its beliefs and codes of conduct, which are held by major segments of the one billion Muslims of the Islamic Middle East, against any and all detractors. The antagonism is not, strictly speaking, against Christianity per se, but rather against Western secular beliefs in individual rights and freedoms (especially sexual freedoms and feminism) and the rampant materialism of the two billion plus people of the West. Conflict arises in that the Western secular mindset and even some of its religious views seem, to Eastern fundamentalists, not only to tolerate but also to value unrestrained hedonism, including the right to blaspheme, and a widespread lack of sexual inhibitions. Western values appear to some fundamentalist Muslims to promote a society where women flaunt their bodies and their sexuality and where people are free to disparage Allah, his prophet Muhammad, and his doctrines with impunity.

In the Christian West, as well as in the Muslim East, the vast majority of people support or are at least sympathetic to fundamentalists in their midst. They tolerate and even endorse the beliefs, practices, and prejudices of their more strident coreligionist even though they themselves behave much as secularists in their private lives and may personally regard the ultrareligious as extremists who go way too far.

My Approach

I believe that explanations of the origin and the nature of religion must lie with consideration of evolution as it has formed the human brain and its processes of thought. Admittedly, the specific paths of evolution, which occurred over hundreds of thousands and millions of years, are, to a large extent, discerned only by means of reasoned speculations. Nonetheless, I contend that they can reveal the nature of religion and that biology is the basis of religion. I appreciate that those who dismiss evolution will accuse me of prejudicing the result of the study from the outset by attempting to force notions of religion to conform to what they regard as speculative evolutionary theory and of not considering other options. So be it. I am not aware of any other options that are open to critical investigation and unconstrained logical analysis.

Belief, in the general sense, is important for animals in making sense of their environments and therefore in facilitating survival. Religious belief is a subset of general belief. It is fashioned by the same evolutionary processes that serve to generate pragmatic beliefs in general.

> Religion and spiritual beliefs [as Andrew Newburg has
> written] have had a particularly profound influence over
> human history, and yet we hardly grasp how they work
> at the biological behavioral or psychological levels. As

20

a neuroscientist, I have come to believe that the study of beliefs may be the single most important quest, both scientifically and spiritually. Furthermore, I think we must begin this exploration by examining the very part of us that does the believing—the human brain.[10]

Both religious apologists and evolutionists agree that a critical feature of humans, one that has provided a great advantage with regard to their current superiority, is the human brain. It is generally held that the brain has evolved as an organ of survival for all creatures, but it was especially important for humans, who have relied most extensively on their superior brainpower for survival and their ultimate dominance in nature.

It must be the human brain that plays the pivotal role in religion, since belief or faith, the critical element in religion, is by its very nature an outcome of thinking, and thinking is a product of the mind. As such, an examination of the evolutionary development and operation of the human brain is critical to the analysis of religion. The application of theories from biology, neurology, evolutionary biology, and evolutionary psychology will be used to explain the operation of the brain and its role in religious belief.

CHAPTER TWO

Can Animals Think And Reason Without Language?

The Magic of Human Language

Humans are unique in their mastery of declarative symbolic language. Although language requires certain physical capabilities it is largely a product of brain processes. By three years of age human toddlers that are merely exposed to the haphazard casual conversations of their parents and siblings, learn to speak naturally. The youngsters are able to express complex thoughts using meaningful sequences of words that they have never been taught or even heard.

According to Michael Tomasello, "Infant research ... suggests that coordinating visual attention may have provided the foundation for the evolution of human language. Babies begin to acquire language through joint activities with others, in which both parties are focused on the same object or task. That is the best time for a toddler to learn the word for the object or activity in question." Young apes exposed to language and systematically taught language do not learn to speak although they do attain a limited amount of receptive language. Apes can learn to recognize and respond to one word or short phrase commands that are often and unambiguously repeated. Using "Bliss" picture boards they can even rudimentarily communicate with humans. However, even under the protracted, controlled and systematic methods used in training animals to acquire language, none has come close to the language level that three-year old humans attain informally.

Despite their lack of language, animals can be intelligent in that they are fully capable of negotiating and exploiting their environments in order to stay alive. The basic physiology and functioning of both the human and primate brains were developed over eons by the same evolutionary processes and remain quite similar in most respects. After all, the human genus only split from the ape genus between five and ten million years ago.

The neurons and neural networks that are basic to the thought processes of apes and humans are similar in configuration and in operation. Apes and other mammals lack the physical structures of throat and mouth that would enable them to speak. Their brains also lack certain neurological structures that are required for learning and using the grammar and syntax of symbolic language. However, like the differences among the different makes and models of the internal combustion engines of automobiles, although their complexity, use of materials, organization and power may differ, the basic operating principles and functions are the same for all of them.

The Mind-Brain Dichotomy and the Soul

Until relatively recently the Cartesian explanation of a dichotomy of mind and body (the mental and physical aspects of the brain), was held to be unique to humans. All other animals possessed a physical brain that determined their actions but they did not have a mind capable of reason. The Cartesian hypothesis implies that animals are, in essence like biological meat machines, which respond mechanically to external stimuli. The classical mind-brain dichotomy has largely been scientifically discredited. However, hubris demands that the human mind simply can not operate like a constrained biological mechanism, in a manner similar to the animal brain. Apologists vehemently insist that we humans are not merely meat machines. We have powers of will, personal choice and self-determination that animals do not, and can not, possess.

For most religious, and some non-religious, people it is inconceivable that there is not a special God given spirit, a soul or a special area of the brain that is possessed by humans but not by "lower" animals. This area transcends the physical human brain and body. But if there is some mysterious element that categorically differentiates the "human mind" from the "animal brain", it has yet to be discovered or even objectively inferred from empirical observations of the operations of the human brain as contrasted with the animal brain. (Recently, the counter theory, that if humans have souls then other animals, and especially primates, must also have souls, has been revived and is gaining currency. This notion goes back at least to Rudolf Steiner at the beginning of the 20th century.)

If we accept that the human mind/body dichotomy does not exist, then critical differences between human and animal minds must be found elsewhere than the fundamental operations of their brains. Human reasoning is convincingly and obviously much superior to that of animals. But, by virtue of many animal experiments that have been conducted over the last half century, the once widespread certainty that animal thinking is entirely emotional or mechanistic and non-rational has lost any sliver of validity.

Coping Without Language

If we can accept that reason, in the broadest sense of the term, is not exclusive to humans it also follows that we must also accept that reasoning is not entirely language dependent. Both reason and emotion are capable of being changed by experiences but the processes are not without some measure of intervention by internal mental processes. This is as true for animals as for humans. Scientific experiments have demonstrated that, far beyond simple operant conditioning, animals can learn from complex natural experiences.

Animals have achieved this reckoning ability without possessing natural symbolic language. Unlike carefully controlled learning in a 'Skinner Box' animals do have the ability to assimilate unfocused past experiences and to use their memories and reasoning abilities for improving future performance in circumstances that are only similar but not identical to past experiences. The storied ability of elephants to remember past events and react accordingly years later is not fiction. Animals have the ability to interpret cues in order to determine where food or water is likely to be found or to follow long, arduous migration routes.

Birds with very tiny brains can learn complex song patterns including those that communicate danger or the desire to attract a mate. According to John Mooney, swamp sparrows can not only learn new songs but they learn them with regional accents and they can remember them for up to a year without using them.[11] Experiments where young zebra finches are taught songs that they will sing all their lives, but which are different from those they would naturally learn from their sires, demonstrate that specific bird songs are not innately programmed. It is only the ability to learn the songs and to produce the sounds required that are innate. Once zebra finches reach maturity, however, they become incapable of learning new songs. Canaries and parrots though, can and often do, learn new songs every year. Alex, an African grey parrot is alleged, by researcher Dr. Irene Pepperberg, to have had a working vocabulary of 100 words. Moreover, she claims that Alex was able to use his large vocabulary in context.

Jane Goodall, after years of extensive observation of creatures in the wild, convinced the world that chimpanzees have individual personalities, temperaments and complex cultures. They make and use tools and communicate instrumentally with each other. Recently Tetsuro Matsuzawa of Kyoto University performed number recall experiments with chimpanzees which demonstrated that their non declarative memory on the experimental tasks was significantly superior to that of humans[12] for the same tasks. Many animals can communicate effectively by means of sounds and gestures. Ordinary dogs can be taught to respond to fifty or more oral commands.

Animal Learning Experiments

Indirect research on the operations of the animal brain were conducted in the first half of the twentieth century by experimental psychologists, who studied animal behavior. Principal among these so-called 'behaviorists' were B.F. Skinner and his followers. The behaviorists' experiments studied the overt behavior of small animals, such as rats, under carefully controlled conditions. The trials were characterized as 'learning', 'conditioning' or 'stimulus-response' experiments. No attempt was made to infer or to speculate about internal brain processes that might drive or be associated with the observed behavior. In fact, Skinner disparaged all those who might attempt to link external behavior to internal brain processes as posing fanciful theories that could not advance, and would likely retard, the cause of scientific enquiry. In Skinner's view, only that which could be; objectively observed, controlled, accurately measured and replicated, was worthy of scientific inquiry. Given the state of brain research and technology at the time Skinner was doing his experimental research, this was not an unreasonable position. It is no longer as tenable.

The Skinnerian view of animal behavior is richer, more sophisticated and empirically grounded than the Cartesian notion that animals act mechanically out of pure emotion. None-the-less it attempts to finesse the obvious. It is the internal brain processes of the individual animal that control its behavior. These are the processes that should be studied to truly understand behavior, learning and belief. Fortunately, modern neuroscience has developed a number of tools that can assist scientists in penetrating the 'black box' that is the brain.

Today many scientists are exploring the internal workings of the neural networks of the brain. Others are studying complex animal behavior in the wilds. For example, Dorothy Cheney and Robert Seyfarth are studying Moreni baboons in their natural habitat in Botswana in field experiments to determine how they think[13] when not constrained by the artificial and narrow environment or the directed and severely limited response choices of the Skinner box.

The 'Skinnerian learning experiments' indicate that there must be residual changes to the neural organization of the animal brain as a result of experience and these determine future behavior. But what if the animals could talk? What are the relative roles of language as compared to experience in creating such residual brain changes and what is the effect of the verbal neural organization on consciousness and on declarative language? This topic will be explored at length.

Subconscious Drivers of Behavior

Perversely, despite humans vaunted cognitive abilities, many if not most, of the ordinary decisions that we humans make on a daily basis are made at a subconscious, non-verbal level. These decisions could be regarded as emotional or non-rational and similar to the purported source of the actions of our animal relatives. On first meeting, some individual we sometimes have an instant dislike for him or her. Other people that we are introduced to are liked and trusted immediately. People are not aware of the source of such subliminal 'prejudice', although they may attempt to rationalize it after the fact. In many cases when required to make decisions we very often 'go with our gut' rather than conduct a deliberative analysis. Such common behavior, often described as being done without due deliberation, appears superficially to be like simple stimulus-response reactions. Yet many if not most of these situations are highly complex and seemingly call for far more sophisticated thought processes than that required by an experimental rat in pressing a bar that it knows will yield food.

On reflection, one must conclude that there are many unanticipated and random variables involved in all but the most trivial instances of such first impression or snap judgment situations. As Malcolm Gladwell asserts, actions taken using snap judgments in complex situations are often more effective than similar decisions made after lengthy deliberation.[14] It follows that there must be a prodigious amount of thought that goes into such decisions which takes place in a very short time. Learned past experience is a major factor for snap judgments, but since no two situations are exactly the same, an inability to tailor internal thought processes and consequent decisions or behavioral responses to new situations would be disastrous for survival. This must be true of other animals in the wild as well.

For humans, like other animals, the remarkably complex and rapid amount of thinking required to make complicated decisions very rapidly is done at the nonverbal level where thought processing proceeds in thousandths of a second. Such extensive thinking is, however, inaccessible to our verbal consciousness.

Abilities Enabling Animals to Survive

Steven Pinker[15] provided what he called " ...a defensible list of cognitive faculties and the core intuitions on which [actions] are based ..." Although Pinker primarily addresses the brain functions of early hominids that lacked modern symbolic language, observation of higher animal behavior indicates that many present day language-less animals also possess similar mental faculties, though usually to a lesser extent than modern humans.

With bracketed italic comments supplied by me, Pinker's list (from The *Blank Slate*) includes:

- "An intuitive physics, which we use to keep track of how objects fall, bounce, and bend. Its core intuition is the concept of the object, which occupies one place, exists for a continuous span of time, and follows laws of motion and force... [*Anyone who has watched the skill with which a dog chases and catches a frisbee recognizes that some animals excel at aspects of this so-called intuitive physics faculty*]

- An intuitive version of biology or natural history, which we use to understand the living world. **Its core intuition is that living things house a hidden essence that gives them their form and powers and drives their growth and bodily functions.**

27

[*This is the notion of an agent. Stalking and hunting, avoiding predators or tending babies would hardly be possible if animals were completely oblivious to this faculty. Why would male lions kill the cubs of their new consort's previous mates if they did not have some elemental intuitive grasp of biology?*]

- An intuitive engineering, which we use to make and understand tools and other artifacts. Its core intuition is that a tool is an object with a purpose – an object designed by a person to achieve a goal. [*Many animals, birds and even insects make and use tools, although they are not very good at generalizing, that is devising new uses for existing tools, or of continuously improving existing tools – but tool making and tool use is not uncommon in the nonhuman world.*]

- An intuitive psychology, which we use to understand other people. Its core intuition is that other people are not objects or machines … Minds contain beliefs and desires and are the immediate cause of behavior… [*This also involves the concept of agency. A rudimentary possession of this faculty is necessary to establish and maintain status orders among social animals. Animals, such as dogs, that make good pets are quite adept at reading the moods and intentions of humans as well as their fellow dogs. The lessons of the so-called "Horse Whisperer[16]" and dog whisperer, attests to the highly sophisticated ways in which animals relate to their fellows. Hans, the counting horse in nineteenth century Germany was so good at picking up subtle cues from his trainer that he was able to fool large crowds of people into thinking he could actually do arithmetic.*]

- A spatial sense, which we use to navigate the world and keep track of where things are… [M*any birds, animals and even insects are capable of incredible feats of migrations over hundreds and even thousands of kilometers. Many animals have excellent memories with respect to the location of hidden food caches. Recent experiments have demonstrated that chimpanzees are superior to humans with regard to short term memory of spatial objects.[17]*)

- A number sense, which we use to think about quantities and amounts. It is based on an ability register exact quantities for small numbers of objects and to make rough relative estimates for larger numbers. [*Higher animals such as apes can demonstrate this faculty. Other animals such as dogs can readily distinguish*

between one, a few and many, even if they do not register numbers as digital quantities.]
- A sense of probability, which we use to reason about the likelihood of uncertain events. It is based on the ability to track the relative frequencies of events that is the proportion of events of some kind that turn out one way or the other. [*Again this is a requisite skill that animals develop to assist survival by determining recurring patterns such as the likelihood that food, prey or predators will be found in a given location or when hunting in packs that their prey may run in a certain direction*]
- An intuitive economics, which we use to exchange goods and favors. It is based on the concept of reciprocal exchange ... [*Experiments and anecdotes with capuchin monkeys by Franz deWaal and others clearly demonstrates that animals possess this faculty. Monkeys get very angry when they believe thy have been cheated. This is also an indication of a sense of distributive justice and rudimentary sense of morality in the animal world*]
- A mental database and logic, which we use to represent ideas and to infer new ideas from old ones. It is based on assertions about what's what, what's where, or who did what to whom, when, where and why. The assertions are linked in a mind-wide web ... [*Animals certainly possess memory and can respond to new situations by comparing elements of a new situation to their memory banks and then responding in novel ways based on the similarities and differences of these comparisons. Semi-permanent pecking orders and status hierarchies as well as devious cheating behaviors have been observed among animals and birds. Higher social animals certainly act based on reciprocity of favors and of disrespect. Dogs and elephants will remember those who have been kind and those who have been mean to them*]
- [p. 220 of <u>The Blank Slate,</u> by Steven Pinker – my italics]

Thinking about Experiences

Humans and animals learn from experience but they also learn by thinking about the experience. Although the evidence is indirect, from their subsequent behavior it can be shown that many animals without benefit of language are capable of interpreting events. Actions taken that result in positive, beneficial experiences are *replicated* to fit new circumstances rather than being repeated exactly. With each replication the nominal behavior is naturally improved as the animal continues to improve its performance. Circumstances associated with negative consequences are avoided. The most adept hunters among lions, hyenas and other predator species may have been blessed with good genes and superior physical potential at birth but their outstanding hunting skill is honed by their experiences of success and failure, which are influenced to a degree by pure luck. Improvement in performance takes place at the cognitive as well as the physical level.

An advantage possessed by many social species is a tendency to specialization. Individuals tend to gravitate to those activities at which they are 'relatively better' than their fellows and to discontinue activities done better by others. Thus there is a naturally induced specialization of individuals and a resulting division of labor in a group that is based on experience. Specialization and division of labor promote the survival of a social species. The larger the group and the more complex their lifestyle the greater the potential benefit of specialization and division of labor. Although they are both greatly aided by language, a fair degree of specialization and division of labor can be achieved by language-less species.

Experiments to highlight this process of natural experiential specialization were undertaken with Carapacys birol, a species of ant[18]. Experimenters contrived a situation where some ants of a new generation of worker ants were allowed to find food or prey when they went out to forage while a control group of ants, by arrangement, could find nothing. After 30 days it was observed that the successful foragers continued to go out and hunt for food while members of the unsuccessful group remained in the nest caring for the new brood of infant ants. Although there are obviously many confounding factors in Nature, the experiment did establish the possibilities of a natural tendency for experiential specialization and division of labor among even the smallest social creatures. To what extent, if any, and how, the tendency for such specialization becomes widespread and innately stable over many generations is unknown. The nature of gene coding or gene regulation for specialization and its connection to inherited genetic characteristics and behavioral instincts remains for further study.

Non-verbal Reason and Emotion

For humans, with their exceptional cognitive abilities, hubris has demanded that our prodigious ability for reasoning should be regarded as a principle difference between humans and other animals. Rene Descartes, with his famous dictum, "I think therefore I am", declared that humans alone are capable of reason and self reflection, while all other animals are driven to act mechanically by using pure emotion.

On the contrary, however it has been determined that, with respect to most behavior, both reason and emotion are present to various degrees and are critical for the survival of other animals as well. As stated by George Lakoff, "Reason is commonly assumed to be conscious; disembodied; dispassionate; literal (fits the world directly); logical (leads from facts to correct conclusions); universal; and self-interested." But, he asserts, *"the cognitive sciences have shown that reason really is mostly unconscious; physical (uses the brain); requires emotion*; uses frames, metaphors, and melodramatic narratives; varies depending on worldview; and is used at least as much in the service of empathy [rationalizing emotionally driven behavior] as self-interest."[19] (Bold italics and bracketed material are mine).

Events, conditions and objects in the environment are of infinite variation. They change continually through time and location. If all individuals of an animal species did not have some capability for cognitive thought that is capable of driving specific behavioral reactions, which are attuned to changing or unusual conditions, their species would soon become extinct. Whenever members of a species encountered novel situations they could not effectively defend their lives or offensively locate or catch food or attract mates. Although cognitive mental processes are often contrasted with emotional processes, as Baruch Spinoza realized in the seventeenth century, they are both necessary and both involved to varying degrees with respect to dealing successfully with a complex environment.

Dog owners often experience the situation where their pets *decide* that they want to go for a walk or to play. The pet brings its master a leash and paces back and forth between the master and the door until the master understands the dog's 'request'. Or the dog will bring a ball and drop it at its master's feet and nudge her to pick up the ball and throw it so as to initiate a game of fetch. The dog may only wish to play with certain people or it may not always be in a mood for such play. Various smells, sounds or sights may distract the dog so that it breaks off the activity even though its master may wish to continue. In this sense it is not the master but the dog that *decides* on the time, nature and duration of play.

The myriad of atypical, or unique, specific situations that present either life threatening dangers or life enhancing opportunities to an animal in the unforgiving wilds may be infrequent when taken individually. In the aggregate however, some novel critical event is an almost weekly if not a daily occurrence. If animals were unable to reason and they acted only by means of operant conditioning or emotion responses, they would be unable to cope with altered or unusual situations on a case by case basis. Such limited response to environmental challenges would swiftly lead to individual demise and consequently to species extinction. This is especially true for large, slow-reproducing species such as hominids.

In addition though, if creatures did not instantly react to common, critical, threatening events by means of so-called emotional reflexive responses, their species would not survive very long either. By means of genetic adaptation, prior generations of a species, including hominids, have developed instinctive or preprogrammed emotional responses. Once triggered, when confronted with a potentially calamitous circumstance, the instincts provide instantaneous reactions without lengthy deliberation. For example, when we are startled by sudden movement or loud noises we involuntarily flinch to protect ourselves.

At the neurological level, the brain's native facilities for reasoned deliberation and emotional reaction overlap. Although an area of the brain called the amygdala is often cited as a center of emotion, most of the areas or organs of the brain, that is, its neural networks in general, are involved with what are thought of as both reason and emotion. Conceptually, reason and emotion might be thought of as a continuum in thought and behavior that operate by means of common processes rather than a dichotomy. The brain appears to have a natural mechanism for the conservation of demanding thought or reasoning processes. Events that are commonplace, even those that might have had a threatening or opportunistic potential in the past are handled by preprogrammed – but not automatic - responses based on experience or emotion and non-deliberative thought response so as to deal with them quickly and efficiently. In the transitional case, an animal can 'control' the degree of deliberative reason or reactive emotion to be applied in the situation.

At one extreme, there are those highly critical situations where a delay of even an instant in reacting can mean certain death. In such cases the animal reacts instantaneously and impulsively, as soon as the threat is perceived. For humans this threat reaction can occur even where there is no conscious awareness of it[20]. If the instantaneous reaction is appropriate, say the animal jumps right, it lives. If the reaction action is wrong it may mean death.

Visiting a zoo, we flinch involuntarily when a snake strikes toward us even though we are aware that we are separated and protected from the snake by an impenetrable wall of glass. Somehow, over many generations such instantaneous involuntary reactions to immediate critical threats became instinctive because they were often effective for survival. Individuals without such instantaneous reactions simply did not survive. As an example, mice will become immediately motionless on detecting the presence of a nearby cat because as a species they have learned that cats instinctively react to relative motion and will wait before pouncing on a motionless prey. Immobility gives the hidden mouse time to evaluate the situation including the exact location of the cat and the best route or means of escape. Other species tend to reflexively flee. When confronted by a bear in the wilds, people are advised to remain motionless but few can resist the urge to ignore the advice and to run like hell.

I am not attempting to revive the Lamarckian notion of pangenesis or even Stalin era biologist Trofim Lysenko's theories about the direct inheritance of acquired behavioral characteristics, although some modern biological-geneticists are speculating about processes that may tend to work along such lines. However, aspects of temperament or traits such as aggressiveness or the tendency to risk taking behavior can be inherited and these do affect the probability of survival of offspring relative to prevailing short term and long term environmental conditions. The balance of temperaments in a social species affects the continuing nature of interaction among individuals in herds or packs - that is, its culture. The word 'culture' is generally not used to describe the nature of styles of frequent interactions in groups of social species, but it is descriptive of the phenomena. Culture can affect the survival rate of social groups and of entire species. Under some environmental conditions and cultures individuals with certain temperaments will flourish while under others they will decline.

A Harvard study of shyness of infants indicates that some children are born shy. They exhibit shyness long before they could have learned the behavior from their environment. If shyness is a native characteristic for some but not all babies in the same family, it appears that such shyness (and by extension other traits) may not be a consequence of either straightforward physical inheritance or of environment and experiential learning. The remaining explanatory possibility is that some aspect of the inherited genome, in some unknown way, perhaps operating by means of gene regulation as influenced by the environment, determines mental processes that affect behavioral expressions such as shyness.

A conclusion of the Minnesota study of identical twins reared in different families from birth is that, as compared to regular siblings or even fraternal twins reared in different families, identical twins show a remarkable predisposition to make similar life choices that cannot be attributed simply to random chance, environment or even overt physical inheritance based on traditional theories. It seems that many reasoned decisions are being subtly influenced by subconscious internal brain processes.

Applications of Non-verbal Thought.

Both verbal and nonverbal thought processes have been determined to occur by means of the firing of neurotransmitter proteins across synapses along vast networks of neurons in the brain. This describes the mechanics but not the nature of the thoughts themselves. It is a tall order indeed to discuss in words a process of thinking which does not use language. However, the nature of this theory dictates that some effort be made to at least illustrate the process, if indirectly.

The processes of non-verbal thought can be differentiated from automatic stimulus/response notions implied by Skinnerian learning theory. Some pertinent examples are included in the book, Blink by Malcolm Gladwell. Gladwell provides numerous illustrations describing how unconscious processes of thought are employed in certain instances to make very sophisticated decisions much more quickly and effectively than could be achieved by the use of deliberative, conscious thought processes.

Recently a man, who had been a Swiss physician, was left without vision by virtue of two strokes which had destroyed the visual lobes in both hemispheres at the back of his brain[21]. His visual system apparatus, that is his eyes and optic nerves, were not impaired but he was unable to process the received visual stimuli that normally would have enabled him to see, because of the damage to his brain.

A neuroscientist, Beatrice de Gelder, asked the man to walk a maze constructed of various obstacles that were placed at random in a hallway of her Institute. Astonishingly, the man was able to negotiate the maze, slowly for certain but with little difficulty. It was as though he had the power of vision even though many tests had established his total lack of sight. More astonishingly he himself had no idea of how his "blind sight" operated. Scientists have determined that visual stimuli travel not only to the visual lobes but to other areas of the mid-brain as well. There the visual stimuli are processed below the level of conscious awareness but, as illustrated by blind sight, such unconscious non- deliberative processes can none-the-less influence behavior.

We are all amazed by people who are labeled "savants". These people are often unable to perform many of the simple intellectual tasks that are routinely required in daily living. But the savants can perform certain prodigious mental feats, often in the areas of memory, mathematics or music. Some of these savants can multiply three and four digit numbers in their head and get the correct answer within a second or two. Others are able to remember the day of the week, the prevailing weather, or news headlines for any date in their past. Savants are able to perform amazing calculations, which greatly exceed the performance of even the smartest individuals, though they appear to have very limited overall intelligence. Like the Swiss physician, the savants themselves cannot explain how they perform such incredible mental feats.

Intuitive Chess

Some years ago the polymath social scientist, Herbert Simon in his studies of human decision making, studied the extraordinary ability of chess grandmasters to play a large number of reasonably accomplished chess players simultaneously[22]. The grandmasters generally win or draw most of the games. In this exercise, twenty to one hundred or more, good but not expert, players sit at tables in front of chess boards. The opponents all play black and they have little restriction on the time they take to make moves. The grand master moves in sequence from player to player and table to table making a move at each player's station, usually taking only a few seconds or less than a minute at each board.

Part of the grandmasters' ability is deliberative but without conscious verbal deliberation. He can see at a glance which of his white pieces might be at risk in the next one or two moves and which of his opponents black pieces might be vulnerable in the next one or two moves. If you asked him why he made such moves that are for immediate advantage or to obviate short run threats he could easily explain it in words even though his original internal diagnosis was non-verbal. This is an ability that is possessed by any reasonably expert chess player and does not explain an ability to play 50 or more experienced players and win or tie most games. The grandmaster does not appear to use 'brute force' like the IBM computer, 'Big Blue', that is programmed to eliminate unreasonable moves and to explicitly test out all reasonable moves for seven or eight rounds in advance and then select the best from the many millions of possibilities. Such a process would take the grandmaster hours if not months to complete for each move. And even Big Blue only plays one game at a time.

According to Simon, the grandmaster can sense or quickly assimilate the overall pattern of the pieces on the chess board at a glance. He intuitively grasps where he should concentrate his forces for offence or for defense. The grandmaster has a "feel" for which general areas of the board an attack on the opponent is likely to succeed over the next moves and which pieces are best used in the attack. The grandmaster also sizes up which areas of the board his men are vulnerable and how to marshal his men for defense. This 'feel' for the situation in each of the different games is acquired in the milliseconds that it takes his brain to assimilate the sensory information from each board. Unlike his explanations of potential threats and opportunities in the next two or three moves, the grandmaster generally cannot fully articulate his strategy except as a sense or a feel for a given situation. The sophisticated processes of requisite thought by the grandmaster occur at the nonverbal level that is inaccessible to his conscious awareness.

The nonverbal reasoning skills of animals are hardly comparable to chess grandmasters but if it has validity, the above anecdotal discussion is an illustration of the potential capabilities of the nonverbal reasoning process in its speed and complexity. What we call intuition is actually a significant amount of non-verbal thought which takes place at the lightning speed of brain processes operating at speeds in the order of thousandths of a second.

Subjective Evaluation

The nonverbal thinking process is somewhat like an art expert's evaluation of the merits of a painting. The artist's draftsmanship, her use of light and shadow and composition are briefly considered but the determination of whether or not the painting is great art, schlock or simply pretty good is more of a holistic process derived from the overall emotional impact of the painting on the expert. Another analogy would be music. The art of composing beautiful music is not an exercise in putting music theory into practice but rather the implementation of preconscious processes. Musical geniuses such as Irving Berlin or George Gershwin initially became successful without formal musical training. Music lovers get deep visceral pleasure from listening to certain music. Tastes may vary but enough individual fans agree on classical, jazz, rap or other genres of music to make it a billion dollar industry.

An ability to excel at chess or music does not invariably equate with the ability to excel at every other human intellectual endeavor or even most of them. Thus this spectacular intuitive ability of chess grandmasters appears to be an example of the potentially awesome power available to other people from developing and harnessing their preconscious, animalistic, thought processes.

The Development of Human Language

It has been said of computers that they greatly amplify the power of the human brain or intellect just as machines greatly increase the power of human muscles. Long before the invention of computers, however, the development of speech using natural language magnified the power of Homo sapiens' native animal brain processes and lifted the fortunes of a struggling species to a degree that has as yet to be matched by applications of the computer.

But why among thousands of animal species, that might have been potential candidates for the evolution of symbolic language, was it only in the Homo sapiens species that speech did develop? (Although there is speculation that other Homo species such as Neanderthals and others, including Homo erectus could also communicate by some form of natural language, it is only certain that our own species, Homo Sapiens, did develop a language ability as we know it, since all the other Homo species are extinct.)

The specific evolutionary paths to the development of language are unknown, but if we assume that it was stimulated by a need for adaptation in order to survive, it is possible to speculate about the nature of the adaptations and the environmental conditions that gave rise to them. It is a consequence of the enhancement of native mental processes produced by language that religion has come about.

The mystery of when natural oral language began and how it developed has been pondered by many linguists, evolutionary biologists, evolutionary psychologists, anthropologists, and philosophers[23]. There is some evidence that the precursors and the drivers of natural language were brokered by sexual specialization, the critical need for close, complex cooperation and the division of labor by a species transitioning from the forest to the savannas of East Africa. Sophisticated communication was advantageous for male hominids foraging in groups over the vast and hazardous savannas as well as by female hominids cooperating in rearing helpless babies. Babies that were in essence born seventeen months prematurely as compared to most other large mammals. The relatively defenseless hominids, their fragile babies and dependent toddlers could not have survived without some compensating ability which allowed them to survive the rigors of nature and competition with other creatures. In particular, the need for cooperation in order to keep hominid babies and toddlers alive, was a critical impetus for the development of language[24]

On the basis of biological and genetic studies scientists have determined that several mutations enabled speech that somehow led to language. A gene, called the FOXP2, associated with the language organs of the brain, appeared less than 200,000 years ago, another MCPH1 emerged only 37,000 years ago. The exact relationships between these genetic changes and improvements in natural languages remain a subject of debate, study and conjecture.

There is some agreement that before they had fully developed natural language, predecessor hominid species, such as Homo erectus, were sophisticated with respect to their non-language oral and gestural communication. Paleoanthropologists surmise that some rudimentary form of oral communication, that was more advanced than that used by modern apes, had been developed over a million years ago. The basis of this theory is that hand axes, that have been dated from that time, bear clear evidence of uniformity in shape and manufacturing processes. The proponents of the theory maintain that teaching this craft, that is instructing others in consistent production of hand axes over generations, must have required some form of language.

Standing upright with their flexible arms and hands free to make a variety of motions, early hominids would have had the potential to communicate functionally with complex hand/arm gestures as well as with a large variety of non-language sounds such as grunts, clicks, howls and a large repertoire of other sounds. A group of theories posits that language developed from such gestures not for tool making but because of the social needs of hunter-gatherers in the field and in congested camps where complex interaction was necessary.

Whatever the path of development, many of the phenotype and genotype mutations required for natural symbolic speech are estimated to have existed and were likely common in the Homo Sapiens species before the beginning of their migration from Africa sometime around 100 - 70 thousand years ago. At that time Homo sapiens began its transformation from a sparse species under stress and struggling to survive, into a thriving species that could readily establish itself as dominant in many and diverse new territories.

According to the above scenario for the first 50-100 thousand years of its existence our species, Homo sapiens, lived a precarious existence barely surviving as a poorly adapted, ape-like creature, on the savannas of East Africa. Hominids, however, had superior functional communication skills, if not fully developed modern language abilities. The species, with their thin skin, poor sense of smell, and inadequate claws and jaws would have struggled, but still they managed to survive on the savannas of Africa by dint of brain power, social organization, task specialization, use of fire, and their superior communication abilities. They competed in ecological niches with other hominid groups and species and with various other animals that were by nature better adapted physically to life on the savannas of East Africa. The major breakthrough, with respect to survival, was the development of natural language which gave rise to their adaptability and their success as a species. Superiority in communication promoted greater coordination and specialization, which ultimately led to their migration from Africa into many other environments.

CHAPTER THREE

The Brain At Work

Brain Functions and Behavior

Before we take a step, move a muscle or say a word, even before we are consciously aware that we have decided to act, there is activity in the brain which initiates and directs the action. According to M. Spinella and O. Wain[25], "Most of the neurological phenomena associated with religious experience involve some *'over activation*[26] of the limbic system' [of the brain]". Both the religiosity and the spirituality dimensions of religion are products of the human brain regardless of whether or not they are ontologically determined. That is, even from an ontological perspective a creator must have determined the operations of the brain and the brain determines spirituality and religiosity.

Since the current theory about the source of religion involves internal brain processes, some familiarity with modern brain research and the operation of the brain will be helpful.

All of the basic operations human of thought occur at an unconscious neurological level as opposed to a language-mediated conscious level. We are unaware of our basic internal thought processes. The brain operates the body by sending signals traveling down the spinal cord to the muscles of the various limbs. In turn, feedback and sense data from the environment travel in the opposite direction and cause neural activity in the brain. The processes include, visual and olfactory signals as well as overt physical behavior and in the case of humans, speaking and listening to language

A critical function of the animal brain is to discern and distinguish among patterns and associations of and among 'Objects, Agents, Conditions, Events, Relationships and Emotions' in the environment (OACEREs). By such means threats to, and opportunities for, the individual can be assessed and acted upon. To survive and to thrive, a creature must avoid potential sources of pain, injury or death as well as to recognize and to seek situations that maximize the acquisition of food, shelter, mating opportunities and comfort. For most individual animals in the perilous and unforgiving wilds, survival is precarious. Sudden, violent death can occur at almost any moment. The possibility of a lingering death due to disease, injury or starvation is ever present. Survival demands continual alertness as well as unreserved and unremitting physical and mental efforts throughout an animal's waking hours.

The basic physical and processing aspects of an animal's brain and its sensory faculties have had hundreds of millions of years to develop. As a consequence, for every species of animal, they have become almost seamlessly integrated (although some glitches remain and others were created, as shall be discussed.) Perception, sensory transmission as well as cognitive processing by an animal's brain and the resultant control of its bodily functions and overt physical behavior are all effectively coordinated. Survival requires it.

Animal (and Human) Brain Research

In the last half of the twentieth century, researchers have performed neurological experiments using rats, apes and other animals. Many of these experiments consist of stimulating tiny areas of the brain by means of inserting a thin electrode through the skull to touch a specific location in the brain. A small electric charge, delivered via these probes, can stimulate a precise area of the brain. The animals so treated are subjected to certain physical situations or tests. Their behavior is compared to the ordinary behavior of similar animals whose brains are not electrically stimulated. This process is used to infer the functions of the stimulated parts of the brain.

Another technique is to use an electrode to deliver a stronger electrical charge in order to ablate or lesion a specific area of the brain, thus rendering it inoperative. As in the first case, the animals' behaviors are observed and compared to a control group in order to deduce what changes might be associated with the loss of use of the lesioned areas. Recently techniques have been developed using chemicals to make certain specific neurons in the brain sensitive to light so that they can be identified. In this way a thin fiberoptic probe can either stimulate or ablate a single neuron.

Two technological developments toward the end of the twentieth century have greatly aided brain research. The first was the development of very high powered microscopes that could image details of the brain at the cellular level. The other was the development of fMRIs or functional magnetic resonance imaging machines. Using fMRIs the effects of various thinking processes on the brains of humans could be studied without the trauma of invasive surgery. Another, similar modern technology is SPECT or single photon emission computed tomography. SPECT is a tomographic imaging technique that uses gamma rays in order to provide true 3D information in real time. Typically, the 3D information is presented as cross-sectional slices through the brain. The set of images can be reformatted or manipulated electronically as required.

In experiments, human subjects are placed inside the cavity of an fMRI machine and are given various mental tasks to perform. The fMRI device pinpoints the location, timing, extent and intensity of the blood flow activity generated within the subject's brain by the task. The researcher can then associate the nature of the thinking required by the task with the area of the brain shown to 'light up' on the video screen or imaged output of the fMRI. In this way non destructive but limited experiments on humans can be conducted that associate various parts of the brain with various major functions such as sight, hearing, smell or speech. It can even capture the effects of more subtle phenomena such as different sorts of reasoning on problems or reactions to different images.

The fMRI machines effectively measure the small aggregate blood flow associated with by electric charges generated in the brain that 'fire' the neurotransmitter proteins across synapses. By doing so they register the intensity and the location in the brain where the specific thought processes have taken place. The more rapid and the more extensive the firing of neurotransmitter proteins, the more electrical energy that is required. The images produced as output by the fMRI show areas of such greater brain activity as being brighter contrasted with areas of non-activity which are darker.

The results of the procedure are meaningful although indirect. Like the advice of the Oracle at Delphi in ancient Greece, their meanings are not always clear and they depend on the questions asked. Recently[27] for example, on the basis of such brain scans, some researchers were reported to have concluded that people enjoy paying income taxes. fMRI is merely a tool that provides an indirect measurement that is subject to interpretation. It hardly captures the richness and complexity of the thinking process, and it can yield seemingly outlandish results. But the method has also yielded important insights into the operation of the brain and the nature of the thinking process.

The Structure of the Brain

The basic unit of thinking in the human (animal) brain is the neuron or nerve cell. Neurons are all similar in their basic structure but they can differ in configuration and function[28]. Estimates are that there can be as many as two hundred billion neurons in a human brain. According to Michael Craig Miller, "The mind arises from an array of mindlessness, [from] billions of linked [neural] cells, each one alone no smarter than an amoeba."[29] Like all cells, the nucleus of each neuron contains 23 pairs of chromosomes which contain the genome of the individual. The genome comprises approximates twenty to thirty thousand genes of which only two percent are exonic or protein coding genes.

Neurons or nerve cells develop filamentary protrusions called dendrites and another type of protrusion called an axon - as illustrated in the drawing below. The root-like dendrites anchor the neuron in place but their main task is in acting as information conduits into the nerve cell. There can be as many as ten thousand dendrite tips extending from a single neuron. Information from a neural cell is passed to other cells in the brain and to the muscles of the body by means of the other type of neural appendage, the axon. Each neuron has only a single axon but it can reach lengths of several feet as it connects to distant parts of the body via the spinal column. A single axon can have thousands of terminal buttons. Along their length, axons are coated with myelin sheath material which insulates the signal that they carry from the millions of other neurons and axons along their path as they connect to the dendrite of a particular neuron or neurons. Damage to the myelin sheath destroys the neuron's ability to communicate.

There are also estimated to be between two hundred billion and a trillion other non-neural cells in the brain called glial cells or glia that serve as support for neurons. Glia provide nutrition, maintain homeostasis, form myelin and are also theorized to assist in signal transmission in the nervous system[30].

The interior of the human brain contains a number of interacting specialized areas (acting like organs) whose major specialized functions are involved in processing sensations such as sight, hearing, smell and touch, send signals to the muscles initiating behavior and they control autonomic functions such as breathing, and digestion.

Sensations from the environment enter the brain via the eyes, ears, nose and tongue or up the spinal column from the sense of touch etc. Sensations acquired from the environment are converted to neurological activity. For example, sounds, which enter the ear as physical waves, are converted to electric waves and then to biochemical activity as they are processed by neurons in the brain. At the other end of the process, the neurons' biochemical processes produce and transmit electric signals that cause muscles to contract and determine bodily activity. The major route for such neural flow in creating bodily motions in the arms, torso and legs is via the brain stem and down the spinal cord.

The brain's neurons are not physically attached together. Instead neurons communicate by firing proteins across minuscule gaps called synapses from a terminal button of an axon to the tip of a dendrite.

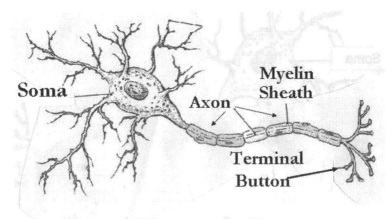

Figure 1. Diagram of a Neuron

DNA codes for the production of one of the many neurotransmitter proteins, enzymes or hormones which carry out distinctive missions in the operations of the brain. Although new neurons can be produced in the brain and axons can grow, especially in young children, the main mechanisms for thought processes in adults occur due to the variations of transmission of neurotransmitter proteins across synapses in neural networks.

Thought data in neurochemical form is transmitted from one of the thousands of terminal buttons of an axon of one cell to the tip of a dendrite of another cell. Estimates are that the two hundred billion, or so, nerve cells in the brain with their estimated 500 trillion to quadrillion synapse connections can require up to 6 - 12 watts of peak electrical energy to power electric pulses across the neurons and to drive protein molecules across synapse gaps between the axons of neurons and the dendrites of others in the brain.

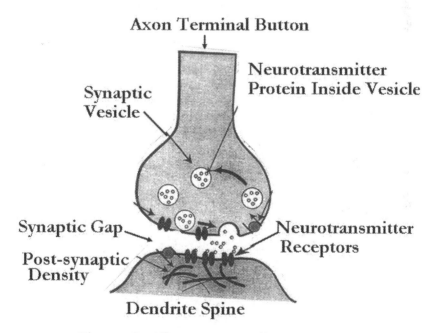

Figure 2. Diagram of a Synapse

When an electric charge causes a neurotransmitter protein to burst out of a synaptic vesicle at the tip of an axon, it enters the fluid in the synapse gap. The dendrite (at the bottom of figure 2) has receptors that 'key' for particular proteins. If the protein fits the particular receptor it is absorbed into the dendrite and initiates a reaction that generates a very tiny electrical current. In wavelike fashion the current travels across the neuron toward the axon. As it travels it weakens so that it may peter out before it reaches the base of the axon. Where there have been many and/or rapid proteins received at the tip of a dendrite a stronger current is generated and it is more likely that it will reach the base of the axon.

Once the electric current has moved down the dendrite across the neuron to the base of the neuron's axon it encounters another biological device called a 'hillock'. This hillock has a degree of sensitivity to electrical currents and acts as a kind of a toggle switch. Some hillocks will allow a small neural current to trigger a current that flashes down the axon to its tips while other, less sensitive, hillocks require greater electric force before they initiate transmission. Once the hillock is toggled, the electric current zips down the axon to its tips or terminal buttons where it pushes neurotransmitter proteins to break out of their vesicles and enter a synaptic gap opposite the dendrite of some other neuron. If there is a match between the protein fired from an axon and a dendrite receptor, the process starts all over again in the receiving neuron.

There are a number of subordinate processes by which cells can become more easily excited or sensitive or to neurotransmitters. For example creatures exposed to risky situations release more adrenalin which heightens the flight or fight response of the amygdala of the brain. With continual exposure to danger the amygdala becomes more sensitive to small amounts of adrenalin. But, beyond a certain point however, more adrenalin can lose its stimulative effect.

The neurotransmitter chain reactions traveling over networks of many millions of nerve cells occur in the order of milliseconds (as compared with microsecond execution of instructions in an electronic computer.). At the start of a chain of a neurological transmission there are hundreds of millions of potential pathways that neurotransmitter proteins might take. The process by which an initial stimulus to a given neuron sets off the transmission along one selected pathway and then branches across associated neurons has yet to be fully understood.

Chemicals, classified as proteins, enzymes and hormones, which are used as neurotransmitters in mental processes and which determine their functions, include: dopamine, serotonin, cortisol, glutamic acid, gamma aminobutyric acid, acetylcholine and many others. The total number of neurotransmitter proteins is in some dispute but is estimated to be between twenty four and one hundred.

At the level of neurons and synapses, mental processes are dependent on a large number of factors. One or more of dozens of neurotransmitters in a thought circuit can fire into millions of synapses along millions of neural paths simultaneously. Such an arrangement provides for the brain's rapid processing of complex phenomena in a parallel fashion. To compound the complexity of the way the brain processes information, different dendrite receptors may accept only certain types of neurotransmitters proteins. Further, the effect of a given neurotransmitter protein in one area of the brain may be very different than its effect in another area of the brain. Since not all proteins are used by a given nerve cell or network, it greatly increases the possible permutations and combinations of the process.

Surrounding the interior area organs of the brain, butting up against the skull wall, is crinkled gray matter, called the cerebral cortex, as depicted below. If unfolded and laid flat, the cortex of the human brain would be equivalent to a sheet covering a 3 foot by 5 foot table top. Gray matter cortex is commonly found in most animals but it is most extensive in primates and especially in humans. In addition, the frontal area, called the neocortex or prefrontal cortex of the human brain is much larger and more developed as compared to our ape cousins. It is this prefrontal cortex region of the brain that has been experimentally determined to be implicated in judgment, decision-making, planning, complex cognitive behaviors, personality expression, and moderating correct social behavior as well as in deterring antisocial and inappropriate behavior.

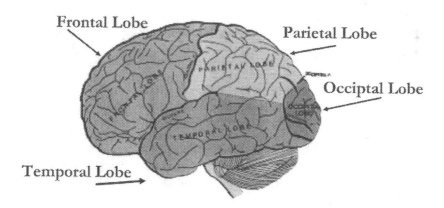

Figure 3. Areas of the Cerebral Cortex.

The Effects of Experience

fMRI studies indicate that changes to the brain's neural networks as a result of frequent repetition of particular activities are semi-permanent.

That is, they remain until changed by some subsequent activity. In fMRI studies, for example, when an individual plays the piano, certain areas of the brain consistently light up and these areas therefore can be associated with the activity of piano playing. This reflects a situation where piano playing activity generates the firing of neurotransmitter proteins by axons and they lock into dendrite receptors of neurons. The more one continues to study, practice and to play the piano the larger these 'lit up' areas become. This is a permanent change in involvement of more of a brain's neurons which roughly parallels increased involvement and ability in piano playing, over time. Similar effects can be shown for meditation, chess, bridge or other endeavors that require significant physical or intellectual development and skill, for proficiency

This type of 'brain plasticity' effect, as D.O. Hebb predicted in the 1950's, is logical. The performance of any behavior requires brain activity in various neural networks. The more difficult or complex the task, and the more often it is encountered, the greater is the neural involvement. Repeating the particular behavior in slightly different circumstances or contexts involves extending neural network activity because new factors are involved. The greater the perceived significance of a behavior, the more often it is used or repeated, the more neural involvement there will be each time it is executed. This is the mechanism of learning and remembering.

fMRI studies of beginners and of veteran professional musicians clearly indicate that even though the tyro may seem to struggle more with the activity, the area of the brain associated with piano playing that lights up for a veteran musician playing a piece on a piano is more extensive than the area lit up for a novice when they play the same piece of music. A significant amount of such experimentation has been done by Andrew Newburg with respect to meditation[31.] As in the case of the musicians, Buddhist monks who have seriously practiced meditation for many years produce far greater areas of their brain that light up to that activity than neophytes. When veteran Buddhist meditators focused on different emotions, different areas of the brain lit up. Journeymen meditators achieved a higher level of mediation and induced greater brain activity which persisted after a session.

A given routine behavior such as the physical coordination required to, say, put on our shoes and tie the laces becomes second nature, its execution highly efficient and it becomes an activity we can perform at the preconscious level so that it does not extend neural networks unless some unusual event occurs that is associated with it. This provides for great efficiency with regard to routine tasks. Such ability greatly enabled the survival of many thousands of predecessor species.

All behavior originates from biochemical brain activity. In circular fashion, behavior can also result in changes to the production of hormones that result in changes to brain circuitry. Post traumatic stress disorder is one of the more extreme examples of permanent changes to the production and use of neurotransmitters that can result from severe external conditions and reactive behavior.

In addition to functional activities, which are necessary for survival, there are activities that relate to entertainment and amusement that only indirectly can be regarded as functional. Human children as well as young animals have been observed engaged in playful activities with their fellows. Evolutionary biologists have argued that for Paleolithic humans, earlier hominids and other anthropoids such activities work to socialize the youngsters and provide preparation or support for various important functional group activities at a later date. That is, such activity helps to train brain circuits that will be useful in adulthood. Playful combat among youngsters not only develops them physically but also establishes brain circuitry that will provide them with physical and mental skills that prepare them for contests with other males for mates as well as coordination in hunting when they mature. Among young human children, social play has been demonstrated to greatly enhance social skills which will be important in adulthood. Such frivolous activities among the young serve to strengthen, group cohesiveness and bonding or reciprocal attachment among adults.

Memory and Neural Networks

Until recently it was assumed that each separate memory was somehow represented in the settings of a finite group of neurons located somewhere in a given area of the cerebral cortex. Efforts were expended in attempting to match learned facts to their brain locations. Human biological memory was regarded as analogous to a filing cabinet or to a computer's memory. Data can be retrieved verbatim from the address of the spots where it is stored. Complex reports can be assembled by the retrieval and assembly of discrete data from many known addresses (locations) in a computer's memory, transforming and integrating them into human readable or useful form.

To the contrary, as Karim Nadir was able to demonstrate, as intuitive and appealing as conceiving of such memory storage and retrieval processes might seem, it is not the way biological memory works. Composite memories do not exist intact or as discrete scenarios in the brain. Rather they are reconstructed by means of neural associations as they are needed and recalled.

Biological memory is composed of complex networks of many millions of neuronal connections that are associated according to many aspects of some experiential reality. Memory retrieval starts with the trigger of a single neuron that then flashes along neural pathways branching in ways that are dependent on established neural connections or associations. These chains of neural activity continue through a network until a memory is formed. In this way the memory is not so much retrieved from a specific location as it is reconstructed from millions of associated or connected neurons that might be located at somewhat separate areas of the midbrain or the cerebral cortex. Some of the involved neurons may be in the limbic system as newly formed from current sensory experiences. The same neuron that is involved in a given memory might also be involved in other memories.

The neurons associated with elements of chance events that are regarded as similar to those that have occurred most often in the past, or those that are regarded as most important, will come to be more easily excited in future. Thus, the most likely neurons to be triggered are associated with those events that happened most recently or those primal events that are deemed most critical as well as those that have been triggered most often in the past because they are the most salient or the most likely to apply in a particular situation.

Actions, whose associated outcome events, tend to increase pleasure or obviate pain will be repeated as appropriate. In this way, over time, as an animal survives and has many experiences, certain neural pathways that are most beneficial will be most frequently used. They will become most prone to excitation and along pathways of neurons in the neural network that are most readily traced when one of the associated neurons is triggered. It is a self- reinforcing cycle as over time chained paths, through the neural networks that are most beneficial, become most prominent and the triggering neurons all along those pathways become most sensitive. These neurons become most likely to become part of a neural pathway chain reaction that produces beneficial behavior. The implementation of support or associated behaviors will also become practiced and effective

Where Does Belief Reside in the Brain?

Human behavior is not always based on deliberative or even reflexive responses to environmental stimuli. It can be a result of conscious self-stimulation. An important element in forming intent and initiating deliberative behavior is the memory of past experiences. Human memory is represented in the brain by particular patterns of millions of networked neurons that are 'loaded' with various neurotransmitter proteins. These neurotransmitters are in vesicles at the terminals of axons. They represent potential memories rather than actual memories. When fired, neurotransmitters fit into corresponding dendrite receptors across the synaptic gap between the axon terminal and dendrite tip. The neuron is excited and sends an electric pulse to its axon where the process is repeated.

Neural memories are not eidetic, that is, they are not discrete, faithful representations of particular events that have been experienced in the past. Rather they constitute associations of sensations that are linked to, and conflated with, neural loadings of current and past events that are themselves products or settings of brain circuits remaining from past experiences. In general, the more familiar one is with the same or similar events or objects, the more the detail that will be remembered because the more neurotransmitter proteins and neurological circuits that will be involved with the patterns of the events.

Experiences and the interpretation of experiences can change the loadings and configurations of the neurons along neural pathways and in consequence the likelihood that they will be triggered and then trigger a chain reaction with respect to particular events. Therefore, unless conditions are stringently controlled, as B.F. Skinner attempted to do, different individuals will respond more or less differently to almost any given stimulus or each of a series of nominally similar stimuli. The same person may not respond exactly the same way to what seems to be a similar stimulus, especially if a significant time has passed between stimuli. The balance between reflexive stimulus/ response and adaptational response is critical to survival.

Experiments have shown that if pictures of a monkey, a banana, and a panda are presented to Japanese and British subjects, the majority of Japanese will say that they believe that the monkey and banana are most similar while most British will say that they believe the monkey and the panda are most similar. It seems that association memories of functional relationships are the most salient to Japanese, that is, monkeys eat bananas. The British by contrast will key in on the fact that the monkey and the panda are both mammals[32]. This tendency is an example of the flexibility of unconscious neuronal 'brain 'wiring', which is the result of unconscious conditioned learning and the nature of belief construction.

Belief involves output from various neural networks that results from some historical procession of experiential stimuli. Just as memories are a reconstruction of past experiences, beliefs have no coherent physical manifestation in the brain but rather are reconstituted and applied in the context of a given situation at hand. Belief is an interpretive function of: the memory of past experiences: cognitive and emotional analyses of past experience and consequential expectations about the future. Values are generalized beliefs.

In this view, belief is a composite of several, to many associated memories combined with learned or experiential values, that is, emotional valences. Belief is to memory somewhat as information is often considered to relate to data. As neutral data and combinations of data can have different interpretations, i.e. information, depends on some context. Chains of association of axons and dendrites in the cortex of brain may yield variations of beliefs that are articulated as they relate to some current context being experienced. Beliefs are conditioned by an emotional valence with respect to short term and long term benefits and detriments to the individual. The more extensive and intensive the neural associations of a belief structure, the stronger the emergence of the belief in various situations and the more potent its effects on behavior.

Despite religious assertions of a set of timeless, immutable and unconditional religious beliefs, even core beliefs and values are, and need to be, customized to current situations that do not exactly fit prior models. Even strongly held beliefs can be rationalized or modified so that they can be applied in different contexts or similar, but not identical, circumstances. General beliefs are important for survival in that they are suppositions, based on experience, of how matters came about, how objects, events, processes and states relate in space, time and function and what is likely to happen under various future circumstances. Religious beliefs can also be important to welfare as presumed intermediates that are used in developing more functional beliefs.

CHAPTER FOUR

The Relationships Between Thought And Language

The Power Conferred by Language

Whatever the prevailing environment was that fostered the development of symbolic natural language among *Homo sapiens*, language was clearly very advantageous. The development of language in one, or possibly a few, species of speechless hominids remains mysterious. Innate grammar and syntax may have developed quickly, within a few generations, after some genotype adaptation, or it may have taken thousands of years. Language as it presently exists required many biological adaptations that developed over hundreds of thousands of years, but conceivably, after some critical tipping point, it flowered and catapulted *Homo sapiens* to dominance in a very brief time span—between twenty thousand and seventy thousand years. Language has also provided the critical platform on which religion developed. The symbologist Ernst Cassirer contended that, without language, religion as we know it would not and could not exist.

We humans are unique in our prodigious abilities to make extensive functional use of sophisticated symbolic or natural language. Language has powers beyond its utilitarian, communication functions. The psychological effects of language go well beyond simple functional communication among individuals. Beyond its fundamental applications in the service of survival, one of the major uses of language has always been in creating and telling stories.

From the time of late–Stone Age cavemen to the modern era, people's fascination with stories, and recently novels and movies, goes well beyond any practical uses of their content. Listening to stories can be an emotional experience. People are mesmerized by spellbinding preachers or actors. Many people are in thrall to written scripture regardless of whether it is written in archaic language and its meanings are outdated, unclear, illogical, or even contradictory. It doesn't matter. Even in cases where it is known and obvious that translators have, for various reasons, altered the text and the meaning of scripture so that it is not faithful to the original, the translation itself is generally considered to be sacred. The language in scripture is not only susceptible to misinterpretation but also often calculatedly ambiguous and designed to encourage readers to adopt a wide variety of interpretations—many of which are at odds or contradictory. Importantly, rather than undermining its credibility and validity, it seems that inscrutable language is one of the strengths of scripture. Such a phenomenon requires explanation.

The Beginnings of Speech

Noam Chomsky, one of the pioneers of academic linguistic studies, has declared that language ability, including grammar and syntax, is physically embedded as part of a deep structure of every human brain at birth. Steven Pinker, currently a major researcher in the field, does not go as far as Chomsky. Nonetheless, he does declare, in his book *The Language Instinct*, that a predisosition to language is innate.

If a child for some reason does not learn to speak (or to use sign language) by the age of eleven, he or she will never be able to learn to speak or sign properly and fluently. Those who learn a new language after the age of ten or twelve will likely have a lifelong accent in the new language no matter how fluent they become. fMRI studies confirm that second languages learned later in life excite a different area of the brain than do languages learned early in life.

Why does the ability to informally acquire language peak before the age of five or six and then fade after eleven? Genetic factors are no doubt involved. The original adaptations had their origins hundreds of thousands or millions of years ago. Development of natural language in the form of speech was accompanied, over eons of development, by genetic mutations and phenotype changes that altered the structures of the human larynx, mouth, nose, and brain.

The Progression of Evolutionary Adaptation

By definition, the nature of evolutionary adaptations, such as the finches' bills that were observed by Charles Darwin, are adaptive changes to an existing phenotype. Need dictates adaptation in the sense that some stochastic phenotype variations and random genetic mutations are beneficial while others are disadvantageous. Those that are beneficial result in a higher proportion of offspring that survive and thus their genes are inherited and spread over the succeeding generations of a species. Those changes that are deleterious may result in death before maturity or limit progeny because of adverse sexual selection, infertility, or pathological behavior by the individuals who have inherited them. Their genetic lineage is truncated within a few generations. Major changes take place by means of incremental progressive adaptations to phenotypes over many, many generations. These often follow tortuous paths and most often end in blind alleys of extinction because past changes, which cannot be undone and become maladaptive as environments change.

Though minor stochastic changes do occur regularly in chromosomes, there are never global or comprehensive overhauls to the genotype and phenotype of creatures that occur in a single step. As Gregor Mendel noted, the vast array of inherited traits are inherited independently of the others. Reptiles don't suddenly become birds. Natural selection tends to preserve the vast majority of genetic traits that have proven successful for survival in the past. Subsequent adaptations are constrained and shaped by the nature of the preexisting traits and the sequence of prior adaptations.[33]

Together with the slow pace of evolution, such progressive incrementalism serves to produce an almost (but not completely) seamless integration with regard to a long sequence of adaptations. In the short run, the vast majority of phenotype traits continue to operate much as before an incremental adaptation. Beneficial physical and mental attributes that support abilities and survival strategies are honed over hundreds or thousands of years. These positive traits tend to be conserved, with enhancements imparted by further adaptations as the environment changes. Sometimes, however, adaptations that ameliorate one aspect of a harsh new environment prove to be an Achilles' heel with respect to other factors or later environmental changes, and so they serve to hasten the extinction of a species. It is an infinitely complex byzantine process

Genetically derived mutations that are incompatible with established phenotype traits invariably result in the birth of individuals that are not likely to survive. Some organs and functions atrophy over many generations of disuse. In the main, however, especially in the nearer term, evolution tends to be an additive process, as those physical attributes and abilities that have been useful for survival in the past are built upon and their uses extended. By this logic, natural language, too, was an addition that was superimposed over the established mental or thought processes of the languageless hominid species in which it developed.

Though a rudimentary language facility was superimposed on the primeval animal thought processes of hominids, they nonetheless continued to think, reason, and form beliefs nonverbally, as other animals do. As is obvious from surgical experiments, microscopic examination, and fMRI studies, speech and the use of symbolic language has not radically changed the biology of the brain. It does not eliminate or even displace nonverbal thought processes. As with other evolutionary adaptations, language is a supplement to primal processes that were in place before the development of language. In this sense, declarative language can be said to be built over or grafted onto the preexisting thought processes that are carried out by means of the operations of neural networks in the brains of animals and humans. Just as the amygdala (which first evolved in reptiles hundreds of millions of years ago) remains a vital part of modern human thought processes, some of which are critical for survival, so too does nonverbal thought remain vital. Languageless thought continues to operate and drive behavior. Importantly, and paradoxically, such "animal" thought can generate behavior that is semi-independent of deliberative language-based decisions and actions.

It is also in the nature of evolutionary adaptation that there can be many paths to a similar outcome. Animals and birds that outwardly resemble each other in appearance and behavior may have started out as very different progenitor species. Many of the adaptations that increase probabilities of survival relative to some particular environmental threat also have other significant properties that affect the lifestyle or culture of animals. The ability to climb trees with alacrity combined with inelegance in running on flat ground doubtlessly had many major effects on anthropoid lifestyles. Coincident outcomes and concurrent properties of adaptations may result in either advantages or disadvantages relative to less-critical threats or opportunities in the short run. Whether or not an opposable thumb originally evolved to assist in grabbing fruits and nuts from high branches or for carrying food to females, over the millennia it has been put to innumerable other practical uses, such as writing. Whatever the origin or purpose of humans having ten fingers, it later determined the base of the number system.

Sometimes adaptations that enhance survival in one area have harmful effects in another. Constructive adaptations can become negative factors that serve to reduce survival probabilities. The development of an upright stance, resulting from bipedalism, pitched the hominid spine in an unnatural position. This has resulted in painful and chronic back problems for many humans as well as difficulties in the coordination of breathing and swallowing simultaneously. To this day about three thousand people a year die by choking on their food, thanks to the adaptational developments of upright stance and changes in the esophagus to accommodate language. It has also been argued that the biological changes necessary for speech weakened the jaw muscles of *Homo sapiens* from that of predecessor hominid and ape species. This diminished their physical offensive and defensive capabilities, although not to the extent that the survival benefits of speech were offset.

Symbolic language developed as a highly effective survival tool. The brain's basic neurological processes for receiving sensory perceptions, and the resultant neural processes involved in cognition, are roughly similar for all higher animals. Yet until now no other animal species has evolved, or, presumably, has needed to evolve, the incredibly advantageous ability to spontaneously learn, and to extensively use, natural symbolic language in intraspecies communication.

Manufactured tools as well as physical adaptations have inherent properties that often enable the extension of their basic functional uses. The discovery that stones could be hurled to drive off predators or to disable prey improved survival in the short run. Over many generations it brought about anatomical changes to the design of the hominid shoulder that facilitated overhand throwing. These changes may have improved throwing ability, but they also made the shoulder more susceptible to rotator cuff injury and reduced a hominid's ability to climb trees and swing from vines. Later on, hominids also learned to sharpen stones so that the stones became more lethal. This led to new uses for them, such as cutting meat and scraping skins. In this way biology instigates and enables tool use, which in turn affects lifestyle and culture, which further affects tool development and use, and in the long run, circularly, can affect biology.

A Computer Analogy

FMRI images show consistent activity in the human brain at the cellular or electrochemical level in response to declarative language, whether heard, spoken, or merely thought. An illustrative albeit imperfect analogy comparing the relationship of declarative language thought processing to nonverbal neurological thought processing is the relationship between computer programming languages and computer machine language.[34]

In order for computers to run and to process data, higher-level computer programming languages, such as BASIC or COBOL, which are necessary for human programmers, must be translated into the patterns of pulses, or square waves of high and low voltages, which constitute the "machine language" that internally directs the operations of computers. Similarly, if our so-called native thought is mediated by electrochemical neurological processes, then what we perceive as our inner thoughts in the form of declarative language must inevitably be transformed or translated into patterns of electrical pulses and neurotransmitter proteins flowing through the neural networks of our brains. Like electrons in a computer, these electric pulses that drive messenger protein molecules must course and back and forth again in the neural networks of the brain with regard to the process of thought. It is analogous to the computer's translation of higher language into the electical pulses of binary machine code for processing and then back to natural language or arabic numerals for an on-screen readout or a printout.

A major difference between the two processes is that the computer translates code once for input and then again for output. Internal processing takes place entirely in machine code without transformation until output is required. By contrast, received verbal language or internal monologue requires the brain to translate back and forth from its neurological systems to its declarative language systems continuously. Continuous transformation from verbal representations to electrochemical, biological processes and back requires, in effect, enormous biological computing power, which slows the operations of verbal thought. Biological transmissions across the neural networks of the brain occur in milliseconds, while the basic operations of the computer occur in microseconds. The brain, however, can overcome this huge speed disadvantage in various ways so that, in many respects, it is a superior language processor.

Language and the Senses

Natural language requires an existing primary sensory carrier such as audio or visual systems of the brain. Speech, for example, is perceived just as other sounds—in the form of vibrations that enter the ear and are transformed to electrochemical processes in the brain. Writing is perceived visually by means of images formed on the macula, at the back of the eyeball, and transmitted via the optic nerve to the visual cortex and other areas of the brain, where it is also transformed for electrochemical processes.

The interpretation of language sound in the brain does not result, as do other sounds and sights, with straightforward biological reactions to the raw nature of the sensations themselves. Broca's and Wernicke's areas of the brain have been shown to be dedicated to further processing perceived language sounds. Language cognition involves a more nuanced, secondary analysis of the particular sound patterns or sights in the brain. If this were not the case, there would be no equivalence between language transmitted by sound and received by hearing and language transmitted by light and received by sight. Parsing of syntax and prosody, the intricate patterns and nuances of sounds, in order to render them the biochemical equivalent of declarative language, requires a great deal more brainpower than simply interpreting the raw sounds in nature.

FMRI studies confirm that coding and decoding oral language in the brain engages a great deal more of the brain's "real estate" and takes far longer than does the mental processing of raw sounds, such as thunder or the roar of a nearby lion, or sights, such as the sudden lunge of a snake. Our basic sensory processes were developed over hundreds of millions of years. Sounds critical for the survival of animals and early homonids are processed very efficiently. Production of raw sounds for intraspecies communication also developed over millions of years. But, protolanguages leading to declarative language speculatively developed more recently, over hundreds of thousands of years. Finally, modern natural symbolic language is estimated to have existed for only tens of thousands of years—relatively few. The course of the development of modern natural language, unique to humans, remains largely a mystery.

Our native ability to discriminate among the finer details of most things seen is, in general, relatively modest. For example, if asked to discriminate among the facial features of several unfamiliar dogs of a given breed and of similar size and color, or two fir trees of similar height, unless we have had special training, our descriptions will be very general and superficial.[35] However, humans have developed neural organization to support an ability to quickly discriminate among hundreds of different human faces that are only subtly different with respect to the sizes, colors, and gross placement of features. Even more spectacularly, as a result of the evolution of a high density of sensors at a spot on the retina called the fovea, along with other developments in neural organization, the human species has developed the ability to discriminate among tiny letters and sequences of written letters Even though they initially may be cursive, printed, of different sizes and colors, or even distorted variations of what we are used to.

Without specialized training we do not have the ability to recognize, describe, or differentiate the subtle differences among thunderclaps, similar odors, color shades, and other natural phenomena. However, when it comes to speech, human powers of discrimination are amazing. We can interpret and process the speech of a wide variety of speakers with different voice characteristics and accents. We can remember verbatim in working memory much spoken communication for a considerable time and the gist of a verbal communication for a much longer time. In the case of the Chinese language, words whose meanings rely on the subtleties of the tone of voice and that are spoken by a wide range of speakers can be routinely learned by children. These exceptional powers of discrimination and memory with respect to language are routinely and spontaneously acquired by the very young.

Humans have a facility for readily adding new words to language, using the same word to mean different things in context, and making up new localized languages. Subgroups of humans create special jargons on the fly. Informal youth gangs routinely devise peculiar expressions for their own internal use. Individuals who speak different languages, if thrown together in relative isolation, will in short order invent a new pidgin language with which to communicate. If the group remains stable, they will then go on to develop a creole language with a standardized grammar and syntax within two or three generations.

Two Different Modes of Thought

Language—originally a highly effective mode of functional communication—has, over many generations, changed the nature of human thought. Language is perceived just as other ordinary sound—in the form of vibrations, or analog signals. As with all animals, it must be transformed to neurochemical thought processes. Of course, all processes of thought are integrated in the brain, but for purposes of explication they can be thought of as being of two different types. Language sounds must be received and transformed into neurological effects, as with other mammals. For humans such neurological effects must be further processed into "language-mediated thought" (LMT) in the brain. Two areas of the brain, Broca's area and Wernicke's area, have been identified by fMRI studies to be significantly involved in the transformation of speech to neurological thought.

Just as opposable thumbs and the use of hand axes led to extensions of old activities, and to entirely new types of physical activities, the properties of language extend rudimentary native thought processes of animals. It is by means of symbolic language that the human mind can conceive of metaphors, abstractions, recursive thinking, and metacognition. Language greatly enhances the ability to categorize discrete memories sequentially. These functions are all beyond the limitations of the native neurological thought processes and associative memory of languageless animals.

The two modes of thought processing generally, but not always, work in tandem. An emotion or decision that is generated by neurological thought may be expressed and communicated to others by means of declarative language. Conversely, declarative language may give rise to emotion or convey metalanguage that stimulates preconscious thinking and emotion in ways that are not apparent from its overt content.

An enabling aspect of language communication is that language also provides a vehicle for efficient "time shifting" with respect to explicitly remembering the specific nature and sequence of events that have occurred in the past. By contrast, the associative nature of neurological thought processes tends to blend prior events by their salient associations, blurring the sequence or the time of occurrence. As memories fade, their less salient aspects or associations are forgotten first. The more critical or important factors linger. Language-mediated thinking enables the recall of discrete memories whose time of occurrence and sequence tend to be preserved for a time. In this way declarative language enables thinking about and planning for the nature and sequence of events that are to come as well.

Like other tools, such as the use of hand axes, whose nature or properties must be physically accommodated for optimal usefulness, there is a downside to language. There are important disjunctions, mismatches, and discontinuities that mar the seamless integration of the complementary operations of basic neurological thought and language-mediated thought processes.

The Relationship Between Thinking and Thought

Speech, or external declarative language, can also be manifested as internal self-talk or conscious thinking. It is clear though that, despite a facility for declarative language and conscious verbal thought, much human thinking also occurs without self-talk in the preconscious neurocircuitry of the brain. Thinking occurs in humans in a manner that is similar to that found in other higher mammals.

In the past, language-mediated conscious thinking was regarded as rational while languageless unconscious thought was regarded as emotional and irrational. To the contrary, modern neuroscientists consider that subconscious thought, formerly referred to as implicit or emotional thought, can be rational. Implicit nonverbal thought determines much of our daily functional behavior.

In *A Theory of Unconscious Thought*,[36] Dijksterhuis and Nordgren have proposed six principles of unconscious (nonverbal) thought as follows: [37]

1. There are two modes of thought, unconscious and conscious. Both of these modes are used depending on circumstances.

2. Conscious thought is constrained by the low capacity of consciousness. Unconscious thought does not have this constraint. [The authors cite studies that estimate the bandwidth of conscious thought (verbal internal monologues) as equivalent to between 10 and 60 bits per second, while the bandwidth of unconscious thought is estimated as equivalent to about 11,200,000 bits per second.]

3. Unconscious thought works bottom up or aschematically while consciousness works top down or schematically. Conscious thought is guided by expectancies and schemas and prone to stereotyping [deductive emphasis] while unconscious thought is guided by experience [inductive emphasis].

4. The unconscious naturally weighs the relative importance of various attributes. Conscious thought [does not, and] often disturbs this natural process.

5. Conscious thought can follow strict rules and is precise whereas unconscious thought gives rough estimates.

6. Conscious thought, and memory search during conscious thought, is focused and convergent. Unconscious thought is more divergent.

A significant advantage of unconscious or neurological thought is speed. The brain receives, processes, and interprets sights and sounds in milliseconds. Even at these speeds, declarative, language-mediated thought (LMT) may take seconds or more to fully develop. We are all familiar with some person who laughs minutes after a joke has been told because he has just gotten it. This is evidence that innate neurological thought processes (INP) were working furiously in the background of his mind until the humor of the joke was determined. In part this is because of the linearity of language and language-mediated thoughts, while processes of neurological thought can be construed as operating in a manner analogous to the random-access parallel processing of computers. Words must be spoken in sequence, one after another, often in long, complex sequences. Individual words can have more than one meaning or subtle shades of contextual meaning. The particular meaning of a word in a phrase may depend on the verbal syntax, tone of voice, facial expression, and gestures used by the speaker, as well as the environmental context of a statement.

The contextual meaning of a word or phrase can turn on another word or inflection that may be either at the end or at the beginning of a sequence of words or phrases. The sentence, "It would be a shame for anything bad to happen to your beautiful children," can take on a very different meaning if spoken by a Mafia don rather than an insurance salesman or your mother-in-law. This puts a burden on working memory to remember and analyze an entire chunk of spoken prose where the meaning of elements (words or phrases) may depend on other parts of the chunk and even on other chunks not in working memory that were heard minutes earlier, that will be heard minutes later, or that depend on an analysis of the situational context in which the words are heard.

The Unconscious, Subconscious, and Preconscious

Sigmund Freud hypothesized unconscious thought processes. But what he called the subconscious, composed of id, ego, and superego, was largely a negative force believed capable of creating psychological problems and dysfunctional behavior at the conscious level. For Freud, traumatic events and desires that are socially unacceptable are repressed from consciousness but nonetheless tend surreptitiously to affect behavior in dysfunctional ways. Dijksterhuis and Nordgren's concept of the unconscious and my ideas about nondeclarative or preconscious thought are a different concept in that they form a large portion of the normal thought processes that are routinely and continuously used in everybody's normal daily life. For the most part, such preconscious thoughts are positive and necessary even though they may, at times, be the source of problems.

A most intriguing question is the correspondence between conscious verbal thought and unconscious, neurological thought. Dijksterhuis and Nordgren define conscious thought as thought with awareness, while unconscious thought as thought without awareness. The two modes of thought are not always in harmony. They diverge without causing mental confusion. By definition we are not aware of our preconscious thoughts or thought processes that are carried on without verbal self-talk. However, it has been estimated that over 80 percent of our day is spent negotiating our way around in our very complex environments quite adequately without conscious self-talk directing our actions.[38] This state can hardly be described as being truly unconscious or unaware.

We typically drive our cars on what has been characterized as autopilot when traveling familiar routes. We steer the auto in traffic, accelerate, decelerate, signal a turn, change lanes in traffic, and brake all without verbal thinking or self-talk. It is misleading or at least imprecise to say that the thinking behind such sophisticated behavior is unconscious in the sense that we are oblivious to or completely unaware of it.

When something out of the ordinary happens during autopilot behavior, we can immediately shift into an internal monologue or dialogue with others to share the experience. Under many circumstances, including during hypnosis, subjects are able to remember and to verbalize events, statements, or written words that they experienced while engaged in a distracting nonverbal activity. The autopilot state may be nonverbal, but it is not unconscious in the sense of a total lack of awareness, like breathing or digestion. Under Dijksterhuis and Nordgren's hypothesis then, driving a car (provided we are not distracted by performing some other task at the same time) will be a manifestation of conscious but nonverbal thought. It does not involve declarative language or verbalizations. It seems to me that such nonlanguage autopilot thinking is best described as preconscious, rather than unconscious, thought. The use of the word subconscious might be appropriate, but this would confuse it with the Freudian subconscious.

I experienced a minor example of the divergence between the two modes of thought. Several years ago I attempted to make a left turn at an intersection on a busy highway in an unfamiliar city. My view of oncoming traffic was partially obscured by cars lined up in the oncoming left turn lane. When the light turned green, I hurriedly began a left turn. The driver of an oncoming car, who did not have to stop for the light, and who I had not seen because of the oncoming cars in the left turn lane, was unable to stop, and his car hit my vehicle. It was not a major accident (though you couldn't tell by the cost of repairs), and I was able to drive away. However, for the next two years I found myself hesitating for an inordinately long time before turning left from a side street onto a main street. While waiting, I would tell myself that there were breaks in traffic that were easily of sufficient length to make the turn. Before the accident I would not have hesitated to use such breaks to complete a left turn safely. Still, I hesitated. The hesitation and unease in making left turns into traffic gradually faded, but it took a long time.

Categories of Thought

I propose three useful categories of thought: declarative conscious, which is language-oriented thought, either spoken or internal; preconscious or nondeclarative-language thought, which is characterized by awareness but without language; and finally; truly unconscious thought, where there is no awareness at all. In nondeclarative preconscious thought, a person is able to recall perceptions of objects or events and, after the fact, apply language to describe, explain, or rationalize them if called on to do so shortly after the event. After a minor automobile accident, we can verbally reconstruct much of what occurred immediately before the crash even though there had been no pertinent self-talk or analysis prior to the crash. Most preconscious thought is not transferred to long-term memory and is lost to declarative memory after a short while.

By contrast, without preconscious thought a person may make inferences about her thought processes based on outcomes or observations, but these are not memories. For example, in the case of the auto accident used above, a person may note the damage and the skid marks and make other observations. Based on these after-the-fact observations, she may say, for example, that the other person must have run a red light. But this is merely self-serving conjecture, not declarative memory. She has no way of reconstituting the actual events from short-term memory with respect to her firsthand coherent descriptions. The third level, unconscious thought, is also the basis of autonomic functions like blushing or sweating when nervous, most implicit first impressions of others, reflexive behaviors, and compulsions, such as the hand washing of those with obsessive-compulsive disorder.

In the preconscious state, many actions are taken that originate from explicit albeit nonverbal internal decisions. These are made on the basis of sense data acquired in real time, using reasoning and memory processes that are not verbalized. In his book *Blink*, Malcolm Gladwell advocates, in some cases, minimizing verbal, conscious distractions so that the mind is free to make decisions on an intuitive (i.e., preconscious) level. His argument, consistent with Dijksterhuis and Nordgren's theory, is that such intuitive decisions can cut through the obfuscation and the dithering that are introduced by verbal deliberations. The results of the intuitive decision-making process, Gladwell asserts, are not only far quicker, but they also generally provide for superior decisions or solutions, since they naturally weigh the relative importance of various attributes from the point of view of self-interest. It should be noted, however, that such is not always the case, and that, in many cases, deliberative conscious decisions are superior.

Preconscious Thought and Decisions

Dijksterhuis and Nordgren experiment with their unconscious thought theory in various decision-making situations in order to demonstrate that the human brain automatically uses a combination of both unconscious (preconscious) and conscious processes in rational decision making. Each is used to a different extent depending on whether the decision to be made is a simple matter of "satisficing" or a complex selection among alternatives with multiple ordinal factors or hard-to-measure attributes.[39] The authors, however, do not discuss the extent, if any, to which their two modes of thinking can combine or, alternatively, can perform as substitutes for each other in some given situation, even if not as effectively. They do not examine circumstances where conflicts exist between the two modes or, therefore, how such conflicts are resolved by the brain. Is there an ideal mix of conscious and unconscious (preconscious) thought in a particular circumstance, given their assertion that the two modes are both used in decision making?

The implication of Dijksterhuis and Nordgren's work is clear. Preconscious (unconscious) innate neurological processes of thought are capable, in many situations, of supporting rational decisions. Nonverbal preconscious thinking is a very large proportion of the normal, day-to-day thought processes of most humans. Furthermore, and significantly, it is not unreasonable to posit that such preconscious nonlanguage thought in humans is not dissimilar to the thought and reasoning processes of other higher animals that do not use spoken, natural language.

Religious belief and behavior are driven to a large extent by preconscious thought processes. People can agree at a conscious, verbal level to such propositions as the validity of evolution while being devoutly committed to fundamentalist religious beliefs that irreconcilably conflict with it. It is because the fundamentalist beliefs are supported by preconscious beliefs that are semi-independent of declarative language. People can agree to the improbability of Bible stories about the Garden of Eden and Noah's ark as being literally true yet still believe in them at a preconscious level. These particular examples of conceptual conflicts do not apply to everyone, but in general such disconnects are a normal, universal product of differences between innate neurological thought processes and language-mediated thought processes.

CHAPTER FIVE

Language-Mediated Thought Versus Innate Neurological Thought

The Verbal-Nonverbal Disjunction

Brain research clearly indicates that both human and animal thought processes involve electric impulses that drive neurotransmitter proteins from the tips of axons, across synapses, to the tips of dendrites in the brain. Such processes of thought in support of intraspecies communication were an early development in animals' adaptation for survival. The ability to communicate by sound and gesture was an advantage when warning others about the presence of predators as well as when seeking out and selecting a mate. Though other animals exhibit various levels of sophistication in their ability to communicate with fellow members of their species with sounds and displays, humans are unique with respect to their use of symbolic language.

A crucial aspect in the present theory of religion is to stress that human declarative, symbolic language must somehow be translated in order to be processed by the same neurological processes that evolved in earlier primate brains.

Language requires external validation. There is an instinct for language; but to be effective, language depends on agreement among speakers and listeners. It is only through usage that different speakers acquire overlapping meanings of words on their own or words in context. Language will not work unless all individuals can discriminate among words and share common notions as to the approximate, if not precise, meaning of each word as it is used in context.

Neurological thought, on the other hand, operates entirely internally by means of neural connections that record and represent data about various associations of phenomena. No external validation is required. Individuals may have similar areas in their brain for processing different types of sensations, but overall the associative neurological connections of each individual are unique. No individual has the exact same arrangement of neurons, dendrites, axons, and synapses as any other. Neural thought processes do not require agreement with anyone else in order to operate satisfactorily. Internal patterns of thought are unique.

This profound difference between innate neurological thought and language-mediated thought presents an almost insurmountable circular dilemma. How do you achieve agreement on the meaning of words in the first place without an ability to use words to establish meaning? Some meanings with regard to tangible objects may be established by means of pointing and pantomime, but this method is idiosyncratic, very limited, and not generalizable beyond individuals who are in frequent contact. It does not fully explain how infants learn grammatically correct language or how groups, whose members lack a common language, quickly arrive at common meanings for new pidgin words. As Steven Pinker has noted, a language instinct is necessary.

At the margin, the nonverbal, neurological thought process evolved by all mammals and the language thought developed by humans are different and, to a degree, incompatible. Some additional internal process is necessary to convert or transform language-mediated thought into neurological thought. Declarative language that is heard is transformed into to neural processes in the brain and in turn neural processes are transformed into declarative language in the form of speech, or internal self-talk in a continuous process.

As with other instances of the translation of languages, there is often no exact one-to-one correspondence between particular concepts in the two modes of thought. People who speak two languages often remark that the meanings of certain words and expressions cannot be exactly translated from one language to the other. As many anecdotes reveal, attempts at literal translations may significantly change the meaning of a word or phrase. An earnest word or phrase can become comical when translated verbatim into another language. By the same token, incongruities also exist with respect to the transformation equivalence of preconscious neurological thought and conscious language-mediated thought. Even a common term, such as the word "cat," may not have exactly the same neurological associative affect for a given individual as it has for others or that which its dictionary meaning implies. Every individual will have a slightly different notion of the category of cat or "catness" that conditions her responses to cats, depending on her knowledge and experiences.

More Language Analogies

An illustrative analogy revolves around differences in computer languages. For example, the computer language COBOL was created to solve accounting and business problems, while another computer language, APL, was created to solve mathematical problems, such as simultaneous linear equations. Each language can be used to perform many of the tasks that the other was specifically designed for, but often only in an awkward or kludgey manner. Similarly, I contend that innate neurological thought processes can handle certain operations of thought very efficiently, but other matters are performed more effectively by language-mediated thinking. Conversely some problems or situations best handled by language-mediated thoughts are poorly performed by purely neurological thinking. This major disjunction in mapping or translation between the modes of thought generates differences between conscious language-mediated thought (LMT) and innate neurological processes (INP) modes of thought. The disjunction is also a major factor in the development of religious belief.

Grammatically acceptable sentences such as "People people left, left," "Farmers monkeys fear slept," and "The rat the cat the mouse chased bit died,"[40] illustrate a language-thought disjunction. These sentences are not amenable to simple or unambiguous parsing with respect to primal thought processing. These anomalies are indicative that the nature of declarative language is, to an extent, independent of the associative nature of neurological, nonverbal thought processes.

Another analogy to the phenomenon of language disjunction is illustrated in the differences between spoken and written language. Despite efforts of grammarians and others to harmonize spoken and written language, significant differences remain. Effective speech differs from effective writing. Pauses, gestures, tone of voice, and facial expression are hardly the equivalents of penmanship, punctuation, syntax, and grammar in writing. We generally do not write exactly as we speak for a variety of reasons. Many spoken phrases do not scan well when written or may not convey the same meaning intended by a speaker. Well-written, grammatically correct language can sound awkward and stilted when spoken. Although there may be substantial correspondence, words may convey slightly or even significantly different meaning when spoken exactly as written (e.g., the book title *Eats, Shoots & Leaves*). Intonation, pace, and prosody, as well as volume, gesture, and facial expression, all impart meaning to spoken words. A spoken phrase often has an entirely different psychological effect on the receiver than the same phrase when written.

By their nature, spoken and written language use different modes of transmission. Sound is the medium of transmission for spoken language, and sight is the medium for written language. Most of us internally voice what we read, and this process accounts for much of the agreement of the meaning of written text with the meaning of the same narrative if it were to be spoken even though the initial processing in the brain of these signals from different senses must also be different, and so some nuanced differences in meaning remain.

Memory and Abstractions

Our innate biological, nonlanguage thought processes tend not to remember specifics. Instead they retain general notions by means of associations of INP thoughts that are recorded as neurotransmitter protein transmission potentials. Complete memories are not retrieved from specific places in the neocortex of the brain in the manner of a computer retrieving a complete document from several specific, linked addresses of a database that is located in its physical memory.

As neural cells fire, human memories are reconstructed bit by bit on the basis of best-match approximations and from associations laid down as a result of experiencing and recording various past events. Memory studies by scientists Karim Nader and Joseph Ledoux indicate that some stimulus will induce a particular neuron to send a flow of neurotransmitter proteins cascading through various networks of associated neurons. These flows result in a reconstructed version of an original memory. The retrieved memory is usually a conflation of several memories, or memories of memories, and so on, whose degree of accuracy or verisimilitude to past memories of objects, agents,. conditions, events, relationships and emotions (OACEREs) depends on many factors.

Specific words, poetry, and prose can be memorized and recalled precisely in sequence, but, except for rare individuals with eidetic, or a so-called photographic memory, this is accomplished with some difficulty by repetition and memory tricks such as association with an explicit series of very familiar related words. The natural thought process of neural networks blends memories of events, places, objects, people, and animals together so that they can be retrieved in many alternative ways through vast arrays of neural connections and their many associations.

Although we are in awe of those with eidetic memory, it can nonetheless be argued that the far more common blended associative memory processes were far more useful for survival in the wild. Associative memory is much better for successfully carrying out everyday activities. It is analogous, in a way, to finding a particular phone number for a name whose spelling is uncertain, in a printed phone book where a range of similar names can be seen at a glance, as compared to typing variations of the spelling of the name into a digital computer lookup in the hope of hitting the exact correct spelling. Associative memory was certainly more useful in early Paleolithic times, where the association of an object or event with prior benign or else life-threatening experiences was a matter of life or death. Computerized relational databases only allow the retrieval of specific records whose relation is predefined. The forte of human associated memory is the ability to quickly and intuitively reconstruct and determine meaningful associations on the fly even though the associations had not been deliberatively contemplated at the time that the memories were stored.

To further illustrate a difference between neurological thought processes (INP) and declarative, language-mediated thought (LMT), take the sophomoric quandary of "What happens when an irresistible force meets an immovable object?" This poser exists only because of formal language, and not in the underlying neural, nonverbal thinking processes, because it depends on a formal definition of the terms. In innate neurological thinking processes, various known and experienced objects may be regarded as belonging to a class that is large or heavy and therefore very difficult or even impossible for the thinker to move in a personal sense, but not, as defined in language, as absolutely and categorically impossible to move under any circumstances by any one, any thing, or any force. Such hypothetical abstract constructs exist only in language. Natural thinking is based on neural networks that are altered by experience that is, conditioned by subjective reality. Formal language is premised on formal or informal definitions, which may be agreed-upon abstract constructs or invented operational definitions. They may have little or nothing to do with experience or empirical reality.

It is by virtue of language-mediated thinking that those phenomena which are not found in nature, and are not possible in nature, can be conceived of and manipulated according to some imaginary, arbitrary characteristics. There are no natural pathways of association in the brain that ordinarily support such artificial or, in Immanuel Kant's term, "synthetic" reasoning. Formal recursion and the logical canonical branching and the power that it gives to thought are strictly enabled by language.

Conscious, declarative language is an artificial creation born of agreed-upon, human-made verbal definitions and artificial constructs. A particular language that has been developed and is recognized by one group can be gibberish to another group unfamiliar with it. Teenagers delight in using neologisms - words and phrases - that are unintelligible to their parents. Artificial constructs may describe natural or unnatural phenomena, and they may describe or convey either realistic or fantastic experiences. We can have far-fetched pseudoexperiences that are purely verbal, as when we read a book. The same neural networks in the brain that process empirical visual experiences process secondhand, synthetic experiences acquired visually from reading, watching movies, or hearing stories. In a sense, emotions and synthetic experiences gained from seeing a movie or reading a book are real. They receive similar neural processing treatment in the brain.

Advantages Derived From Symbolic Language

There are many aspects of human advancement that would be impossible without symbolic language. Language is a means of sophisticated intraspecies communication that is many times more efficient and effective than the modes of communication used by other animals. Language enables a much greater specialization of functions among members of a human group. It tends to greatly multiply the overt native intelligence quotient of individual humans, both in terms of their store of knowledge and their reasoning potential. Written language multiplies the effectiveness of spoken language because of its permanence. Writing is available to those who may be far away from the originator in distance or in time. Written text can be analyzed and pondered at length.

That portion of our thoughts that uses declarative language promotes ruminating and evaluating past experiences. It also facilitates sharing and comparisons of ideas expressed by language among groups of individuals. Language enables cooperative speculation and foreplanning that is based on the present, past, and the probable future. Although languageless animals can learn from and use past experiences to guide them or anticipate immediate future events, by and large, they live in the present, function in real time, and act based on their current situation. Coordinated activities are possible and practiced by animals, but without language these are limited to activities that are of obvious and immediate benefit to all.

By virtue of the time shifting ability conferred by language, the development of language ability also led to the development of long-term memory in humans. Human long-term memory is phenomenal to the point of being unique as compared to other animals. Even without writing, with language thoughts, lessons of the past can be recalled clearly, and discussed and compared with others, and the details can be fleshed out and well-learned with respect to their many different aspects and possible consequences.

The animal (and human) neurological memory works by melding associated past experiences. Prompted by the senses of sight, sound, smell, taste, and feel, animals can, in a sense, connect to past experiences in their minds. Humans can also render these memories in specific terms using declarative language (e.g., Marcel Proust and the smell of madeleines). But most memory tends to be fuzzier or less specific, especially with the passage of time. Memories of past events and actions can be analyzed for what might have been done differently to achieve greater benefit.

Social animals may gain status by aggressiveness, intimidation, and physical contests. Individuals in language-enabled human groups may gain status by means of their verbal fluency in language-mediated activities. Some late Paleolithic and early Neolithic humans could earn high status by means of specializing in activities that catered to language-dependent religious needs, as broadly defined. These included healing activities, rain ceremonies, rites for successful hunts, identifying food that could be eaten, keeping oral history, remembering kinships and genealogical ties, and regulating some aspects of personal conduct. Such specialists would also naturally promote the value of religious rites and ceremonies among their people to build their status. The beginnings of formal religion came about as individuals sought status within tribes by performing such language dependent services.

Modes of Thought and the Reconciliation of Discrepancies

Daniel Gilbert refers to a study where American subjects were asked which countries were most similar to each other[41]—Ceylon and Nepal or West Germany and East Germany.[42] Most of them picked East and West Germany as most similar. Later, after an intervening exercise, when the same subjects were asked to pick the countries most dissimilar to each other, many again picked the same pair of countries. That is, East and West Germany were selected as both the most similar and the most dissimilar to each other. Behavioral economists Daniel Kahneman and Amos Tversky also have demonstrated that such inconsistencies of humans in making rational choices among complex alternatives are common.

Had the subjects of the study Gilbert referenced been in a "language, logic" frame of mind, they, of course, would have realized that the formal definitions of the words similar and dissimilar preclude using the same pair of countries in both instances. But they were not. Operating at a preconscious, nondefinition thought level, there is no conflict for the human brain to determine that the same countries are both the most similar and the most dissimilar. In the two instances, different sets of key characteristics were preconsciously selected for comparison. Such a state is anathema for the explicit definition process, which is the basis of formal language and logic. It is an illustration of how we use both LMT and INP thought simultaneously without realizing that we are doing so. Artificial dictionary definitions or constructs that are not native to the neural processes of the animal brain did not play a part in the decision about the Germanys, though they might have had the subjects been apprised that definitional consistency was important.

Another illustrative example of the effects of language-mediated thought versus neurological thought is a study comparing exemplar versus rule-based theories of categorization. An experiment was performed by psychologists Rouder and Ratcliff using fMRIs.[43] One group of subject radiologists was given a set of standardized x-ray examples as references in order to classify x-rays as showing either benign or malignant tumors. A second group was given a discrete set of rules for classifying the sample x-rays as benign or malignant. The experiments clearly showed that different areas of the subjects' brains lit up consistently, depending on the method used. It can be postulated that the rule-based classification used formal language processing and primarily lit up the language-processing areas of the brain, while the exemplar-based classification uses preconscious neurological thinking and so lit up other areas. Even though the overall process was combined at the front and back ends by means of language, internal processing differed between the groups. Humans naturally use both methods of decision making. The best method will depend on the situation.

Dictionary definitions of words may change as a result of reported usage, but this is a sporadic deliberative process performed by experts. As such it differs from the often subtle and gradual changes in preconscious referent matching due to repeated usage in various contexts by informal groups of individuals. Before the invention of writing, humans were unable to look up verbal definitions of words in dictionaries and thesauri or get discreet sets of rules so as to use them in a conventional, prescribed, consistent manner. As Steven Pinker notes, today, even with ready access to dictionaries, much of common colloquial speech continues to be determined by the same empirical processes that were used before writing was invented. [44] There is a plethora of examples of words, such as enormity, whose common usage differs from their dictionary definitions.

Differences Between Self-Talk and Basic Neurological Thought

We humans perceive our inner thinking as being composed of an internal monologue or self-talk even though it is evident that, at its most fundamental level, our basic thinking must originate with nonverbal, neurological processes in our brains. We are oblivious to this biological thinking process at the conscious, verbal level. One might even say that we only think that we only think verbally. It is an illusion that is promoted by our consummate facility with language, the impenetrable subtlety of our natural thought processes, and the *almost* seamless integration of the two. This appears to be the basis of our hubris concerning acceptance of philosophers' pronouncements about the inability of animals to think or to reason. Much of the analysis of the nature of religion has, in the past, been examined with respect to conscious, verbal thought. Although there are many insights to be gained from such an examination, it falls short of a complete explanation of the power and resilience of the phenomenon of religion. The widespread acceptance of miracles cannot be explained rationally. A comprehensive explanation of religion as a phenomenon must also include effects of neurological, preconscious thought processes.

Rational analysis using verbal thinking explains neither how nor why some people can practice birth control themselves while wholeheartedly supporting their church's uncompromising ban on birth control and family planning. It does not explain how some of those who believe in the unconditional sanctity of life can also be uncompromising proponents of the death penalty. Belief in rationality fails to deal with how lifelong, dedicated ministers and priests can rail against homosexuality even as they engage in homosexual practices themselves. As the new academic discipline of behavioral economics indicates, understanding of human behavior lies not entirely with rational, conscious thought but also with the operation of preconscious thinking. Preconscious attitudes, which serve private or selfish needs, are not necessarily consistent with the advantageous public positions of an individual. Moreover the inconsistencies may not be apparent to the self. The studies of behavioral economists provide vivid examples of discrepancies between LMT and INP modes of thinking.

As with the example of declaring East Germany and West Germany as being both most similar and most dissimilar, preconscious thinking does not necessarily eliminate or even recognize such seeming contradictions. People who appear on the surface to act contrary to their professed doctrines or even their own self-interest may have other preconscious, nuanced agendas that influence them. When they act contrary to positions that they have publicly espoused, they do not necessarily feel like hypocrites or suffer remorse. Much of our religious thinking resides with our preconscious thought processes.

Neurological Studies of Religion

One avenue for exploring the nature of religion by modern scientists has been to artificially induce religious experiences while examining the subject's brain with an MRI device. In one series of experiments, Michael Persinger attached electromagnets inside helmets and then put them on the heads of volunteers. He found that turning on a weak magnetic field close to the subject's head triggered bursts of electrical activity in the temporal lobes of their brains. The volunteers tended to describe their resultant feelings during these bursts as "supernatural or spiritual," "an out-of-body experience," or "a sense of the divine."

In 1997, neurologist Vilayanur Ramachandran reported that his research suggested that depth of religious feeling [spirituality] might depend on natural and not helmet induced enhancements in the electrical activity of the temporal lobes. He noted that this same region of the brain is important for speech perception. "One experience common to many spiritual states is hearing the voice of God. It seems to arise when you misattribute inner speech ... to something outside yourself. During such experiences, the brain's Broca's area ... switches on."[45]

Language Orientation and Religion

It is time for a thought experiment. It postulates two types of people having different orientations with regard to language. One group, LMT, relies entirely on language-mediated declarative language, and the other, INP, entirely on neurological, nonverbal thought, in dealing with their respective environments. Animals do conform to the latter category, but there is no such dichotomy with regard to humans. Even the most extreme individual is not that different with regard to using both modes of thought in dealing with the environment. But assume, for purposes of the thought experiment, that such a bifurcation does exist for different humans.

At one extreme are those people who theoretically live completely in a conscious, language-oriented, rational world. Such people's interactions with the environment, including with their fellows, is mediated exclusively by means of deliberate, defined language. They believe that every word has a precise definition. Words and their referents correspond exactly. They maintain that words should be used in a manner that is true to their formal definitions. They believe, as did Humpty Dumpty, the character in Lewis Carroll's tale of Alice in Wonderland, that they say exactly what they mean and they mean exactly what they say. The thought processes of these hypothetical people will be precise and definitional. Psychologically, they will have a low tolerance for ambiguity and a high need for control. Many will be described as "not suffering fools gladly."

These people, whose dealings with the world tend to be mediated primarily by declarative language rather than intuition, have a need to determine the precise nature of OACEREs (objects, agents, conditions, events, relations, and emotions). They perceive that survival and achievement depend on discovering defined relationships and finding unambiguous meanings in patterns of events that are coherent and consistent with respect to declarative language. Explicit-language people become anxious if they are negatively impacted by some vague mysterious force or factor that they believe they need to, or should be able to, explain or control. Anything perceived as potentially significant that they don't fully comprehend can produce angst.

Because of the nature of their definite or explicit thinking processes, language-oriented people are loath to either attribute or accept unknown causal factors or gaps in their understanding to some vague and unknown mystical or divine force, even if it purports to reduce their anxiety level or deliver other social benefits. They are skeptics. God, the afterlife, and other religious metaphysical notions are slippery concepts that are not amenable to precise, unvarying definitions capable of consistent logical manipulation. Acceptance of an afterlife, for example, requires the acceptance of a very wide range of undefined possibilities, even though authors, such as John Milton, in his *Paradise Lost*, and religious authorities might propose some notions of it. But for our hypothetical highly verbal people, which are oriented to precise definitions, such nebulous religious theology is not intrinsically or doctrinally appealing. Explicit language-oriented people reject explaining a mysterious unknown by postulating some alternative vague unknown or a fanciful scenario as simply tautological thinking. It is unreasonable and unacceptable to them. From their writings on religion, Richard Dawkins, Sam Harris, and Christopher Hitchens, for example, appear to strongly hold this type of verbal orientation.

The other group in this thought experiment is composed of people who deal with the world by means of preconscious, nonverbal thought processes. They are intuitive and far more credulous. They simply accept the evidence of their senses as they perceive it. Short of a perceived direct threat, the unknown causes little anxiety. For these nonverbally-oriented people, there is no compulsion to preemptively reconcile discordant or conflicting elements in nature for the sake of curiosity or symmetry. Intuitive people have little compulsion to seek a mystical or divine force as an explanation for otherwise unexplained events. They easily accept of the limits of their knowledge without worry. Psychologically these people tend to have a very high tolerance for ambiguity. Using the preconscious, animal aspects of their brains, they tend to operate at an intuitive real-time level that simply accepts their experiences at perceived face value (or what they are told is face value).

Paradoxically, these nonverbally-oriented people, though highly credulous, are also not likely to be committed devout religious fundamentalists for the very reason that, with ready acceptance of the unusual in nature and a very high tolerance for ambiguity, most existential questions do not produce anxiety. They have no need or compulsion to reconcile or explain discordant elements in nature unless they pose an immediate threat. (On this basis, I contend that nonhuman animals do not have or need God.)

The hypothetical preconscious-oriented people behave like creatures in Skinnerian experiments, which learn and unlearn through the acquisition and extinction of habits by means of repeated trials in controlled environments. They do not tend to generalize or to consciously analyze patterns of events. They tend to mostly live in the moment, with learning coming after only a short and finite number of trials, and extinction of learning the same. Preconscious-oriented people accept the mysteries of nature and the unexplained as matters of fact or even as "magic," but they don't reflect on the role or the motivation of some magician who might be causing the events. Such people, operating at a neurological level, tend to seek pleasure and avoid pain in a straightforward, stimulus-response manner. Their efforts at determining patterns in nature are strictly pragmatic. They repeat behavior that works or is perceived as beneficial. They avoid behavior that doesn't work or is not beneficial, and even more so if it is harmful or counterproductive. The more practiced a behavior, the more efficient it becomes, resulting in quicker, more consistent payoffs, and thus the more likely the particular behavior is to be repeated in perceived similar circumstances.

Individuals in this second group are pragmatically oriented, as they tend to deal with reality by means of neurological, or preconscious, thought. They are not likely to be religious.

People under hypnosis have no problem accepting conflicting propositions without becoming anxious. Although the hypnotists' suggestions are verbal, they somehow go directly to the preconscious, neurological processing areas of the brain. The suggestions appear to slip past the dissonance-registering processes of the brain's thalamus and its working memory. An amusing part of many hypnotists' acts is to convince people under hypnosis that objects or events that are logically impossible or incompatible with each other are present or are happening. The subjects do not show signs of internal conflict or anxiety. Subjects can be convinced that they will not remember anything that they did under hypnosis. An inference that can be drawn is that although the nonverbal aspects of the brain are also determined to make sense of the environment, it is oriented to immediate or near-term patterns that will benefit survival and therefore does not contemplate some abstract "ultimate reality." Many logical and apparent incompatibilities that do not affect near-term survival can be accepted and isolated or compartmentalized by the neurological, nonverbal processing functions of the brain.

Just as people under hypnosis exhibit no anxiety in behaving as ducks and quacking accordingly, or in accepting that an object can be in two places at the same time, our hypothetical nonverbally-oriented people can accept without deliberation the proposition that there is some vague,

80

metaphysical factor or force that reconciles inconsistencies even though they cannot fathom it with their limited level of rationality. They do not have a prerequisite need to scrutinize, pin down, or define the exact nature of such an inscrutable power or to generate and pass along stories that support it.

A Real-Life Example

In the 1990s, a program was instituted at Syracuse University to train helpers for severely autistic and neurologically impaired children based on the theory that many of them have normal mental abilities but are stymied because of physical impairment. To overcome their physical limitations, intermediaries called "facilitators" were trained to hold an autistic child's hand over an answer board and, by reducing their shakes, help them respond to questions that were asked. When the facilitator "discerned" that the autistic student wished to point to a particular answer box in response to a question, the facilitator would steady the child's hand so that he could touch the desired answer box. The program was a great success with the children and their parents.

Autistic children, along with their facilitators, were mainstreamed into schools and colleges, and they performed satisfactorily. However, after some time, critics of the procedure were able to conduct experiments where the facilitators were unaware of the questions being asked of the autistic children. The results showed conclusively that the autistic children could not answer the questions by themselves. The entire procedure was bogus (though proponents of the research continue to insist that it has some value).

For our purposes the most interesting aspect of these experiments is that apparently the facilitators themselves were not "faking it." These intelligent, university-trained people seemed to honestly believe that it was not they, but rather the autistic child that they were helping, who was actually answering the questions. As the autistic child's hand would waver over the answer board in a jerky, seemingly random manner, facilitators really believed that they could detect subtle hand movements or differences in pressure when the child's hands approached a particular answer box, which was often, but not always, correct. Facilitators in training who expressed doubts about their ability to discriminate among jerky movements of the autistic child's attempts to push an answer key were dismissed from the program. But many others with higher tolerances for ambiguity and the ability to function at a preconscious level remained and were "successfully trained." These facilitators honestly believed that their charges were supplying the answers to questions.

Compartmentalized Thinking

All human beings use both modes, that is, language-mediated as well as innate neurological thought processing. Because of this they are driven to find stable relationships and valid defined meanings among objects, agents, conditions, and events of nature while also being able to accept fuzzy, inconsistent, and unpredictable forces as causal agents in nature in those cases where cogent explanation seems unreachable.

People can, in effect, compartmentalize their thinking and their lives. At times, to a greater or lesser extent, most people can believe that metaphysical forces are real, and they behave accordingly. At the same time, in different contexts or aspects of their lives, they can behave as hard-headed empirical scientists, rigorously searching to prove reliability and validity of each and every concept in order to establish relationships and meanings in nature so they might learn how to control it. Though they are in a small minority, a number of accomplished natural scientists, such as William Behe, are also, at the same time, proponents of intelligent design or creation science. Their published works bear witness to the fact that these people are sincere in their belief that there is little or no fundamental conflict in the two endeavors—except as they try to deny or to reconcile what they regard as a perceived conflict between the two worldviews that exists only in the minds of others who are, to their way of thinking, wrong.

It is the interplay of the two modes of processing experiences that allows for the process of reification, where widely accepted supernatural abstractions and inexplicable natural phenomena come to be regarded as real. Mysterious forces are accepted preconsciously, but then there is a penchant to describe and define them declaratively. It is a neat accommodation of the two modes of mind wherein both the definitional needs of conscious language processing and the need for acceptance of mysterious empirical phenomena are simultaneously satisfied with respect to the same situation. This ability also promotes the explicit satisficing and rationalization that have greatly assisted in the ascent of humans.[46]

Like most natural phenomena, human thought processing also falls along a normal curve. At one extreme some people refuse to accept or to reify supernatural or divine powers that are claimed to explain the unfolding of the universe, but for which they have no acceptable reasonable explanation. These people do not acknowledge any objective benefit from worshipping, obeying religious creeds, or behaving in accordance with what others presume that a divine entity requires. They are unlikely to conceive of, or accept, an amorphous metaphysical God to which they are exhorted to sincerely pray and even to dedicate their lives. Sometimes however such people do succumb to social peer pressure, overt coercion by others or for pragmatic reasons. At the other extreme are those highly spiritual people that have such a high tolerance for ambiguity and uncertainty that they have no need to empirically define the unexplained or to reify metaphysical forces.

In between the extremes of the thought mode continuum are the vast majority of people who accept the unknown and seemingly irrational aspects of nature and reality but have a compulsion to rationalize them as well, so as to create logical extensions of nonlogical propositions. These people are not satisfied merely to simply accept the proposition that there must be a God that created or controls the unfolding of the universe. They need to know the nature of God, how She operates and what She wants or doesn't want from mankind, in order to reduce the anxiety these propositions induce. And of course some people who are desperate for a miracle or the intervention of some metaphysical power also tend to believe, but this type of belief comes as a result of their desperation.

This basic human need is also found in the sciences, as scientists go beyond their data or rational proofs to speculate on wider implications. It is exemplified by theoretical scientists who, for example, extrapolate findings from the study of particle physics in order to propose string theory. Such is the manner by which new knowledge is often formed. The phenomenon also explains the appeal of fantasy computer games in which a character is given supernatural powers and then the particular powers are used in a rational manner by a player to overcome obstacles and enemies in pursuit of winning the game. Similarly we tend metaphorically to project aspects of humanness as well as supernatural powers on mysterious metaphysical forces that are presumed to control nature.

The existence and perpetuation of religion depends on the interplay between preconscious thought processes, which ingenuously accept experience and declarative language processes, which attempt to speculate and to formulate scenarios to explain the mysterious or irrational. Much of the appeal of religious fundamentalism is emotional or social and nonrational, though it uses, to great effect, glib explanations and the fabrication of logical scenarios to explain the mysterious or unknown. We have a need to make sense of the unknown. All men need Gods - as Homer said three thousand years ago.

83

CHAPTER SIX

Social Animals And A Theory Of Mind

Social Conformity

As has been noted by sociologists, religion can be studied as a function of the desirability of individuals to cooperate for their mutual benefit. Intelligent primates, with sophisticated communication abilities, would have realized early on that delegating absolute leadership to a single individual (king), rather than enduring the perpetual chaos of physical contests for dominance, would be beneficial for all. Furthermore, hereditary kingship, in many cases, tended to ensure the continuity of effective leadership across generations. In essence groups of early humans allowed kings to have the power over the life or death of the rank and file in exchange for his control in ensuring relatively harmonious intramural relations and effective coordination of the group in dealing with nature and other, competing groups.

Emile Durkheim, the father of sociology, has suggested that cooperation, brokered by religion, was the key to the ascent of humans. But conversely, is religion merely a consequence of the formation of cooperative tribes to ameliorate continual detrimental struggles for leadership? That is, is religion the source of effective and enduring group cooperation and group cohesion, or is religion merely one useful cultural device, among others, for maintaining group cooperation?

Many social animals cooperate for mutual benefit. Baboons form into troupes of up to two hundred individuals. These troops roam the open savannas of Africa and mingle peacefully with other troupes. Female baboons remain in the troupe their entire lives, along with their mothers, aunts, sisters, and offspring. Males, except for the alpha male or males, leave the troupe as they mature. Young males often team up with their close kin to take over an existing troupe from the aging alpha male who has remained in the troupe, or cooperate to entice females into starting a new troupe with them.

By contrast, in chimpanzee society it is the males who remain in the band and cooperate with their male kin. Young, maturing females leave to join other bands. Unlike baboons, chimpanzees are highly territorial. An innate tendency to kinship cooperation among males in a troupe does not extend to those from outside their territory. They recognize strangers both on sight and by behavior. Members of each chimpanzee troupe patrol the boundaries of their territory. Interlopers are chased off or killed. As a result of the amount of the troupe's energy that is spent on being vigilant as well as their aggressiveness, male-centered chimpanzee troupes tend to be considerably smaller in number than the female-centered baboon troupes.

Although there are present-day primates, such as orangutans, that live a mainly solitary existence, most early hominid species were likely highly social animals. Evidence indicates that early human societies were similar to the chimpanzee model. Genetic analysis indicates that as late as seventy thousand years ago, there may have been as few as five thousand humans, all of whom lived in East Africa. According to Sam Bowles, there was not much of an increase in the population until about ten thousand years ago, when agriculture became common. According to Bowles this was because of continual territorial wars in human hunter-gatherer societies.[47]

Given the living conditions postulated for Paleolithic humans, where all the males and females lived in close proximity, there would have been a tendency for aggressive males to engage in battles for female consorts. As with other social animals, intramural combat for breeding rights among early humans was likely minimized by means of the creation and maintenance of a status order among the males of a group. Still, as young males matured, dominance contests would have caused many deaths or the breakaway of small groups from a main tribe. Such small groups would have to move out to a territory not claimed by a larger group if they wished to survive.

The chances of survival on the savanna for a small group of hominids would not have been high. A single male accompanied by two or three female hominids would not likely have survived for very long under the harsh environmental conditions or against territorial challenges from larger groups of hominids. A small group would not likely have initiated a line of succession that lasted beyond two or three generations. Before *Homo sapiens* could dominate the earth, they had to learn to accept exclusive male-female bonds, to cooperate in rearing infants, and to overcome the adverse effects of their natural xenophobia.

Promoting Group Cohesion

Scientists have observed that species of apes and other primates spend a considerable amount of time picking fleas, ticks, lice, and burrs from the backs of their fellows in a process called grooming. Since primates cannot scratch their own backs, they have to rely on others to give them relief from such nuisances. Grooming is a practical exercise that gives relief and improves the health of the groomee. It has been observed that the touching involved in grooming appears to be enjoyed by both the groomer and the groomee for its own sake. This practice serves to cultivate a web of reciprocal obligations among members of a primate subgroup that grooms each other.

As with grazing animals such as gnus, hunter-gatherer hominids discovered that maintaining larger groups on the savanna held advantages that had not been as important in the primordial forests. Larger numbers afforded them the ability to better protect themselves and their offspring from increased dangers of predation, gather food, and defend their territories from other groups and competing species of hominids. Disease, drought, predation, and famine were not as likely to cripple larger, more numerous troupes to the point where they would be significantly weakened and then inexorably dwindle to extinction over a few succeeding generations.

Paradoxically, in social species larger groups tend to be unstable. Grooming activity promotes reciprocity, which helps to make a group more cohesive and so can sustain a group. But grooming requires lengthy one-to-one interaction. Because of this it tends to be effective in maintaining reciprocal cohesion among small groups of up to twenty adult individuals who are part of a stable group.

The larger the group, the greater the tendency toward interpersonal conflict, the creation of competing factions, and the emergence of other forces that create dissention and split a larger group into smaller, competing groups. Despite such obstacles, the size of the groups of humans likely continued to grow larger. Such growth meant that kinship bonds and frequent face-to-face interactions were diminished. Obviously language and religion played major roles in balancing intramural cooperation and interclan competition. A case can be made that some form of religion can foster groups greater than twenty individuals to remain stable and to cooperate over many years. The larger the group, the more necessary and potent religion becomes as a means of brokering cooperation.

But we are getting ahead of the story. There were other evolutionary developments as well that came into play to foster cooperation in larger groups of Paleolithic humans.

The Mirror Neuron Effect

Human beings have a proclivity to imitate the behavior of others. This imitative tendency, which begins in early childhood, appears to be natural rather than learned. It has been observed that if a mother sticks her tongue out at her month-old baby, the baby will often respond by sticking out her tongue as well, even though the baby cannot see its own tongue.

In a recent article, Michael Tomasello, of the Max Planck Institute for Evolutionary Anthropology, in Leipzig Germany, discussed the unique tendency of humans to pay attention to whatever other humans are paying attention to.

Our research team has shown that even infants—at around their first birthdays, before language acquisition has begun—tend to follow the direction of another person's eyes, not their heads. Thus, when an adult looked to the ceiling with her eyes only, head remaining straight ahead, infants looked to the ceiling in turn. However, when the adult closed her eyes and pointed her head to the ceiling, infants did not very often follow … Humans are sensitive to the direction of the eyes specifically in a way that our nearest primate relatives are not. This is the first demonstration of an actual behavioral function for humans' uniquely visible eyes [i.e., because of the large white areas of the eyeball].

Why might it have been advantageous for some early humans to advertise their eye direction in a way that enabled others to determine what they were looking at more easily? One possible answer, what we have called the cooperative eye hypothesis, is that especially visible eyes made it easier to coordinate close-range collaborative activities in which discerning where the other was looking and perhaps what she was planning, benefited both participants ... If we are gathering berries to share, with one of us pulling down a branch and the other harvesting the fruit, it would be useful—especially before language evolved—for us to coordinate our activities and communicate our plans, using our eyes and perhaps other visually based gestures ...

> ... If I am, in effect, advertising the direction of my eyes, I must be in a social environment full of others who are not often inclined to take advantage of this to my detriment—by, say, beating me to the food or escaping aggression before me. Indeed, I must be in a cooperative social environment in which others following the direction of my eyes somehow benefits me.

The tendency to follow the direction of gaze of others is conjectural evidence indicating the advantage for early hominids to have lived in very close colonies. These hominids were vulnerable to predation. Their very young were especially helpless. For reasons of safety, convenience, and efficiency in breeding and childcare, as well as for cooperation in hunting, living close together in extended clan groups would have been very advantageous. In the hurly-burly of a crowded lair, with a cacophony of noise and difficulty in communication, direction of one's gaze would have been an important indicator of where to direct another's attention.

Barriers to Effective Cooperation

The potential number of social interactions among individuals in a group increases factorially as their number grows. This means that by the time there are over one hundred members in a group, there are many millions of possible interactions among the many combinations of two or more different individuals. Among social insects such as ants and bees, the problem is solved by constraining the range and complexity of interactions. For hominids struggling to survive on the savanna, complex and variable cooperative interactions among individuals was critical.

Both status-order coercion and reciprocity rapidly become ineffective as means of maintaining peaceable cooperation in such large groups with regard to complex social interaction. Even where large tribes are organized into self-governing clans led by dominant patriarchs, the potential for chaos, leadership challenges, disagreements, jealousies, cheating, shirking, adverse selection, and other dysfunctional practices grows geometrically with the size of a group and a population.

The alpha male or patriarch of a small troupe that is composed mainly of his wives, his offspring, and his grandchildren is respected and feared. The traditional patriarch of a very large group of loosely related individuals may, however, become simply a burdensome old male and the daily or weekly target of some of the more ambitious younger males. Under such circumstances large groups will be highly unstable. Such unstable groups would not likely enhance the probability of survival of their members by means of cooperation and specialization. Some other force for cohesion and cooperation is required.

The Solution: Development of Mirror Neurons

For the above reasons, the development of a mutation to the hominid genotype in the form of mirror neurons in their brain would have been advantageous and so was propagated genetically. Though controversial, the existence and effects of mirror neurons in humans and other animals have been studied by Michael Arbib and Giacomo Rizzolatti at the University of Southern California and discussed in a book by Marco Iacobni.[48]

Mirror neurons are not exclusive to humans. At their most fundamental level, mirror neurons function so as to induce and facilitate animals in imitating the behavior of others of their species and to react to the others' emotional displays. Infant humans in particular tend to observe the actions of their mothers and other humans with whom they are in frequent contact. These agents are regarded as being the most salient aspect of any situation. The youngsters tend to replicate or "ape" behavior as they observe it in these significant others. It is not known exactly when or how such mirror neurons began to evolve, or even whether they are somehow learned very early rather than inherited, but as the verb "ape" implies, the brains of our cousins, the great apes, also possess these nerve cells, though not nearly to the extent that humans do.

Imitative behavior initiated and supported by the mirror neuron effect also promotes empathy by prompting individuals to identify with the behavior and the emotional responses of others in various situations. On observing a male being hit in the crotch by some object on the TV show "America's Funniest Home Videos," a typical male response is involuntarily flinching and grimacing and then laughing nervously. Many humans react emotionally not only to the violent mistreatment of other humans but also to mistreatment other higher humanlike mammals such as apes.[49]

The existence of mirror neurons in other animals indicates that some form of mirror neurons first emerged, before the species *Ardipithecus afarensis* diverged from the ape genus more than eight million years ago. Mirror neurons appear to be mutations of the genes that code for recognition and attraction to other members of a species, most especially with regard to mating or recognizing and raising their own young. The primitive origins of the type of gene that codes for same-species recognition must go back hundreds of millions of years. We also know, from fMRI experiments, that there is a distinct area of the human brain that is specialized for facial recognition.

Though other apes tend to imitate observed behavior, their brains contain far fewer mirror neurons than do the brains of humans.[50] Mirror neurons likely became more numerous among social, cooperative hominids, since they were especially beneficial to their survival. Having many mirror neurons, coupled with an extended childhood, greatly improved the ability of young hominids to learn from their parents and peers.

Arguments Pro and Con

In modern times, generations of sophomoric pranksters have gone onto a crowded street and stood motionless while staring up, and sometimes pointing, at some inconsequential object high up on a nearby building. Then they get a big laugh as many other unsuspecting people walking down the street stop, look up in the same direction, and, generally without asking, try to discern what the pranksters and the others are staring at. This is an inborn tendency and a critical attribute unique to humans that is related to the operation of mirror neurons.

Alas, although the behavior ascribed as being triggered by mirror neurons is unquestioned, the existence and precise nature of mirror neurons in humans is in some dispute in the scientific community. It is not settled science. This is because it is very difficult to stipulate the exact operation of a particular neuron or group of neurons as opposed to their general modes of functioning. As a result, even some scientists who accept the existence of mirror neurons in other animals have questioned their existence and/or their functions in humans. However, whether or not mirror neurons exist in humans, the effects attributed to them are especially pronounced among humans. For purposes of the present exposition, it hardly matters whether there are specific mirror neurons or the effect is due to some combination of neurons, neurotransmitter proteins, and hormones. The penchant of humans of all ages, but particularly the young, to emulate and imitate others is very strong and it is obvious. For this reason we shall continue to refer to the phenomenon as the mirror neuron effect.

A Theory of Mind

A result of the mirror neuron effect is that when observing the behavior of others, a human can infer the thoughts and the emotions that the other may be experiencing. By observing a particular situation, and empathizing and projecting, a person can speculate with respect to what another might be feeling and thinking. Moreover, because of the mirror neuron effect, we humans can not only hypothesize what another person is thinking about us but also what she is thinking about what we are thinking about her. This is a basis of a theory of the mind. So important are mirror neuron effects considered to be in supporting human social interaction that defects or overt failure in the operation of this effect is suspected by some to be a major culprit in human autism and Asperger's syndrome. The inability of people with these disorders to "read" other people and therefore respond appropriately is socially crippling.

Recent experiments using fMRIs were performed on ten-year-olds who had been tested as either high or low with regard to susceptibility to peer influence. Some subjects were shown angry hand signals and angry facial expressions. Results indicated "highly coordinated brain activity in neural systems underlying perception of action and decision making. These findings suggest that the probability of resisting peer influence depends on neural interactions."[51] Sensitivity to peer influence is determined, in large part, by neurons and preconscious thought processes (as opposed to conscious, deliberative decision processes).

Overall, the abilities that are dependent on mirror neuron effects, coupled with language abilities, support the cultural forms for cooperative living. These abilities allow humans to live successfully in cooperative, highly coordinated colonies of many hundreds of individuals. Disruptive forces of aggression and competition have not been eliminated, but the ability to read the intentions and anticipate the actions of others allows for implicit group pressure and the threat of group sanctions that keep most individuals in line by deterring antisocial behavior.

It was the ability to form large, stable, cooperative groups as a result of the mirror neuron effect and the development of language that played a major role in promoting the survival and eventual dominance of humans. In this view religion is a consequential supportive mechanism rather than the initial impetus for perpetuating large, stable cooperative communities, as is postulated in some sociological theories of religion. What some regard as the innate tendency to religion is more accurately depicted as a particular consequence of the mirror neuron effect and the need for cooperation and specialization in large groups among a naturally aggressive species that was poorly endowed for survival on the savanna.

The Dark Side of the Mirror Neuron Effect

The potent mirror neuron effect genie came with a darker side when paired with another major boon, language. Mirror neuron effects have increased both social manipulation and individual self-doubt. Although primates have been observed to engage in manipulative behavior, humans, equipped with language, are quantum leaps better at it. We humans have the ability to contemplate others' thoughts so as to anticipate their actions and statements. This ability presents a potent means for attempting to influence others.

By behaving in certain ways or suggesting things that we believe, we can induce others to alter their future actions and statements. We can hope to induce them to act or speak in ways more sympathetic to our own interests. If we are being mean or selfish, we can use such manipulation to their detriment as well. Since others also can infer what we are thinking about what they are thinking, they can counter our counter of their anticipated actions, and so on. (It is a little like the circularity of the old spoof "Spy vs. Spy," in *Mad* magazine, where each spy anticipates the measures, countermeasures, and counter-countermeasures of the other spy in an infinite regress.)

One human can't really know for certain exactly what another is thinking except in special or extreme cases. Inferences about the thinking of others are generally erroneous to some extent. Erroneous inferences can cause a great deal of dissention and conflict in a group of humans. (This effect is a staple in comedy, farce, romance, and mystery literature.) Fortunately, unlike plots in theater and in literature, in the real world such misunderstanding or dissention tends to be limited because of the ability to ask for clarification and to compare actions and impressions with others.

Social Control of Individual Behavior

Antisocial actions are punished by a majority of a group. The mere internalized threat of severe social repercussions precludes antisocial behavior in most cases. Actions based on egregious errors of inference by ordinary members of a group, especially if they are injurious to group cohesion or hurtful to significant members of the group, are unequivocally corrected or summarily punished by other members of the group. As observed in studies of interactions in groups of primates, concerted group censure does not require language. But it is greatly facilitated by language.

Social censures include verbal reprimands, ostracism, and physical punishment or the threat of it. They become part of the internalized culture of a group. Only infrequently will an adult member of a group push the envelope of personal self-interest to behave in a manner that is overtly inimical to the interest of the group. In some cases social sanctions, or the threat of them, can be more effective in behavior control than corporal punishment or its threatened use. This is not to say that self-interested activity that is dysfunctional to the group or other individual members is never pursued, but it tends to be carried out surreptitiously by means of cheating, sneaking, or shirking.

Unlike other social animals, such as various species of apes and monkeys that punish only observed, egregious acts of antisocial behavior, human groups also punish antisocial language, overt psychological attitudes, and deemed intent, as well as mere hearsay about such conduct and anticipated actions. Complex norms of public behavior are socially enforced at all times and in most places by members of groups. In circular fashion these enforced behavioral mores serve to affect inferences about the thinking of others. As such the existence and enforcement of social norms produces a certain degree of comforting certainty as an important aspect of a culture. This establishment of acceptable behavior and mores is a basis of human morality as well as religious behavior.

Interpersonal Influence and Social Manipulation

Much interpersonal influence is benign or beneficial, and it has been critical to the arc of human survival and dominance in nature. When interpersonal influence is calculated to garner unwarranted benefit for the influencer and/or is to the detriment of others, it is regarded as manipulation. Manipulative language or behavior, whether successful or not, most often leads to hard feelings, which are destructive to group harmony and threaten its continued existence. Groups develop social norms and strictures to deal with such manipulative behavior.

The term "Machiavellian mind" has been coined by Andrew Whitton and Richard Byrne to describe such manipulative behavior,[52] which is supported by abilities that are enhanced by the mirror neuron effect. Despite the potentially punitive effect of social pressure, adverse manipulation is nonetheless commonly practiced to some extent by various members of groups of humans because they believe that their implementation of manipulative behavior will not be detected. Even if their duplicity is eventually detected, the reward from a successful outcome will justify the consequences, either because punishment will have become moot or else their penalty will be minor compared with their gains.

The needs and wants of every individual member of even the most cooperative of groups of humans will differ somewhat, and this can be a source of social friction. Zero-sum competition is especially true with regard to mating and, often, the desire for status or recognition. An individual's needs and desires will inevitably conflict with the desires of other individuals. To the extent that all individuals are to some degree selfish and competitive, they will act in the interests of their own welfare. In most cases this will not coincide, or it will even overtly conflict, with the welfare of others or with the group as a whole. In the distant past this was especially true where female mates were in short supply, a condition guaranteed to be a source of friction among the males in a hominid group, who may have lusted after several females. For this reason isolated groups of human are inherently unstable. There had to be some countervailing force that maintained cohesion and cooperation.

In addition to the problems caused by manipulation, contemplating that others with a different worldview are engaged in thinking about and pursuing their own self-interests can lead one to question the appropriateness of one's own thinking and behavior. Thus there tends to be a degree of tension in the innermost thoughts of individuals in terms of the desirability and the extent of either cooperating or competing with others.

Self-Doubt

Another consequential dysfunction of mirror neuron effects and language is that the knowledge that others are pursuing their own interests, even to one's detriment, can lead to self-doubt. Individuals want to believe that others' thinking is consonant with their own and that they are accepted and respected by others in their reference group. Others may exaggerate the value of their own abilities and contributions so as to elevate their status. Some individuals may accept these claims or even exaggerate the value of others' abilities and possessions compared to their own, even though the claims may not be objectively true. (Recall the biblical injunction against jealousy.)

Because we can only know our own declarative thoughts, some individuals may come to believe that their own thoughts are different, strange, of low caliber, or transparent to others. Even those who are not suffering paranoia may nonetheless sense that they are the subject of covert deprecation or even ridicule by others, whether it is true or not. It is often the case that people have negative reactions on being around strangers who are speaking a language they do not understand. It is not that they want to be part of the strangers' conversations but rather that they wish to be certain that derogatory comments about them are not being bandied about. Negative reactions occur even though those speaking in a foreign language overtly pose no threat.

Self-doubt is not totally a bad thing. Admittedly, it can incite an individual to take some dysfunctional action, as in the extreme case of suicide. Mostly, though, it inhibits individuals from going off half-cocked, testing or defying social convention, and taking rash actions that are not well thought out and that will tend ultimately to have negative consequences for themselves or their loved ones. Doubt can be a major element in careful planning to ensure positive outcomes. The range of the effects of self-doubt can go from caution in planning and hesitation in taking risky or precipitous behavior all the way to feckless dithering, submissiveness, and a paralysis from taking any actions that might in any way affect or displease others.

We are all keenly aware of our own problems and limitations, but not nearly as aware or knowledgeable about the insecurities, shortcomings, and troubles of others. To paraphrase an old adage, "Everyone thinks the other fellow has it made. But if you only knew, you'd realize that he has problems that are similar to your own." As the longshoreman philosopher Eric Hoffer wrote, "When people are free to do as they please, they usually imitate each other." There is a psychological safety in conformity that ameliorates self-doubt.

As with many other matters, the bell curve of probable variation is a factor in self-doubt. Not everyone is insecure or acts from insecurity. Many believe that they truly are superior to their fellows. Of course, as Carl Jung pointed out, often what appears to be a superiority complex is usually only a desperate bravado covering up for a greater degree of insecurity. There is a wide range in the quality of self-doubt as well as in the resultant behavior. Individuals act and learn to either overcome or finesse various disadvantageous aspects of their self-doubt. The range of this effect includes mild paranoia, depression, constant feelings of low self-worth, expectations of critical treatment from others, having a chip on one's shoulder, self-deprecation, defensiveness, overachievement, and insistence on always having one's own way.

Consequences of Self-Doubt

Sometimes an individual believes that things are not going well because of uncontrollable external forces that conspire against her. In this case, a presumed awareness of the negative thinking of others about her can lead to profound self-doubt, even a form of paranoia, where all of one's woes are attributed to others.

Resentment can occur even when things are going reasonably well but a person believes that he deserves to be in a better position in comparison to others. It is easy to come to believe that others may have a natural or an unfair advantage or that they are somehow thwarting legitimate efforts to increase one's welfare. Even for so-called normal people, it is sometimes the case that there are subtle indications that others are conspiring against them or think they are better, and these conditions are reflected in their language.

Those who do deem themselves to be superior to others and have a need to prove it may also be disposed to harbor disrespect or attempt to manipulate the others and take advantage of them. At the other margin, some people, such as skinheads, supremacists, and others, have come to believe that their birthright has become fraudulently usurped by foreigners and members of minority groups that do not deserve it nearly as much as they. For these people, other groups are denigrated and loathed the more they are perceived as successful. The feelings of being taken advantage of and suffering injustice, that is, being a victim, may lead to protests and violence.

Other individuals believe that they must join forces with like-minded people to beat the devious, undeserving others at their own game, within culturally dictated limitations. (The Internet is a boon to such people.) For most people in a civilized culture, lashing out overtly at those deemed to be taking legal but unwarranted or unfair advantage of the system is unacceptable except in obvious or dire circumstances (but such issues can still be used by politicians to attract votes).

Animals that experience their lives mainly in the present can react angrily to being harmed by others or take umbrage if they believe that they are being denied their due by their fellows. To an extent they can develop differential attraction and dislike for their fellows or, as in a case of capuchin monkeys, as reported by Frans deWaal, band together to punish others for past behavior.[53] Animals can have, and can display, aggressive or submissive temperaments. But without language, the mirror neuron effect in other animals relates only to immediate perceived reality and not an internalized, subjective version of summative thoughts and experiences or acts to forestall conjectural future events. Enduring behavior that is predetermined, or that is conditioned by internalized beliefs of low self-worth, group prejudice, or obsessive mistrust, simply has no meaning with respect to other animals, but it certainly does with respect to humans.

Synthetic Experience

Individual animals must interpret sensations from their experiences in order to react. The lessons of past salient experiences are remembered and applied to future experiences. Survival demands it.

For humans, certain language that is heard from others results in what has been described as synthetic experience. Hearing and reading about a situation that one has never encountered may have a somewhat similar effect on the neural networks of the brain as actually having experienced the situation. For example, reading about camping and survival in the wilderness can greatly alter the behavior of a tyro survivalist. Such synthetic experience can obviate painful real-life experiential lessons, some of which might even have proven fatal. Having a mental framework that regards as benign behavior the treatment of medical personnel or the lessons of a boxing coach, which otherwise might have been construed as threatening or dangerous, makes all the difference in the reactions or the responses to such treatment.

Synthetic experience can be divided into two types. The first is an organic synthetic experience. This is illustrated by the example above with regard to preparing in advance for camping in the wilderness. Human behavior is determined both by direct experience as well as past synthetic experience, and it is applied to future situations.

The second type is externally originated synthetic experience. When others are present or share an experience, their interpretation of the experience, as transmitted by language, can determine an individual's internal interpretation of the experience. When there was an outbreak of disease in a medieval village, and people were told by their leaders that the source of the disease was the arrival of a stranger, a dybbuk, or an eclipse of the moon, it tended to have the effect of a synthetic experience. Synthetic experience extends beyond a mere acceptance in the particular instance. It is generalized. Those who have absorbed the synthetic experience will subsequently attribute disease to the appearance of strangers, witches, or eclipses. The experiential concept of a link between disease and some proximal occurrence that is maintained as being evil, if accepted, is generalized. It tends to affect future behavior in many other situations that are construed as similar or having some important element in common.

Synthetic experiences may not have the force of direct experience, but they do have a semipermanent effect on neural networks and affect behavior in the same manner. Synthetic and direct experiences tend to be concatenated in the neural networks of the brain. The behavioral and expressive effects of most synthetic experiences generally do not make as deep an impression as direct experience, which can even be traumatic.

In general, neural impressions of synthetic experiences can be altered more easily than those created by direct experience. However, they do tend to persist and to significantly affect future behavior. In addition, direct experience tends to be somewhat singular and situational whereas synthetic experience can be repeated and repeated in various situations until it defines future behavior in all situations that have some common element.

An ability to learn from experience, which evolved in animals as a survival trait, can be said to have been directly extended to similar effects of the sensations derived from language on the neural networks of human brain.

Using Language to Negotiate Interpersonal Relations

Language is an effective medium by which humans, as social animals, can negotiate interpersonal relationships, especially when they first establish the relationship. Professor Alan Fiske, of UCLA, has categorized the relationships that are brokered by language into four basic categories: communality, dominance, reciprocity, and sexuality. Manipulation and self-doubt are major factors driving these interpersonal communications.

On first meeting, people often do a little conversational dance to determine whether they have friends or acquaintances in common, to find out what trips to domestic and foreign lands they have visited, and so forth. It is a conversation for relatedness. In the southern portion of the United States, one of the first questions strangers are asked by Christians is, "What church do you attend?" For Orthodox Jews it is, "What butcher do you use?" Such information, along with jewelry and clothing worn and automobiles driven, establishes communality.

Often a form of verbal jousting also takes place in the initial stages of a relationship. This jockeying to determine dominance can take many forms. Sometimes it is in the form of name dropping or asking pointed questions. Dominance discussions can also be masked in humor, as one individual pokes "innocent" fun at another to assess the other's reaction. As with communality discussions, the dominance conversations that take place at the beginning of a relationship are critical because they will generally define the entire course of the relationship. Of course, events can change relationships. People get angry with others, and relative economic fortunes change. Changes in established relationships, however, generally involve a great deal of emotional angst.

Conversations for reciprocity take place in ongoing relationships. Each party attempts to informally assess what potential benefits the other is able and willing to deliver. Probing for potential reciprocity greatly affects and reflects the states of communality and dominance, and can be anxiety producing. Over time reciprocal acts can change the balance of communality and dominance, depending on the relative importance of the acts to the parties. Sometimes reciprocal arrangements are explicitly negotiated up front before some benefit or assistance is rendered. Problems arise when the receiver of a benefit does not pay back the favor in the manner the giver thinks he should. The problem is exacerbated when the original act is performed with only a vague understanding of what is required by way of reciprocity.

One of the most subtle and complex conversations is between a male and a female with regard to romance. Because the emotional stakes are high, much of the conversation involves indirection. Males, fearing rejection, will try to get females to evince interest in them by means of romancing them with attention and sometimes gifts, but without asking direct questions that might elicit negative responses. The males will use double entendres and "keep it light" in building a relationship. In that way, if a female is not interested, his ego is not bruised. Females will covertly inivite unfamiliar males to approach them by using non verbal cues such as hair smoothing, smiling and eye contact. Females will attempt to determine the degree of commitment and the long-term potential of a male without committing themselves. Even if a female is interested in a particular male, she may hide it by using coy circumlocutions until she is certain that the male is sincere lest she be thought of as too eager or too easy.

The Role of Gossip

Once language had been developed for basic communication further stimulus for its development was as an extremely effective means of coordinating hunting and gathering efforts and organizing communal activities to protect vulnerable infants. After these utilitarian uses of language, the next functional impetus for development most probably was the use of language for gossip. Gossip can reduce self-doubt by publicizing and moderating the thoughts and behavior of individual members of a social circle. In this way acceptable behavior is agreed upon and promulgated. By conforming to known acceptable behavior, an individual can be assured that no one in her reference group will condemn her behavior. In addition, the knowledge that others can sometimes behave in stupid and foolish ways can be comforting. Being part of a gossip network gives one the secure feeling of being part of an in-group. (It is unfortunate, however, that in-groups often require out-groups.)

Although the term gossip has a negative connotation, it has played a critical role in the ascent of humans to dominance as well as in the establishment of religion. The effect of gossip is to constrain and regulate the behavior of members of a group so that group cohesion and effectiveness are maintained. For groups of humans, gossip provides a medium for what sociologist Bronislaw Malinowski has termed "phatic communion," or communication among individuals by means of conversation whose practical content is subordinate to its function in indicating and reinforcing social bonds and groupings.

Robin Dunbar has theorized that for early humans, language-mediated gossip became a substitute for primate grooming in so far as bonding or building cooperative networks within a group based on reciprocity. In ape cultures, social bonding and establishing reciprocal obligations by means of physical grooming is limited to very small groups by the nature of the one-on-one application and the considerable time it takes. Gossip, on the other hand, can be transmitted to small groups of intimate friends simultaneously. A snippet of gossip need only take a few minutes to deliver.

While gossip may be less personal than grooming, it deals with a much more extensive range of concerns. If there are interlocking groups, so that each of five friends who hear some gossip spreads it to four or five others who also spread it, the size of a group that can be maintained as a result of gossip becomes much larger.

Uses of Gossip

While gossip in modern times connotes pejorative stories about those who are personally known to the hearer, in early Neolithic times, and as used here, it included all sorts of stories about people known, stereotypical, and unknown. As with primate grooming, humans enjoy gossip for its own sake. They listen avidly even if it does not concern them or if they do not traffic in it. And there is a strong psychological impulse to relay gossip. People are fascinated to be privy to the covert activities of others, even if the others are not known personally. In this way using language for gossip forms and produces a reciprocity held together by phatic communion among an in-group. The maximum potential size of a group facilitated by gossip networks is thought to be in the range of about 150 individuals. There is also some research that suggests that the human brain is not capable of sustaining a network of acquaintances greater than 150 members.

From at least early Neolithic times, and likely much earlier, storytellers would tell fascinating, gossipy stories to those huddled around campfires in the evenings. These tales were entertaining, but they also imparted vocabulary, folkwisdom, and lore. The storytellers might have been older men sharing their knowledge or merely retelling stories that they had heard during their lifetimes. But there is a strong likelihood that ultimately a cadre of professional storytellers arose and they earned their living at it.

Professional storytellers would have enjoyed the handouts and the hospitality of their listeners in exchange for entertainment. The stories conveyed morals, mores, and norms of behavior so that these gradually became the accepted standards of interpersonal behavior for the community of listeners. Professional storytellers might travel among groups within related tribes, or from marketplace to marketplace, spreading absorbing tales that also taught the people what was honorable, what was acceptable with respect to behavior and attitudes, what was unacceptable, and what was punishable behavior and how it should be punished. In this way common mores would be spread among a large collection of interdependent tribes. Itinerant storytellers would have also been a means by which innovations that had been developed in one group were spread to others. In this manner gossip served both as a marketplace of morality and of progress.

Gossip and Monkey Business

Among primates, if capuchin monkeys happen to observe one of their fellows sequestering more than his share of food, they will join forces to punish the cheater. But such punishment depends on the cheating being obvious to several others. Monkeys can get away with a lot of monkey business if they are not noticed—and especially if they realize it. In a tribe of humans, even if someone does not observe the cheating activity directly but has indirect evidence or suspects cheating, she can initiate gossip about the alleged miscreant and so trigger group response or even retribution. As mediated by gossip, the nature of the castigated cheating is far more diverse and subtle than is possible without language.

Those who hear gossip subliminally evaluate whether it is reasonable and interesting (juicy). Interest is determined in part by the skill of the gossiper (or storyteller) and in part by the nature of the story—that is, the appeal of its characters or the events being described. As marginal activities are gossiped about and evaluated, over time a consensus will emerge about what is acceptable behavior, what behavior is simply shameful, and what behavior is despicable. The penchant of Neolithic humans for storytelling and for paying close attention to stories told expertly very likely grew out of the widespread practice of gossip. Many of the stories in the Bible's book of Genesis have a strong quality of gossip in their narratives though they deal with larger-than-life people not personally known to the listeners.

In the modern world, a fascination with gossip as broadly defined, both telling and listening to it, is extended to gossip about famous people, such as athletes or movie stars, who are known vicariously. Large industries are dedicated to, and profit handsomely by, reporting on the comings and goings of famous and glamorous people. For many people, it seems there is an almost insatiable appetite for knowing where and how the so-called glitterati, such as movie stars and sports stars, spend their time and what sort of clothing they wear. People will pay good money to learn about the stars' lives, and they will pay premium prices for mass market goods nominally associated with such people.

In the distant past, one of the reasons that some individuals could earn their living as storytellers was because most people were naturally fascinated by gossip. Favorite stories of a gossipy nature involved the exploits and foibles of people described as important. As is evidenced from biblical stories, most of which were originally oral and were written down at a much later time, anecdotes that reflect pejoratively on the protagonist of a story serve to heighten the dramatic tension in the story, make it more memorable, and increase the stimulus to retell it.

Individuals with an aptitude for storytelling/gossip became better through practice, as they honed their skills by keenly observing the reactions of their audiences. Those who were poor storytellers tended not to be rewarded and remained amateurs. More than mere gossip or pseudo gossip, storytelling was a marketplace of ideas and progress as well as talent and morality. Wandering from settlement to friendly settlement, storytellers told fascinating stories that tended to spread culture, morality, and applications of technology across a wide segment of a population. Many of the stories were cautionary tales having a moral. Such were the beginnings of religion.

Adverse Conformity and Gossip

Much to the chagrin of parents, a teenager's inclination to conform to the behavior of her reference group can be a much more powerful force than her concern for parental dictates, coercion, or logic. Even appeals that pander to her self-interest can carry less force. Such conformity can be driven by self-doubt in the form of the need for acceptance or approval from significant others. Those teenage individuals who do not conform to the practices of their associated reference group are often punished socially by the group. Although the conformity effect of groups of humans is most pronounced in the emotionally turbulent teenage years, it remains potent throughout life. The need to belong is a powerful force.

Evolutionary biologists in Austria and Germany conducted experiments in which human subjects were given the opinions of others with regard to behavior that had been taken by fellow subjects in the course of a game they had played.[54] Subjects were asked to evaluate how ethical each of the other game players had been in their conduct of the game. A summary of the opinions of all the participants regarding the other players was given to them. The subjects were also given objective data about the same game behavior of participants, which was based on a computer analysis. It was found that subjects tended to believe and to act on the opinions of their fellows, even though these contradicted the definitive factual data that had been given to them and which, they were expressly told, was accurate.

A consequence of the conformity effect is an almost insatiable desire not only to consume gossip but to also spread it. People are not only receptive to it, but they also actively solicit gossip as it relates to the activities of others.

One important purpose of gossip is phatic communion,[55] and not the transfer of practical information. Therefore people readily accept and retell gossipy stories without carefully reflecting on their reasonableness or checking them for accuracy. Gossip and urban legends are simply a medium of social exchange. People socially trade on them. Unless gossip or an urban legend is deemed to be obviously bogus or will reflect poorly on them, listeners may have doubts or reservations about the veracity of the stories, but they nonetheless listen to them and pass the stories on to others. In fact, even though the stories may be accepted only with a grain of salt, they may be embellished with new details and with spurious proofs of authenticity as they are spread. Men and women both engage in gossip, as loosely defined, to an equal extent, although the forms of their gossip may be different.

It seems strange that one human being should obtain vicarious pleasure simply by hearing narrative stories about the activities of casual acquaintances or complete strangers. The central characters of the stories may be people who they will seldom or never meet, who do not have any usefully valid lessons to teach them, whose lives will in no significant way impact their own lives. People readily listen to the stories even though they may suspect them of being wholly, or in part, fictive. The incredible amount of time that men devote to idly talking about various sports figures or telling dirty jokes, and that women in beauty parlors and elsewhere spend chatting about the outrageously costly fashions worn by movie stars at awards shows, lends credence to Dunbar's thesis about gossip being the language equivalent of primate grooming.

Gossip—Good and Evil

Gossip can have positive as well as negative effects. Within a village, keeping up with gossip can allay self-doubt, reinforce a sense of belongingness, and help to establish mores. Indirectly, gossip may enable members of a group to keep tabs on the activities of other members of their reference group; to figure out or instill the styles of appearance or activities that are acceptable, unacceptable, outrageous, exceptional, or ridiculous; and to assist in informally coordinating the activities of members of a group as well as to exercise mild sanctions for unacceptable behavior. (Of course in the age of Facebook, what were mild, gossipy sanctions can become traumatic.)

Returning to a favored analogy, it is clear that many, though not all, suicide bombers are rational. They have diverse motivations, but dozens have blown themselves to bits, influenced by a religious zeal, in an act deemed most heinous from the standpoint of most religious creeds. There is little doubt that such extreme self-destructive behavior, which is contrary to the most innate of human instincts, is to a large extent, but paradoxically, driven by a desire for acceptance. As such it flourishes when it is encouraged by the actions of prestigious others and when the suicides are described as being carried out by martyrs who have earned the acceptance of God as well as the elites of their religion. Martyrdom is supported by some clergy and rationalized by the influential press so that, instead of community censure, prospective suicide bombers perceive widespread approval.

Although they were not suicide bombers, John Wilkes Booth, the assassin of Abraham Lincoln in 1865, and Timothy McVeigh, who blew up the Murrah Building in Oklahoma City in 1995, murdering 168 people, had at least one thing in common. Both of them fervently believed that their bold acts would awaken the masses to the oppressive nature of the government of their day. They were absolutely certain that most people, or at least most right thinking people, thought as they did about the government. They believed that their bold act would inspire masses of like-minded people to rise up and overthrow the government (or at least effect major changes). Importantly, when history was to be written, they believed that they would be regarded as heroes.

Status, Leadership, and Religion

Groups of humans seem to implicitly recognize a need for leadership. A leader is seen as not only necessary to coordinate the activities of his followers (or group) but also to provide a climate of certainty and thus moderate self-doubt. As many social science experiments (and the TV reality show *Survivor*) have demonstrated, when a number of individuals come together in a group, specific roles tend to emerge spontaneously. One primary role that tends to emerge in all groups is that of a leader/coordinator. The leader chosen either formally or implicitly by a group may not be the strongest, smartest, most articulate, or most aggressive member. It seems the nature of, and the choice of, a spontaneous leader is highly complex. It is a function of the personality, knowledge, or ability of some individual, the mix of personalities of the group, the group's situation, and the most important threats or opportunities they recognize as being their challenges. In newly formed groups where the leader is unproven, other members of the group may tend to quickly and reflexively defer to a leader and accept direction from him unless or until he clearly proves to be unfit. It is essentially the so-called power of the hat.[56] As a default, people tend to accept rational/nominal authority as, on balance, benefiting them unless shown otherwise.

Religion is a special case of the status acceptance phenomenon. People may have serious doubts about religious beliefs or practices, or have questions about the character or knowledge of a particular priest, minister, imam, or rabbi in their reference community. Nonetheless they still give public respect and deference to these religious leaders in all matters of religion, and even in many areas that are outside of a religious purview. At its base this so-called belief in belief is a desire for an orderly society that will be of benefit to all, but especially in reducing the uncertainty of the believer.

Rodney Stark's exchange theory of religion theorizes that possible gains from accepting the metaphysical and acceding to the demands of a religion are so very much greater than any losses from rejection that most people do not insist on obtaining guarantees. The exchange theory of religion is similar to Pascal's wager, which in essence advocates that by going along and pretending to be religious even though a person has serious doubts, she will either fool God or be excused by God, and gain eternal paradise despite her inner doubts. At a more secular level, belief in belief stems from a desire for the benefits of conformity in producing a strong, potent group and a secure place within it for an individual.

Religion as a Guarantor

Across historic times religion became a kind of guarantor of reciprocity among individuals and a vehicle for achieving social harmony in large groups. The golden rule, to treat others as you wish to be treated, and much of the Decalogue requiring one to honor one's parents and to not lie, steal, murder, cheat, or resent the good fortune of others, are directed at imposing symmetrical and benign behavior among humans. Such precepts were essential to human societies long before the Ten Commandments and the Bible were formulated. In religious communities there are sanctions for disregarding religious dictates, which, depending on time, place, type of transgression, and the particular religion, have varied from minor rebukes to corporal and even capital punishment. For the most part, the rules are internalized by members of most societies so that they are most often routinely observed as behavioral norms. These implicit rules are a major factor in the cohesiveness and effectiveness of religious groups.

As sociologists have noted, religion was, and is, used as a vehicle for differentiating one group or community from others. To the same extent that it fosters intragroup cohesion it also spawns inter group hostility. Individuals might be leery of cooperating with others who do not have the same reciprocal ties to others as they do and who might not respect them. Individuals need to believe that other members of their reference group are of like mind, and are motivated and constrained by the same mores and myths as they are, so that they are roughly equal to one another. Even if outsiders did not pose an overt challenge, self-doubt among some individuals might degrade cooperative activities and social harmony. Those suffering with the greatest degree of self-doubt find the certainty of the religion of their group very comforting in dealing with (or not dealing with, and avoiding, shunning, and persecuting) others from the outside.

Religion asserts the implementation of ostensibly hard-and-fast rules and codes of conduct among all of its adherents. One is taught that following the formal and informal cultural or religious rules is always the right thing to do and the correct way to live. Follow the stated rules and you will never be sorry with respect to engendering the disapproval of others. One need never feel anxious wondering what others are thinking about her if the others are all committed to compatible religious principles. When everyone else in one's reference group is also following the rules, it makes for a very harmonious social order where people have minimal self-doubt or anxiety with regard to their interpersonal relationships and a maximal sense of belonging. By the same token, those who don't appear to subscribe to one's particular religious precepts are not to be trusted. These "others" are assumed to be unfair, devious, or inclined to do physical injury in order to get their way. Such bigotry is often accepted even when personal or group experience does not directly confirm such prejudice. It is an indirect means of delineating membership and maintaining the cohesion of a group.

Religious Manipulation

Religious belief is hardly the only way that individuals can be manipulated by others, but because it is such a ubiquitous and deep-seated cultural phenomenon, it can provide a compelling lever when used for social manipulation. In recent times a number of outrageous financial scams have seen people who were highly regarded within a religious community taking advantage of the trust of their coreligionists. To be accepted by the faithful, one must be familiar and faithful to the rules, tropes, and behavioral forms of a religion. Some of those who are very familiar with the rules and forms of a religion may be able to twist its precepts for their own benefits. Sometimes they do so with implicitly motivated reasoning—that is, without recognizing the boundaries between their own self-interest and the defense of their accepted religious tenets or theology.

The stronger the bonds of trust with regard to religious precepts, religious authorities, and even coreligionists, the more extensive the potential effects of social manipulation on the basis of the religion. Billions of dollars are voluntarily given by those who are themselves needy or relatively poor to support religion and religious institutions. Some religious leaders have no problem with traveling on their own private jets, living an opulent lifestyle in palatial homes, and owning several very expensive limousines, even as they solicit donations from the impoverished. These religious leaders brashly tout anecdotes about others who were broke but nonetheless donated their desperately needed money to God, via the preacher's fund. Miraculously, soon after their donation, the parishioners' fortunes are said to have changed radically and they became rich and happy. In other areas of the economy, such people who similarly prey on the poor might be imprisoned. It is hard to conceive of any other social phenomenon that could induce so many diverse individuals to compromise their economic well-being and, in the extreme, to destroy their very selves in suicide bombings, especially on the basis of purely speculative promises for which there can be no guarantee.

Why Do People Act Against Their Self-Interest?

Is Rodney Stark correct that the vague and highly speculative potential rewards of eternal life are so great that people are willing to exchange much of their time and their wealth, even to the point of impoverishment, for it? Are they fools to sacrifice so much for, in the words of Joe Hill, "Pie in the sky in the sweet bye and bye"? The question must be asked: are religious people aware of religion's potential for manipulation, and if so, why would they then have so much unqualified trust in religion and in religious authorities? The well-known aphorism that "the devil can quote scripture" is one indicator that the religious are fully aware of this possibility even as they succumb to the blandishment of religion. The basic answer to this conundrum is twofold.

First of all, the nature of religious doctrine is such that some of the directives and the actions that might otherwise be construed as being manipulative, because they induce behavior that is obviously contrary or detrimental to an individual's self-interest, can also be viewed by the religious as being virtuous behavior both in the short run and in some undefined long term. Many religious doctrines preach that merely seeking pleasure and avoiding pain is giving in to baser animal instincts. There is virtue and nobility in self-sacrifice, self-denial, and even suffering. Donating money and volunteering time for the benefit of others, especially in serving a religious institution, which will in turn minister to the needy, will be repaid spiritually, financially, in the afterlife, or some other way, many times over, and it also strengthens their religious community in the here and now.

Older people can be induced to give away much of their savings, even if it means personal privation or becoming a burden to their relatives or society. They are lauded for being so generous to the church. There can be a significant social payoff of acceptance and recognition for the overly generous in ignoring one's own needs for the putative benefit of others. The religious unquestioningly trust the leaders of the church, mosque, or synagogue to use their money and their energies wisely, and for temporal and ultimate good. Their own suffering may be great, but there must be those who are in greater need. Such people feel that they are superior and virtuous for having made an unselfish sacrifice for the greater good of their religion, community, and mankind, while also, as is the belief in many religions, advancing their case for their own entry to heaven. In Starkian terms, in a circular manner, the very religious manipulation that provides feelings of value or benefit also justifies the transaction's benefits. Under certain circumstances, as with primate grooming, people enjoy the very activity of giving away money for its own sake when they believe the cause is just.

Another response to the question of why people allow themselves to be manipulated by communicated religious doctrine is that there are presumed strong social sanctions against the abuse of religious doctrine with respect to the faithful of that doctrine. The prospect of being shunned or excommunicated can be dire in cases where everyone in a community refuses to speak to or have anything to do with a shunned individual. Traditionally, loners had a very hard time surviving in a community. Although many people notionally submit to exploitation by religious authorities in order to ensure their own eternal life, there are, nonetheless, very real social penalties and self-serving benefits for them in the here and now of their communities.

Admittedly, in the modern West, the sanctions of shunning or excommunication are far less coercive that they were in the past. When Baruch Spinoza was excommunicated in the seventeenth century, he was forced to become a recluse. In Mohammad's time in western Arabia, being shunned meant certain death within a few months because an individual or even a small group could not survive alone in the harshness of the desert without community resources.

The belief that others share their views about the nature of proper conduct and the purpose of life promotes pseudokinship. It greatly reinforces and strengthens the faith of many individuals. Believing that individuals who are members of other groups are different and undoubtedly unsympathetic further solidifies that bond. All or most of the members of a religious group will cooperate in the censure of anyone of their number who acts or speaks out of line with respect to the beliefs and approved conduct of the religion. Any behavior that is disapproved of by religious authorities is threatening because it is regarded as tempting to the weaker, less-committed members of the religion to wantonly transgress. Such social censure of forbidden behavior for even minor infractions is like the thin end of a wedge with regard to generating self-discipline to resist temptation for offenses of a more fundamental nature. Rather than feeling unreasonably constrained by religious strictures, many people are comforted by the coercive potential of their religion and the certainty and uniformity of social interaction that it promotes.

Language, Self-Doubt, Manipulation, and Religion

The development of language created a powerful tool that enabled a social species of hominids to achieve a high level of cooperation and coordination in dealing with the vicissitudes of their environment.. Language facilitated a normally aggressive and xenophobic species to form into larger groups or tribes. A high level of specialization among individual members of the increasingly larger human groups was also fostered by language.

Along with these benefits, language also introduced self-doubt and the ability to manipulate others through the use of language. Status striving and competition, which are conducted in other animal groups by behavioral means, could also be pursued using language by individuals in groups of humans. One method of achieving social status, available to the old and the weak, was by means of private knowledge as conveyed through language, in advising others on how to better their condition and survive or in convincing them that they could improve their condition by having the adviser invoke supernatural powers. Appealing to self-doubt and using the powers of manipulation afforded by language gave certain individuals an ability to gain a secure position or a high rank in a large group of humans. These language-brokered building blocks of social organization also gave rise to, and continue to support, religion.

CHAPTER SEVEN

Ordinary Belief And Religious Belief

Belief, Knowledge, and Reason

Most of the beliefs that we use in conducting our daily lives are what Justin Barrett has termed "nonreflective" beliefs. These are based on inductive logic. Over the course of our lives, we have observed many events that have occurred in similar fashion many times. By default we tend to believe that certain future events will probably be replicated in a similar fashion under similar circumstances. If we were to spill a cup of hot coffee in our lap, we believe that it will burn and wet our clothes, so, without thinking much about the matter, we are careful whenever we handle hot coffee. The shorthand thinking generated by the nonreflective beliefs is, on the surface, similar in many ways to the Skinnerian learning of animals. It certainly makes survival in given environments much more efficient.

Profound beliefs are those beliefs that are long lasting and influential with respect to many activities. They constitute the internalized beliefs of individuals that generally are reached after some reflection using deductive as well as inductive logic. Such reflection is often based on a human's declarative verbal thought, but it can also take place at the nonverbal, preconscious, experiential level as well. It seems to me, based on reports from primate laboratories, that higher nonhuman animals also act on complex beliefs that might be regarded as reflective if they were human.

Typology of Belief

At a conscious level, as we seek and conceive patterns in order to understand nature, we naturally form reflective beliefs that are taken to be valid. Often we accept the communicated beliefs of others if they seem reasonable in light of our experience. These beliefs seem logically to promote our own welfare as well as that of our kin, humanity, and the world and its ecology. They are the basis of our actions. Belief can be categorized at several levels:

- Validated beliefs are those established facts and concepts that could, if needed, be scientifically confirmed (or at least not rejected), and whose circumstances of applicability have been well-established. Their outcomes can be controlled to a large extent.
- Rules of thumb or heuristics that seem to work well enough are used for common endeavors whose operations are not well understood or under control. Applied heuristic techniques are not always successful, but they are usually "good enough" or very useful under certain conditions. Often, the perception of only a few external cues is sufficient for us to invoke heuristic behavior in complex situations. This can lead to problems.
- Conventional wisdom encompasses those beliefs and propositions that are widely accepted by many people without proof because they seem to be reasonable or can't be rejected out of hand. It is proof by the method of agreement. Some conventional wisdom may become tautologically true as a result of widespread agreement and the acceptance of results that are not challenged. Conventional wisdom is generally supported by anecdotal evidence that is purported to "prove," or at least demonstrate, the basic proposition supporting it.
- Faith is a belief in some overarching, generally (though not necessarily) metaphysical phenomenon in which we have some emotional investment. Faith is something that we want to be true, even if it isn't or can't be validated, and even in the face of illogic or contradictory evidence that must be rejected in order to hold or defend the belief.

Externally there are major conceptual differences between nonreflective secular or functional beliefs and the beliefs of faith. But, with respect to internal neurological brain processes, all beliefs are similar and handled in a similar manner. All beliefs, both secular and faith-based, are supported by associative chains of neurons and the protein loading at the tips of axons. There is no physical "God" part of the brain. There is no specific organ, area of the brain, neural network, or mental process that deals with notions of faith as distinct from secular or functional beliefs.

The Bases of Subjective Beliefs

Particular religious beliefs often rest on well-thought-out selections of some antecedent, plausible events or conditions that are declared to be causal to some well-known and significant outcome. Evidence regarding faith, although appearing logical and often defended with logic, is, as the philosopher Pierre Bayle declared in the seventeenth century, ultimately highly conjectural and subjective at its basis. For example, proofs for the existence of God rest on subjective assertions, such as there must be a purpose for life or the fact that the world exists means that there must be a maker. Although the propositions, on their face, appear to be logical, they are simply assertions. They are products of synthetic reasoning, in a Kantian sense, that cannot be empirically validated. A cynic might counter such asserted belief by challenging the speaker to prove it. Or by asking, Why is it so, and who says? Experiential proofs of faith are based on specious connections of cause and effect and are always after the fact. To my knowledge there never has been an example of an experiential proof of faith that has successfully passed either a prospective scientific test or a double-blind test. By definition faith cannot be proven. Despite this, even the most spiritual of people regard themselves as being rational beings who don't believe in nonsense.

It is widely held that there are no arguments that can be used to trump valid logic. Calling someone—their statements, their behavior, or their beliefs—irrational, illogical, or merely emotional is considered to be a major insult. A healthy ego, or self-concept, demands that we consider our own beliefs to be rational and valid, or else we would have changed them. However, as the old adage goes, "A lot of what we know just ain't so." Many of the beliefs that are accepted as authoritative by many people are simply conventional wisdom that is based on spurious anecdotal evidence or even blind faith. Core beliefs may rest on pure emotion based on what we need or wish to be true, rather than what is true. We are motivated to rationalize them based on post hoc anecdotal evidence. It seems that humans have a need to hold certain beliefs that they know at some level are not functional or practical.

Given the nature of the conventional wisdom, pertinent validating data are often unobtainable or a proposition is much too complex and difficult for an individual to resolve. Conventional wisdom is accepted without critical questioning primarily because respected individuals in our reference group also believe it. For humans, as social animals, there is a need to believe what others believe. However, to a greater or lesser degree, the belief or notion must sound plausible (what social scientists refer to as having "face validity".) To have face validity a proposition or a concept should not conflict with prior beliefs, be consonant with our desires and self-interests and not have apparent negative short-term consequences. The now completely discredited proposition that the sun revolves around the earth had face validity. A person standing on earth could observe the sun dailly travelling in the sky around the earth. What better proof could there be? It was so passionately believed by almost everyone that, as late as the seventeenth century, church officials had no problem excommunicating and even executing those who expressed a contrary belief.

Neural Networks and Belief

Modern humans, as were their predecessor hominids, are pattern-making and meaning-making creatures. Patterns and meanings in nature constitute beliefs. Beliefs are registered in the states of neural networks, and they determine behavior. Neural network states are continually being created, expanded, and reformed through experience. For animals and early hominids, these neural templates of belief promoted both efficiency and effectiveness with regard to complex survival tasks such as hunting, gathering, and recognizing and escaping predators. It is these configured neural networks that contain and reconstruct, when triggered, relevant memories of the map of a territory, including the places where prey, predators, forage, or dangerous obstacles are most likely found.

Subtle cue recognition,[57] such as the sight, sound, or smell of hidden prey or predators, triggers a cascade of neurotransmitter protein flows across a neural network. Representations of the pragmatic beliefs that drove the actions that allowed hominids to effectively locate and pursue prey, and to avoid and escape predators, by directing physical abilities and by knowing and second-guessing the habits and stratagems of the other creature, are embedded in configurations of neural networks. The formation of neurologically based knowledge arrangements as bases of beliefs allowed hominids to project and plan for the future. Practical belief, with respect to the presumption of patterns in nature, is necessary for survival. It is postulated that all higher animals create such neural belief networks with regard to patterns in nature, independent of language, though not nearly as efficiently and extensively as do language-enabled humans.

The buildup of neural networks that give rise to beliefs serves to delineate sense data and thus renders memory, perception, cognition, and preconscious thought more effective. The more often and the longer we look at a picture, the more detail we notice and remember. The more often a situation is encountered, the more extensive detail about it is captured by altered states of our neural networks. Knowledge and belief is acquired by our preconscious thought processes. Because of the buildup of beliefs, ultimately we can quickly respond appropriately to a situation if we perceive only a few decisive cues, thus foreshortening what might have been a tortuous reflective analysis.

Sensations or cues from the environment trigger preconscious thoughts that are considered both emotional as well as rational in nature. In the distant past, the benefits from quick reactions and automatic responses that were implemented by a repertory of practiced behaviors far outweighed mistakes made because of premature actions due to erroneous beliefs. Being able to read a situation quickly was often critical for survival. As the philosopher A. N. Whitehead has said, "Operations of [reflective] thought are like cavalry charges in battle—they are strictly limited in number, they require fresh horses and must only be made at decisive moments."

Learning

For convenience, several types of learning can be distinguished. First, there is rote learning, such as the memorization of a poem or the times tables by a third grader. Then there is simple experiential learning, such as learning to put on a warm coat when it is cold outside. Finally there is cognitive learning, where some understanding or control of various phenomena is gained. In the example of the times table, cognitive learning would occur where a person learns to derive the times tables. Experiential learning is nonreflective. It relies mainly on cue associations to form inductive belief. Cognitive is reflective. It involves the applications of deductive logic in order to discern and understand relationships and patterns among OACEREs. While some limited generalization can be applied as a result of experiential learning, generalization and extension based on cognitive learning are widespread.

The significance of preconscious thought in the learning process is unquestioned. Knotty problems are often resolved after a night's sleep. Almost everyone has had the experience of struggling long and hard to master a concept in mathematics, physics, or some other arcane subject only to later realize that the erstwhile unfathomable concept is really intuitively logical and could have been deduced in a straightforward manner. We reprove ourselves for the struggle to master, by means of rote or essentially brute force, that which we could have thought our way through from the beginning with innate logic. Some teachers are adamant that the best way to learn something is by intuitive logic that builds up from axioms or first principles, rather than learning by rote memorization. But this assumes that the neurological pathways supporting the logic that leads to an intuitive understanding of, or the solution to, a problem either mirror the teaching process or have been in place all along, rather than developing as the nature of the solution becomes progressively clearer.

We (and the teachers) fail to recognize that neurological structures in our brains are changed in the learning process. What is intuitively logical to the instructor, or to the student only after her mental effort to master the material, was not at all accessible before the struggle. It is the very process of learning that produces permanent neurological changes which subsequently allows for intuitive solutions to similar problems.

We are aware of our progress in cognitive knowledge by means of external validation but we are not aware of the effects of the development of internal neurological structures. Teachers and others who have long ago mastered abstract concepts may lack an appreciation for the need to develop the requisite neural structures, and as a result, they are often frustrated when their students cannot comprehend what is obvious to them.

As a form of turnabout being fair play, youngsters take much more quickly and intuitively to the uses of computers and other modern electronic technology than do oldsters because of their brains' much greater plasticity in quickly forming the requisite new neural networks that render multiple-step computer procedures, which are esoteric to the oldsters, as being simply logical and intuitive to the youngsters.

A similar process works for physical task development as well. There is an old adage that goes, "It's just like riding a bicycle: once you've learned you never forget." The centrifugal, gyroscopic effect that keeps a person upright on an unstable platform such as a bicycle is not intuitive. Learning to accept this counterintuitive effect can be easier said than done. For some people it is a difficult and lengthy process to build up the mental structures that will overcome the reflex to stabilize oneself and the bike by putting one's foot on the ground. The older the beginner is, the harder it is. However, once this enabling brain change has been achieved and the activity mastered, not only bike riding but other similar activities become second nature and can be invoked whenever necessary, even after years of nonuse.

Preconscious Learning Effects

The shift in intuitive belief with respect to neural networks is similar to other brain changes that allow us to perform highly complex tasks at a preconscious level. We do not deliberate with respect to the many subtle and complex cues and sensations we receive from the environment as we barrel down the highway in our cars at sixty miles an hour or more. In response to many diverse cues, we perform a complex series of actions—guiding the car, keeping it on the road, not crashing into other cars as they move in and out of our lane—as we progress toward our intended destination, all without reflective or declarative thought.

If we had to rely completely on cognitive deliberative processes, as we do when first learning to drive, we could not drive a car nearly as well or as effectively. Contrary to the admonition to pay very close attention to everything, we would be dangerous drivers if we did because, at the conscious level, we cannot pay close attention to more than one thing at a time. Fortunately the "bandwidth" of preconscious thought is many times greater than that of conscious declarative thought. Safe driving requires preconscious attention to several things in a very rapid sequence and then being prepared to focus on one of them should it become necessary. Restricted to the conscious reflective level, we would be destined to forever drive like rank beginners.

Language and Learning

The interaction of thinking, behavior, and the alteration of the brain's neural networks that affect future behavior and thinking is both circular and serendipitous for all animals. Language performs a multiplier effect. Humans, communicating by means of natural language, can control and structure their environments to an extent that is impossible for other animals. Importantly, unlike animals, people can exert conscious control over some of the structural changes to the preconscious neural networks of their brains.

Not only is it logical but also empirically demonstrable that language, in the form of speech or reading, can, like other behavior, alter neural networks. FMRI studies clearly show that as people consider problems and engage in self-talk, various neurons are activated. One common definition of learning is a change of behavioral response in a given situation as a result of the acquisition of information or experience. A great deal of our learning is achieved by means of language, oral and written, which is transmitted through sense media. Arguably, such language-mediated learning for modern humans, and especially youngsters, is more extensive than their learning from direct experience. Much of learning, particularly among children, is a blend of direct experience and communicated language.[58] Not only, as indicated above, does spoken language that is heard cause neural changes in the brain, but these changes can be long lasting. Some learned notions constitute long-term beliefs that become factors in interpreting or understanding subsequent experiences, including language that is heard.

The brain of a person who hears language is affected by the content of language and by the metalanguage, including the quality of the sound itself. It is also dependent on prior brain structures that are in place. A controversial theory, espoused in the book *Hidden Persuaders*, by Vance Packard, is that certain subliminally received language can also compel behavior even though it is received below the level of consciousness. Although the subliminal effect, presented in the book, is wildly exaggerated, in special cases it can be demonstrated that an individual performing some behavior may indeed be unaware of the source of some suggestive directive that alters its execution or even gives rise to it.

Learning and Belief

In the middle of the twentieth century, learning experiments were performed by behavioral psychologists, such as B. F. Skinner. In some of the experiments, for example, rats were placed in an enclosure that contained a lever. After some time running around, sniffing and pushing things, the rat would eventually press the lever and food would be introduced into the enclosure. In short order the rat would "learn" that whenever the lever was pushed food would be received. After a number of trials, the researcher would change the mechanism to either increase the time lag between pressing the lever and the arrival of food or arrange for no food to be received when the lever was pressed. A conditioned rat would continue to press the lever a number of times before it gave up. Conditions were varied by increasing the number of trials where food was not delivered to see how long the rat would persist in pushing the lever before giving up. In some experiments, after learning to press the lever for food, the food would be dispensed intermittently, and the number of presses until food was received or the rat gave up receiving reinforcement for the last time was carefully noted.

The rat was said to have associated the process of pushing the lever with obtaining food. That is, a mental association was created and remained represented within the neural networks of the rat brain. Put in other words, the rat came to believe that pushing the lever would result in getting food, although behavioral scientists (and others) generally do not use terminology such as belief in describing the nature of an animal's behavior. When the rat became hungry, it looked for cues in its environment that might lead to acquiring food. Based on memory associations in the neural networks of its brain, the rat believed that pressing the lever would yield food. A cynic might propose that if the rat could speak it might be convinced that unrequited presses of the lever were its own fault for failure to live right. The believing rat, therefore, might continue to press the lever forever without obtaining food, until it starved to death.

The pioneers of behaviorism, such as J. B. Watson and B. F. Skinner, made it a point of pride that they only dealt with measurable and highly controlled input as well as observable and measurable resultant outcomes. They disdained any speculation with respect to underlying processes in the "black box" of the brain that might be responsible for what they termed "learning effects." The rat itself was not aware of the nature of the experiment or the mechanisms by which the food was stocked and released. But its behavior was determined by its processes of thought. The behavioral scientists learned about rat behavior. Without doubt, it was a learning experience for the scientists. From the point of view of the rat, however, I contend that the experiential learning experiments are more aptly characterized as belief formation and belief alteration experiments than learning.

At the margin, cognitive learning is a process aimed at acquiring an understanding of some phenomenon so as to be able to gain control of it. Teachers explain a particular technique or phenomenon, why it works, how it relates to other similar techniques or phenomena, and how it can be generalized. Inductive or experiential learning occurs when neural networks are formed that associate some phenomenon with the conditions under which it occurs and its relationships with other salient phenomena. Skinner's rats had no control over the food that was dispensed except in pressing the lever in the belief that food would appear, and no understanding or knowledge of the experiment in which they were participating. If the rats had any notion that they were being manipulated by an experimenter, they might have regarded the experimenter as being a god.

Beliefs can be taught or inculcated. But the focus of belief is the repetition of what works, avoiding what doesn't work, and recognizing the situations applicable to each. At the far end of a continuum, many beliefs are formed as preconscious associations in a natural, nonreflective manner. It is very doubtful that rats reflect on why or under what conditions pressing a bar yields food. Many of our human beliefs are acquired without deliberation or reflection as a result of experiences and input from our senses that create preconscious neural associations. Unlike cognitive learning, beliefs that we hold in certain areas or aspects of our lives need not be logically consistent with those that are operative in other aspects of our lives.

The Brain and Individual Differences

Animal behavior continues to be regarded by many as innate, emotional response to environmental circumstances, rather than being calculated or involving sentient responses to an encountered stimulus. Behaviorists considered the brain to be like a black box. Its internal workings are not directly knowable, but they can be acceptably finessed with respect to the knowledge of outcomes that result from consistent given inputs. All rat brains were assumed to operate in the same manner that is analogous to a the situation of a locked impenetrable device in which fixed mechanisms connect inputs to outputs.

Operations of mechanistic thought are learned indirectly from the objective measurements of inputs and outcomes. The preferred terminology of behaviorists connotes unconscious reflex linkages of cause-effect relationships rather than speculating on the internal thought processes that control the behavior of the individual subject animal. Behaviorists' experimental treatment, it seems to me, leads to belief formation rather than learning in a true sense, and this difference, though it may be subtle, is more than merely semantic.

It was observed in behaviorist experiments that individual animals of the same species of similar age and condition respond somewhat differently with regard to controlled stimuli. The number of trials to learn the behavior and the number of barren trials before the extinction of the learning can differ significantly from one animal to another. Researchers, however, masked such individual differences with statistics, such as the average number of trials before extinction for all subject animals used in the experiment. In doing so a great deal of information was ignored with respect to consideration of intraspecies biological variation.

Individual differences in performance can be due to the experimenter's inability to absolutely control every aspect of the experimental situation, but they may also be due to variations in the creatures' intelligence, physical ability, and individual temperaments. It is difficult to reject the general notion that, before pushing the lever, the rat, at some level of its nonverbal preconsciousness, had an unquestioned unreflective belief that pushing the lever would yield food. Even in rats, experience alters beliefs, beliefs tend to be stable, and they are determined in part by processes over which the subject rat (i.e., its brain), as opposed to the researcher and the experimental conditions, has some measure of control or at least affect.

Rats and humans are both mammals, and their brains share many anatomical and functional similarities despite their differences. It can clearly be inferred that established human belief begins in the neural structures of the brain and is facilitated by the differential production and transmission of brain chemicals that are involved in the learning process. Although the technology was not available to the early behaviorists, fMRI studies clearly confirm neural changes in rat brains as a result of stimulus-response learning experiments. Behavioral psychologists of the 1940s and '50s did not believe that stimulus-response learning in controlled circumstances could be applied to humans as well as to rats. Under certain circumstances it can.

The Power and Limitations of Belief

In general, the longer the string of successful trial presses of the lever, the longer a rat will persist in pushing the lever even though no food is obtained. Similarly the more useful a belief and the longer it has been successfully used, the stronger it becomes and the more resistant to purging. In those situations where the rat intermittently obtains food, interspersed with presses of the lever that yield no food, the result is that the rat will persist in pressing the lever for a far longer time than was the case with continuous reinforcement followed by complete cessation. Similarly, human belief also becomes more resistant to purging if it is useful some of the time. In this sense the lessons learned by behaviorists are applicable to humans.

Every sports coach and boxing manager is well aware of the power of belief in achieving success. Boxing managers often arrange easy confidence-building matches for their boxers. When a boxer believes that he can and should win a match, he will put forth a greater effort and disregard pain inflicted by his opponent. An occasional minor setback can serve to strengthen the resolve and greater efforts of the athlete. Athletes in general build up their confidence and their appetite for winning as a result of success in competitions as well as being told of their superior ability by people they respect.

Seminal, Cascading Experiences

In his book *Outliers*, Malcolm Gladwell pursues the existential theme that it is happenstance or relatively short-lived but formative experiences that are most responsible for producing exceptional people. An example Gladwell uses is that of youngsters whose birthdates occurred right after the cutoff date for enrollment in childhood hockey leagues. They tend therefore to be stronger, faster, and better skaters than those youngsters who were born later in the year. Because of this slight advantage, some of them succeeded early in the first league that they joined, and as a result, they received more attentive coaching. With better coaching some of them performed better and got more positive feedback on their performance. His analysis of birthdates of NHL hockey players demonstrated that many of them happened to be born in January or February, which shows a positive correlation between birth month and hockey prowess.

Independent of fMRI studies, we humans presume that our beliefs are rational, valid, and based on memories of thoroughly vetted propositions. Beliefs are thought to reside as permanent, fully formed entities in our brains, and changed only by being destroyed or replaced by more reasonable beliefs. *But this is not so.* Like other memory, our beliefs are developed over time, and they remain in the form of associations in neural networks. Such memories and beliefs are retained in the form of more well-defined neural networks and a proclivity to trigger certain neurotransmitter proteins in the amygdala or hippocampus of the brain in certain circumstances. Such internal representations of beliefs are malleable. They are adaptable and can be triggered by a wide range of circumstances. At a preconscious level, we can retain incompatible beliefs without mental distress unless we encounter an explicit situation where such different beliefs indicate that inconsistent or incompatible actions needs to be taken.

Just as the rat comes to believe that the lever no longer provides food, new beliefs must also deal with old beliefs, not by simply erasing them but by forming new neural networks that gradually or swiftly encroach over the old networks. For the most part, adults do not just accept new beliefs de novo as though there are no other existing beliefs that impinge on the new one. Previously held associated beliefs must be conflated with new beliefs, altered, or progressively obliterated.

Memory

Computer analogies are limited with respect to the structure and operation of biological memory. In a computer, information exists as discrete data, albeit in representational form as binary code. It is located at specific addresses or places within the computer's physical memory device(s). By contrast, animal memory does not exist as a series of discrete coded entities but rather amorphously, as connections among neural pathways and protein loadings at the tips of axons. There is no one-to-one relationship between a memory factoid and any specific network of neural configurations. When a particular synapse is triggered, it begins a unique chain reaction along networks of millions of neurons. The final or aggregate effect from the output of the many interconnected neurons is the production of a memory. When the recall process is triggered at different times, a somewhat different version of the memory is composed each time, depending in part on context, such as the triggering circumstances, elapsed time, and intervening memories or other neural changes.

Memory research at the neurological level is comparatively recent. In the 1990s it was discovered that a certain chemical erased memory in fish. When the chemical anisomycin, which is a protein synthesis inhibitor, was put into a tank of water, fish that were introduced into the tank became disoriented. They were apparently incapable of learning their way around the physical structures of the tank, something fish normally do with ease. Postmortem examinations determined that the chemical inhibited the production of a protein that is necessary for memory in the fishes' brains. This alerted scientists to look for and to study proteins that are required for the formation of long-term memory in animals and humans.

There is a major advantage to neurological processes that remember by neural associations. Memories that are recalled and reconstructed from long-term memory are integrated with current sensory information in the hippocampus. These reconstructed associated memories from the past are merged with current sensory experiences and become more useful with respect to dealing with a current situation. Memory retrieval occurs at the unconscious level so that a person is completely unaware of the process. Older people commonly experience "senior moments," a condition where they are unable to remember something that they are sure they know. Often after an hour or even a day or more, the answer pops into their consciousness. This often occurs at a time when they are thinking of other, unrelated matters.

The process of merging current information with memories that are recalled allows them to be updated for use in the future before they are stored again in permanent memory. (Aristotle's technique of associating new memories with old over-learned memories supports this view.[59]) The disadvantage of this process of biological memory formation and retrieval is that memories are not so much recalled in pristine form as they are unconsciously reconstructed with regard to the situation at hand. They are reconstructed by accessing a large number of associated neural networks that are integrated with selective sensory information. In this way the retrieved memories may be selective or confounded with memories of other events and otherwise not completely faithful to past occurrences. Reconstructed memories are altered or adapted to a greater or lesser extent to suit current circumstances and uses.

Experiments have been performed where people were asked to draw pictures immediately after seeing a video of an auto accident. After various elapsed times, they were again asked to draw pictures of the accident scene. Curiously, the experiments reveal that in drawing the subsequent pictures, even after a lapse of several hours, the subjects often included accurate details that they had not included in their first drawing. This indicates that either not all information in short-term memory was used, possibly because of various "distractors" of the moment, or further unconscious cognitive searching and analysis determined that other factors were relevant. As expected, with the passage of time, subjects were also more likely to include more erroneous details in their pictures.

The memory of a specific incident can be reconstructed many times, but it will have become blended with, or "contaminated" by, sensory input with which it has become associated in the periodic reconstructions. Because of such conflation with sensory input from intervening and confounding situations, the more often a memory is recalled, the less precise or faithful it becomes with respect to the original event as well as the initial memory. As might be concluded from the McMartin and other preschool sexual abuse trials, people, especially youngsters, asked to recall events that occurred some time in the past are very vulnerable to suggestions and to current circumstances in their recall of past events[60].

For our ancient ancestors out in the African savanna, this process of memory formation was a boon. The continual and unthinking updating of old memories was less confusing and far more valuable for survival than the alternative computer-like method of discrete memory storage, retrieval, and complex analysis. Discrete memories preserved and recalled faithfully must be screened, compared to other discrete memories, evaluated in light of a current situation, and matched to the new circumstances. This is a complex, time-consuming, and inefficient process often requiring external knowledge (analogous to the operations of supplemental computer programs) to bootstrap itself. It requires far more brainpower than the automatic process that has evolved with respect to biological preconscious thinking and memory reconstruction.

In some areas of modern society, however, the biological memory process can be problematic. For example, memories of much earlier events are sworn to be "the whole truth and nothing but the truth" in courts of law. But the unreliability of eyewitness memories that have been recalled many times in the often lengthy interval that has passed between an incident and the trial can be a real problem. To compound the problem, people in general firmly believe that the memory they have recalled is indeed wholly accurate. Under experimental conditions, however, it is demonstrable that invariably many of the details of their memory are incorrect and that the inaccuracies grow with time. This phenomenon, the Rashomon effect, also partially explains why two or more witnesses to the same event may have divergent recollections of the event after the passage of time.

At the preconscious level, primitive beliefs based on associative learning were formed with respect to anticipating or predicting future situations that would or might be dangerous. Our ancestors learned to avoid certain foods believed to be detrimental to their health, to avoid locations where they might be exposed to danger, and to be wary of others, especially strangers who might harm them. To an extent, our attraction, aversion, or psychological sensitivity to certain other people, animals, or situations that we have recently encountered, the so-called first impressions effect, developed as an application of the ancient nonreflective belief formation process, a process that remains operational at the preconscious level for modern humans.

Both the power and resilience of invoked beliefs are increased when they are tailored to the context of a situation that triggers their formation. These are further increased if the beliefs have proven beneficial in the past or if they are known to be shared by significant others. For these reasons religious beliefs are especially steadfast. Belief can be based on a complex blend of empirical experience, temperament, the experiences of others, conventional wisdom, logic, and faith. At the conscious level of language, there is an implicit attempt to impose logic on beliefs. At the unconscious, neurological level, perceived utility and physical and ego self-protection, rather than logical consistency, are most important.

Pattern Recognition

Animals and humans tend to have a penchant (a strong tendency just short of a compulsion) to determine patterns and cause-effect relationships of those objects and events that they deem to be most significant in their environments. Wolpert points to this trait as the basis of a "true understanding of Nature."[61] It is their dazzling effectiveness in discerning and remembering definitions and associations with regard to OACEREs that separates humans from other animals. In particular, the patterns and relationships that are regarded as useful are refined and extended by means of comparison and contrast, metaphors, distinctions, and other evaluations that depend on language ability. New activities are contrived and initiated in order to reveal the nature and usefulness of various beliefs and hypotheses under varying circumstances. Doing so through the use of language improves and extends the range of application of beliefs.

But this gift of superior pattern recognition ability and differentiation of OACEREs can also extend to the presumption of patterns where none exist. Many, if not most, patterns are speculative and tentative when they are first conceived of from experience. Similarities and differences are subjective. Through repeated experiences, comparing and contrasting objects and events, similar and dissimilar characteristics are noted, confirmed, and categorized into sets of OACEREs. The more common and experientially or cognitively confirmed these patterns and cause-effect relationships are, the more they become established with regard to the brain's neural networks of beliefs. The more well-established the nonreflective beliefs become, the more automatically they are invoked when circumstances deemed to be relevant are encountered.

The process of vetting beliefs, with respect to their accuracy as a reflection of reality and their usefulness to the individual, is not foolproof. Logically, where a belief cannot be confirmed by predicting or explaining later occurrences, one might presume that it would be discarded or modified. Just as the rat ceases to press the bar if it does not yield food, useless and especially counterproductive beliefs tend to be abandoned. But the belief may have been, or might be, useful in some other context. Humans can be convinced that beliefs can be useful in some oblique way or at some time in the future. Hasty elimination of all aspects of a belief can leave a void with respect to dealing with irregular occurrences in the environment or learning from the results of certain experiences. For humans, summarily dismissing beliefs that don't seem just right in a particular context is inhibited because of their circular penchant to use belief in order to interpret reality and to extend related beliefs.

Although using nonreflective belief to interpret reality is generally a very positive factor, it can also cause problems. Because of the circularity of interpreting experiences, new experience can be erroneously interpreted so as to confirm and therefore reinforce false beliefs. Of course, in most instances this is a self-limiting or self-correcting process. Over time, as beliefs fail to be useful, the acute human senses of perception and cognition, along with communication with others, will tend to correct false or useless beliefs and reorganize belief structures. But, if such beliefs are by nature difficult or impossible to disprove through direct experience, and are adaptable so as to be related to a wide variety of events, they tend to persist.

The Circular Interpretation of Beliefs

We don't comprehend the cognitive processes by which a rat's thinking operates or its ability to rationalize, if it does, but the behaviorists' experiments have clearly demonstrated that when an animal sometimes receives a reward for performing a particular task and sometimes does not, it serves to actually strengthen belief, as indicated by the extended persistence of the learned causal behavior. Conjecturally, if a human can be convinced that some infrequent occurrence is due to a metaphysical or religious cause, it may also tend to strengthen his religious belief or faith even though, rationally, the cause-effect linkage is highly speculative.[62]

Some years ago Leon Festinger studied a cult that had a deep-seated religious belief that the world would end on a certain date.[63] Cult members quit their jobs, sold and gave away their possessions, and gathered together and engaged in fervent prayer as they awaited the end of the world. When the world did not end as foretold, one might have predicted that these people would lose their faith and their beliefs. This was not the case. In fact, cult members rationalized that the nonoccurrence of the end of the world was a positive sign from God. For most of them, according to Festinger, their faith and their beliefs in their religious doctrines became stronger.

Paradoxically, human commitment to prior beliefs can become stronger because of the failure of the type of belief, characterized as faith, to objectively reflect reality. With our marvelous powers of rationalization, humans can reinterpret an initial situation as well as selected outcomes and their presumed consequences. They may attribute the nonevent to their own interpretation of some intervening event that had occurred. They might conclude that somehow the original belief was misinterpreted or that the tragedy actually occurred but in a different form or place. Like Jonah in the Bible, who was told that the people of Nineveh had repented their iniquities and reformed, they may rationalize that something had occurred to obviate the necessity for God to carry out the tragedy. Cult believers might have concluded that their own piety and their prayers in the face of a possible calamity worked to save the world. They praised God for the miracle for the sake of others even though it meant that they themselves were temporarily denied their share in the world to come.

Complex, Experiential Learning

Unlike the classic behaviorists' animal experiments, where some critical necessity must be obtained by learning a simple, specific task under tightly controlled conditions, most of animal and human nonreflective learning is far more ambiguous and tenuous. Natural learning generally occurs under inconsistent, uncontrollable circumstances. Many concurrent lessons may be learned over the same period of time. The time lapse between behavior and reward can be substantial, with many other intervening events. Furthermore, both the nature of the causal behavior and the rewards obtained, which must be connected for learning to take place, can be vague or ambiguous with respect to several significant dimensions.

We are told that every once in a while a compelling belief bursts forth as an epiphany. For example, on his journey to Damascus, Paul had a dream about Jesus that dramatically changed his life. While it is possible, it is highly unusual for significant life-altering beliefs to be formed de novo in a single eureka moment. This is seldom, if ever, the case. It is far more likely that such eureka moments occur only after some new thought or some bit of new information is suddenly and associatively connected with prior notions that had been bothersome and chewed over preconsciously for some time. After a significant period of either conscious or preconscious rumination on some thorny issue, a comprehensive solution can suddenly pop into one's conscious mind. Especially after periods of sleep or some unusual occurrence, solutions to vexing problems are often realized even though the sleeping or taken-aback person had no inkling that the problem, or its solution, was being considered.

There are stories of ancient and modern holy people and other charismatic individuals, such as the fictional Svengali or the real-life Rasputin, Jim Jones, or Marshall Applewhite, who seemingly could, in fairly short order, profoundly and permanently alter the belief structures of the brains of some of those with whom they came in contact. However, as Rodney Stark argues in his book *The Rise of Christianity*, such examples of rapid, dramatic changes of entire belief structures are very rare exceptions. They are often precipitated only after the convert has been primed for some time by means of thinking and worrying about a personal or existential problem.

Profound beliefs, including religious beliefs, are built up slowly as associations in neural networks continue to be created and expanded from an early age and over many experiences. Such experiences start with the teaching and the examples of parents but then continue on throughout life based on both subjective interpretation of the unfolding of significant events as well as interactions with significant others. The experiences that form our religious beliefs are often coincident with significant or happy events, praise from significant others, particular objects or symbols, and many, many other facets of our daily lives. At the same time, beliefs that are triggered by distressing or traumatic events can often be summarily acquired and compelling.

The Development of Belief

Earliest childhood memories and religious stories are most vivid and significant, but religious concepts continue to develop. Beliefs are not static. Instead they are altered with each new relevant experience, even though such alteration may not be acknowledged or recognized by the believer. Exposure to new ideas and the experience of new events most often are interpreted to reinforce old beliefs. They are, in a sense, integrated with old beliefs so that an inertia, with respect to belief alteration, is developed. Subtle alterations in established beliefs can occur even where an individual is completely unaware of them. In the normal course of events, rarely do new experiences, good or bad, immediately and radically change current beliefs or create entirely new beliefs whose foundations have not been laid for some time.

As discussed earlier, beliefs reside at the neuronal and nonverbal level of the brain and don't necessarily have to make sense with respect to linguistic reasoning. Belief at the preconscious level can be linguistically characterized as feelings or latent predispositions to behave in certain ways, or to express opinions, in response to certain conditions or events. At the preconscious level, like hypnotized individuals, we have little problem in accepting and contemplating logically incompatible or impossible concepts or relationships. However, symbolic language reasoning ability serves to police illogical beliefs at the conscious level, ensuring that public actions and utterances are not inconsistent or logically indefensible. Mirror neuron effects tend to function so as to temper our speech with respect to our perceptions of others' beliefs.

The paradox of how scientists can reject evolution while at the same time work in fields that are dependent on concepts derived from and reliant on evolutionary theory can be explained by the discontinuity that exists between conscious, language-mediated thinking and preconscious, neural network associations. Operations of preconscious thought processes can explain why devout Muslims who are also secular scholars or accomplished scientists can keep straight faces as they insist that the Koran contains all of the scientific knowledge that has been discovered or that ever will be discovered.

Of course, on a case-by-case basis, it is difficult to determine the level of sincerity of people who blithely accept incompatible notions such as a conflict between evolution and religion. Is the individual merely rationalizing to satisfy two irreconcilable groups to which he belongs? Does he truly not recognize the incompatibility, or merely not acknowledge it? Can a person truly believe in striving for peace and charity to one's fellow humans while committing heinous atrocities? Is she genuinely sincere about publicly advocating an extreme belief in one area on her life while espousing incompatible beliefs in other areas?

Internalization of Belief

Fundamental beliefs are those that become reflexive guides to action under various common circumstances. These beliefs tend to be constantly socially reinforced whether or not they can be objectively validated. A salesperson's approach to a new customer may be based on his beliefs about the actions, gestures, product knowledge, or phrases that will ingratiate him with a prospective customer and garner success. If he has had success with sports discussions, shaggy dog stories, or off-color jokes, the salesperson will perfect these approaches and will preconsciously attribute much of his success to such gambits.

Internalization of basic beliefs involves many pathways of association in neural networks, as well a high density of neurotransmitter molecules, which ensures the firing of a chain of synapses when an elicited association is triggered. For the faithful, religious beliefs become well-established at neural levels of the brain's cortex—they become second nature. Since the neural associations exist below the level of language, they tend to be invoked by preconscious triggers as well as by conscious thoughts. The warm, fuzzy feelings that people get from beholding religious symbols or participating in rites are initially and primarily experienced at a preconscious level. For humans, as social animals, contentment can be observed to be associated with being part of a religious community and performing the rites and duties required by the religion. In circular fashion the appropriateness and benefits of the behavior seem to be reinforced daily.

Because religious beliefs are associated with a wide array of experiences—birth, marriage, death, holiday celebrations, good and bad fortune—and with symbolic objects, they have highly diverse effects with respect to various neural networks of the human brain. Since these effects on the brain are at the preconscious level, they are not necessarily coherent or logical in a formal language sense. Our own belief in God, for instance, is tied into who we were, who we are, what we desire, and how we see ourselves and our futures. Our fundamental beliefs are supported at a neural level by, for example, memories of the objects we have associated with belief in God, what we have been told by significant people in our lives, our presumptions about the beliefs of our parents and our pastor, and even an acceptance of a vague idea of some form of life after death.

For belief formation, sensations from events and experiences must have a long-lasting effect on the associative connections of neural networks. It is primarily an inductive process. Sensations create neural associations that can be classified as being either benign or injurious to the individual. These determine future behavior as a creature seeks to survive, seek pleasure, and avoid pain.

Learning, by contrast, has important deductive as well as inductive reasoning components. Higher animals may have inductive powers of belief formation that are comparable to humans. However, without language, their deductive learning ability is limited. When language-enabled humans face a new situation, past deductive lessons are implicitly mixed with inductive associations in determining a solution or reaction.

CHAPTER EIGHT

Religious Behavior And Ritual

Religion and Behavior

Although much of learned discourse on religion tends to focus on theology, scripture, and philosophy, most individuals relate to religion at the behavioral and social levels rather than the intellectual level. People go to church, participate in church activities, and network with coreligionists. They read prayer books, sing hymns, touch their foreheads to the ground five times a day in obeisance to Allah, light Sabbath candles, inculcate their children, and observe holiday ceremonies. Formulaic behavior, such as rites and rituals, is one of the most powerful methods for inducing people to commit to a religion. Every religion has prescribed rituals. Many churchgoers and mosque-goers may not read scripture daily, weekly, or even yearly, and many are unfamiliar with it. Sermons wash over them and are quickly forgotten, experienced more as entertainment than as prescriptive lessons. Ordinary people seldom seriously discuss theology with their coreligionists, and when they do, they often misquote it. Much of religious behavior is initiated from a preconscious level of thought.

In circular fashion, the preconscious brain initiates actions and then, in turn, the effects of the actions are fed back via one or more of the senses to stimulate activity in the brain. As the psychiatrist Eric Berne has described in his book *The Games People Play*, an unconscious, persistent way of thinking can have long-lasting effects that permanently alter our interactions with others. Persistent ways of behavioral interaction become inured in our thought processes, and therefore self-perpetuating. Predominant attitudes and temperament are, in part, the outcome of ways of thinking that have become habitual, but for which we are not aware. Subliminally, they continue to affect our behavior toward others and, in response, others' behavior toward us. Beliefs and attitudes circumscribe our relationships and define "who we are."

Brain Circuits and Behavior

(Those of you who are right-handed and play tennis can perform this thought experiment. Others can adapt it to some other physical activity, such as bowling or golf, or to their left-handedness.) Imagine making a perfect service ace in tennis. Think in your mind about how you throw the ball up with your left hand. With your right arm, you swing the racquet in an overhead arc, and you smack the ball downward just at the top of its travel with plenty of pace and spin so that it just clears the net and curves downward into the corner of your opponent's service court, less than an inch inside the boundary line.

Now try to imagine this same service scenario using your left arm. Your thoughts will not be nearly as detailed and vivid as they were for the right-handed service. This reflects the awkwardness that you might have if you really tried to serve with your left arm. But why is it so? It is only an imaginary exercise, so why can't we conjure up as vivid, detailed, and fluid a vision of being the equal of a left-handed John McEnroe as we can for our experienced right arm?

Those readers who are older and not able to play tennis nearly as well as they once could can still perform the third segment of the thought experiment. They will find that they can still conceive of the perfect serve ace with their right arm, and only awkwardly with their left arm, even though they are now physically incapable of performing the serve with a modicum of grace with either arm.

The answer is that in learning and practicing our tennis serve, we have built neural networks in our brain that direct our behavior. When we think about the activity, we call on these neural networks to imagine actually performing the task. Since we have never learned to serve with our left arm (unless we are ambidextrous or left-handed), the neural networks we call upon to imagine that task are not nearly as extensive or as well-organized. Although physical ability may decline with age or through lack of use, established neural network pathways tend to persist.

As John Dewey pronounced, "I hear and I forget, I see and I forget, I do and I remember." Although seeing and hearing do in fact build neural networks and create memories, the most effective means of adapting neural networks is to act on sense data from the environment and receive sense feedback from the result of the action. We remember because the axons of various neurons have changed so that they communicate with other neurons that are relevant to the performance of a task. The more often a task is performed under varying circumstances, the more neurons are connected, the more proteins are concentrated at the ends of the affected axons, and the greater the potential to manufacture the particular proteins involved. One of the major reasons why smoking is such a difficult habit to break is that, at least for inveterate smokers, it is practiced many times a day and is closely associated with many routine activities, such as finishing a meal or drinking coffee.

Not only is sense-data feedback from behavior capable of configuring neural networks, but language conveyed to the brain as sound or sight data can also affect neural networks, albeit not as effectively. Significant as well, we humans, without performing action or receiving outside stimulus, are capable of adjusting our own neural networks recursively simply by our thinking—that is, by conscious internal monologue. Such internal monologue is also capable of altering behavioral response to external stimuli.

An autosuggestive method for self-improvement was advocated by Émile Coué early in the twentieth century. Using his methods, moods and behaviors are changed by means of daily repetition of a self-improvement mantra, such as, "Every day, in every way, I am getting better and better." The technique does work after a fashion, although not sufficiently effectively or in a controlled-enough manner as to be widely practical. Experiments were performed with basketball players where one group practiced on the courts, another group thought about playing, and a third group did nothing. The results clearly demonstrated that thinking about playing improved a player's game performance—not nearly as much as actual practice, but measurably more than doing nothing.

Three Rs of Survival Behavior

Neural networks are expanded and elaborated by means of the repetition, replication, and recursion of behaviors. Such behaviors are important for acquiring and using survival skills. The predilection of creatures to replicate successful behavior is a critical survival attribute. Replication of behavior involves the ability of animals to adapt learned procedures to related but slightly differing conditions and contexts. This ability is supported by the nature of associative long-term memories (in contrast to the discrete memory of a computer). Behavior is adjusted from past successful learned behavior if it is deemed to be more appropriate with respect to altered variables in a familiar situation. If the altered behavior proves more efficacious, it becomes stored in long-term memory associations and tends to be the basis of replication in future circumstances that are judged to be similar.

Behavioral recursion is the condition where a set procedure or stratagem is used repeatedly as an element of other more comprehensive strategies in various circumstances where it is considered to be effective or needed. Within their overall hunting strategy, cats have learned to wait until prey is totally immobilized or dead before starting to eat it. This results in repetitious behavior, as the cat strikes a mouse and then waits for it to move, and if it does, the cat strikes it again and waits. This is done for the sake of both safety and efficiency. To the extent that creatures were, or are, creative in extending the basic inclination to repeat successful behavior, the more successful the species.

In Paleolithic times, and earlier with respect to predecessor species, activities that were repeated with frequency tended to be those that most critically fostered survival. The more successful an individual creature is at survival behavior, the more adept it becomes. The more adept the animal becomes, the more successful it is at those activities, such as acquiring food and mating, that ensure passing on its genes. The more often a behavior is executed and the more complex the behavior, the more extensive neural networks of the brain become and the larger the brain area becomes that is devoted to supporting it. Within groups of social animals, specialization fosters an increase in the importance and scope of rituals, as well as the differentiation of rituals among various specialists.

As every athlete knows, musculature and body structure adapt so as to enable the execution of repeated behavior more effectively and more efficiently. A top tennis or squash player can practice a particular shot thousands of times until it becomes second nature. The placement of the shot is reflexively and flawlessly executed when needed. Actions are supported by neural changes in the brain that mirror improvements in physical activities. What is called "muscle memory" is located in the brain. Success begets success, and survival results in the enhancement of the ability to survive. In this way, as Malcolm Gladwell suggests in *Outliers*, an initially lucky happenstance that yields a small advantage can be the start of a cascading chain of events that build on the previous events and lead on to great success. Initial success, over time and with repeated execution, improves a creature's future chances of genetic survival. The most vulnerable times for any creature are infancy, before survival skills are enabled, and old age, when survival skills become physically difficult.

Repeated and "overlearned" physical strategies and actions become habitual so that they are executed automatically without deliberation or little conscious thought. As the philosopher A. N. Whitehead has observed with regard to humans, "Civilization advances by extending the number of important operations which we can perform without thinking about them."[64]

Whitehead's maxim is implicitly put into practice in applying the three Rs to the survival imperative that impels individuals to employ all the mental and physical actions, which they deem to be beneficial in the service of their survival. Behavior that is successful in one area is used over and over, but it is also extended and adapted so that it can be applied, quickly and without deliberation, to some new area where it is preconsciously considered appropriate. If individuals are successful, the operations will be further refined and then replicated at the next opportunity. If the replicated practice is unsuccessful, it will be abandoned for that general usage and in time forgotten.

In modern times many complex human activities, such as playing the piano, driving to work, playing sports, dancing, and planning a party, are rarely critical for survival. But the underlying, innate processes of permanent expansion of neural networks in the brain that result from repeated activities persist with respect to the most often repeated behavior, whether serendipitous, studied, or forced, even though the activities are not critical for survival.

The influence of established neural networks works both ways. Established neural circuits in the brain can be called on as needed when a task or behavior is required to successfully interact with the environment. Working in the other direction, neural networks establish the salient aspects of the environment and are a large factor in determining behavior.

It is a subtle but critical difference. To an extent we harness our established neural networks, but we are driven by them as well.

Altruism, Adventure, and Dispersion

If the survival of a species depends on the instinct for individual self-preservation, how is the action of an individual who martyrs himself or sacrifices his life for others to be explained? Can cultural norms and beliefs overcome the instinct for self-preservation for a majority of people, or is altruism an aberration? Philosophers as well as psychologists and evolutionary biologists have long been intrigued by altruistic behavior.

Altruistic behavior is a core value or fundamental belief of most religions. A condition of belonging to most religions is sharing with, helping out, and sacrificing for one's coreligionists. There are numerous examples of altruistic behavior among animals, including other primates, but behavior, especially what E. O. Wilson terms the "hard-core altruism" that goes beyond normal cooperative, reciprocal activities, is most evident in human societies.

Sociobiologists, such as Richard Dawkins and Lewis Thomas , explain altruistic and risky behavior in terms of increasing the likelihood of the survival and perpetuation of certain genes. If a man gives up his own life in order to preserve his brother's life, half of his genes will survive through his brother. Humans do not generally think about gene survival when they undertake to sacrifice themselves for others, some of whom may be nonrelatives or who cannot be relied upon to reciprocate the beau geste.

Sociologists looking at group cooperation as an advantage for survival in the context of the competition in nature and with other groups suggest that religion and other human-made means of generating social bonds create a condition of pseudokinship that invokes deep-seated inclinations. Individuals implicitly recognize that making sacrifices for a group that they regard as kindred will probabilistically result in some benefit for their own blood kin somewhere in the future.

By means of the miracle of language, humans are able to create and sustain an internalized notion of pseudokinship that extends beyond blood relations. Once again, according to the theory, a circular effect is created. The conviction of pseudokinship promotes cooperation and coordination among a group. Such cooperation advances the welfare of the group and in turn strengthens the internalization of pseudokinship. As Milton M. Gordon observed, "Man defending the honor or the welfare of his ethnic group is a man defending himself."[65] It was neither by nature nor by accident that the entire nation of ancient Israel was claimed to be entirely composed of cousins descended from the twelve sons of their patriarch Jacob. Many religious denominations impose notions and practices of psuedokinship on their congregants, for example, by addressing all coreligionists as sister or brother.

Precedence of Religiosity or Spirituality

The two aspects of religion, religiosity and spirituality, though intertwined, can be regarded as having different roles in the origination and perpetuation of religion. Anthropological theorists might argue that although spirituality may have developed very early in order to explain mysterious natural phenomena, it is religiosity that primarily promoted the survival of groups of early humans. By means of genetic drift among populations, a tendency toward religiosity among individuals evolved to become an innate human drive. Feelings of pseudokinship as well as the coercive aspects of religiosity foster cooperation and can be construed as being, in some ways, functional both fot the individual and for the group. Thus, over generations, it has been speculated that spirituality spawned religiosity, and religiosity reinforced spirituality, so that in concert they fostered the survival of groups and ultimately the human species.

The Intrinsic Value of Religion

Is religiosity a cause of human survival, a result of serendipitous survival practices, or merely a concurrent "spandrel" that is only coincidentally related to survival? The scenario described above implicitly posits that religiosity was a primary driver of survival, and spirituality, a secondary cultural device whose purpose was to reinforce religiosity. That is, people had the need to create and enforce certain religious behavior as an effective means of supporting survival strategies and of competing with other clans of humans.

This is contrary to conventional thinking about religion. In conventional thinking, spirituality is most often regarded as the primary driver that is manifested by religiosity. Spirituality is declared to be ordained by God. It is in obeisance to supernatural forces that religious practices are determined. Conventionally, spirituality drives the various forms of religiosity, and not vice versa. It is religiosity and the various methods of exhibiting spirituality that constitute evolutionary spandrels within the context of an elemental and eternal core of spirituality.

In modern societies purely religious activities appear to be nonfunctional in a direct and objective sense (assuming they are not requited by the supernatural). Even those who devote their lives to, and earn their living from, an association with religious organizations do not benefit practically from the intrinsic nature of prayers and rituals themselves. Benefit received by way of comfort or psychological well-being is very subjective and difficult to measure. Benefits claimed for religion, such as social cohesion and mental health, are indirect and tenuous circumstantial benefits.

Religion can and has caused social divisiveness and internecine conflict instead of garnering the benefits from social cohesion. Religion can be a source of mental distress as well as comfort. There is no real evidence that early human groups that practiced various forms of religion had a better survival rate that those who did not. It is simply a supposition. There is no evidence to support the proposition that some debatable tendency of religion to foster effective groups resulted in a higher rate of survival for individual group members, and that over many generations this resulted in changes to human DNA that innately support either spirituuality or religiosity.

Nonfunctional solitary religious activities are widely practiced. For example, time-consuming daily prayer—donning phylacteries, prostrating oneself on the ground five times a day and reciting set prayers, saying silent prayers to the counting of beads, saying prayers aloud at bedtime—do not seem to have any practical payoff except in circular fashion. These rituals reinforce religious beliefs and commitment to other religious behaviors. Even the vaunted benefits of meditation are a result of the act of meditation itself rather than being due to a response of the supernatural or of any particular religious doctrine. In modern times, religiosity is used culturally as an expression of conformity and commitment that is meant to strengthen group cohesion rather than being the root of the functional activity.

A great deal of many a modern human's time and energy can be devoted to prayer and other ritualistic activities that are performed in the vague hope of receiving God's beneficence. Rituals are faithfully performed at the urging and with the assurances of clergy, speaking on behalf of God, of some nebulous form of eternal life. In some instances there is a promise of financial reward in this lifetime. But there is no objective, or even rational, cause-and-effect relationship that can be established between such religious activity and any determinate functional benefit whatsoever except for circular, after-the-fact anecdotal or apocryphal examples.

The religious behavior of performing and encouraging wanton killing of members of one's own species, or seeking martyrdom in the name of some abstract notion, is anathema to survival of a species in the animal world. Such behavior can only be countenanced by dehumanizing members of other groups, and by exaggerating the future indirect payback of pseudokinship or the certainty of life after death.

Ubiquitous and Persistent Ritual and Symbols

A hallmark of most religions is their insistence on ritualized behaviors. Rites, rituals, and ceremonies are replicated over and over with only minor temporal and situational variations. There are daily and weekly rituals as well as various festivals and holy days that call for particular ceremonies. There are private rituals such as morning and evening prayers, public expressions of individual rituals such as blessings over foods and invocations at public events, family rituals such as prayers at meal times, as well as public rites and ceremonies. These serve to promote religion and particular religions by means of public displays and public commitment. It is, however, moot as to what objective practical benefit, if any, is achieved by such behavior.

As ritual behavior continues to be repeated, and as long as there are no overt negative consequences, the neural networks of the brain associated with it are expanded and strengthened. The result is that the activity begins to have a psychological importance for the practitioner as it is integrated with other, positive activities and becomes habitual or, in essence, an addictive behavior. Just as exercise regimens, which may start out onerous, can become pleasurable after much daily practice, and are missed if they are skipped or discontinued, people also get a sense of loss when, for some reason, they do not or cannot practice their daily religious rituals.

The Importance of Symbols

Many rituals and ritualistic behaviors are associated with symbolic objects that become a sort of shorthand reminder of the beliefs and rituals. For the religious, symbols of their religion tend to be everywhere. Symbols extend the intensity and longevity of the impact of religious experiences with respect to the brain's neural networks. Churches, mosques, and synagogues are all decorated with the symbols of faith. Sensations from often-used symbolic objects can trigger certain synapses so that they operate as mental shorthand or reminders of religious doctrines. Some religions promote the use of beads, both as symbols and as mnemonic devices. Catholics and Anglicans use rosaries to guide prayers. Prayer beads are also used by Buddhists, Hindus, and Muslims. Jews use prayer shawls and phylacteries while praying. Symbols such as crucifixes, particular head coverings, and vermillion dots on the forehead can be used to identify coreligionists and even factions within religious group. In addition to social recognition, the effects of such symbols on brain circuitry can be profound.

Religious behavior and rites become meaningful and functional as they are performed repeatedly and thought about often. As has been established, behavior that is useful or meaningful is replicated. But, conversely, it is also true that behavior that is often replicated becomes meaningful, and it often becomes adapted for some use with respect to the actions of daily living. In a circular manner then, behavior that is functional is repeated, and behavior that is repeated is adapted to functional uses. Of course on the African savanna, hominids did not have the luxury of spending a great deal of time on nonfunctional behavior. With the exception of play, and perhaps recreational sex, only the first part of the circular law of behavior would have been observed in Paleolithic times, as behavior that proved useful was replicated.

The Circular Importance of Ritual

Rituals cause permanent changes to the neurocircuitry of the brain in relation to their frequency and intensity as well as their association with other neural memories. The changes tend to become self-reinforcing because the more often the rites are practiced the more they become associated with significant memories. By design, ceremonies are inexorably woven into all of life's major milestone events, such as births, marriages, and deaths, and are structured to intensively involve groups of people. Religious concepts and definitions become reified. Jews, for example, tack onto their doorposts containers holding those passages of scripture that say, "You shall put these passages on your doorposts," and they insert into phylactery cases the passage that says, "You shall bind them for frontlets on your foreheads." At a Catholic Mass, priests and their congregants pray over wine and wafers that are the transubstantiated blood and body of Jesus. Their doctrine asserts that these articles are not really symbols but actually the blood and body of Jesus.

Different religions place different emphases on rites and rituals, but they all use and depend on them to reinforce belief and commitment, to impose group discipline, and to point out others who are also devoted to the particular religion. Devout Muslims are called to prayer five times daily, and Jews three times daily. Religious people tend to form relationships with those they observe practicing the rituals of the religion.. Such practices make it obvious to others who is observant and who is not. These practices serve to spread and to socially enforce the observance of religious rituals through a community.

In most religions, the prayers recited, and the manner in which they are recited, hardly varies from day to day or from year to year over many thousands of occurrences. Once a person is inured to routine prayer or other rites, not performing them can cause anxiety. At most gatherings where religious people get together to enjoy themselves, and especially at festivals, there invariably is a religious invocation, if not a major ritual ceremony or component which tends to elevate and promote the status of a religion, in part by cowing doubters and backsliders.

Buddhism and some forms of Protestant Christianity are less slavishly invariant with respect to rites and rituals, but rituals and ceremonies are definitely factors in perpetuating those faiths as well. Protestants thank God and bless their food before each major meal, and the blessing is often rote or a variation of a standard prayer. Pious Protestant Christians attend church services every Sunday, and they may study scripture daily. Holidays such as Christmas and Easter have their own unique symbols and customs that provide powerful cues and reminders of the faith. Buddhists chant, light candles, burn incense, and offer food to monks as part of their daily rituals.

Design and Implementation of Rituals

As both religion and culture take shape and acquire permanence within a group, they are supported by the elaboration of permanent neural networks. Champions of some cause (i.e., those who benefit either directly or indirectly from the cause) are inclined to identify successful applications of a religion and then extend or try out similar beliefs, rituals, or practices in slightly different venues.[66] If the responses to such augmentation are positive, that is, if they gain traction with respect to the positive responses of others, they are further refined and adapted as recursive stratagems. If unsuccessful they are forgotten or downplayed. In this way advocated causes can be advanced, and individuals can gain status and community resources. Over time most or all of the original sources of the rituals may become lost as they are woven into the daily lives and activities of practitioners and as a result become meaningful to them.

Some examples should serve to illustrate the point. Champions of a religion put its indelible stamp on the seminal life events such as birth, marriage, and death. For most Christians a church ceremony officiated by a minister is the hallmark of a proper wedding. Even those who are not especially devout do not consider themselves or those they care about to be properly wed unless they have had a church wedding. It is important for Catholic priests to administer last rites to a dying man so that he, or his soul, might ascend to heaven. With Muslims and Jews, a married woman cannot get a religious divorce without her husband's permission. Catholics cannot get divorced except by petitioning the church for an annulment of their marriage. By custom, Muslim women in many countries must be entirely covered from head to toe for modesty. Even in the more moderate Islamic and secular countries, wearing a hijab, which covers all of a woman's hair, is a critical symbol of her modesty. The wearing of the hijab has been the cause for a number of political conflicts, some of them violent.

Religious authorities also extend the influence of their religions to other matters, such as what can be eaten and how it can be eaten, matters of dress, type of music that is acceptable, proper conduct of interpersonal relations. Just about any human activity can be clothed in religion. Nominally the champions of religion work to fulfill that which they claim are God's ordained commands, which are received from scripture or from the interpretation of scripture. At the same time, coincidentally and without perceiving its biological effects, religion also works to connect ever larger networks of nerve cells that invoke and associate religion with every aspect of a person's life.

Since the very beginning, when shamans and other religious leaders worked for their food and the protection of their tribe, there has usually been some monetary, status, or other personal benefit that gives the religious leaders an incentive to continue and extend religious processes. The composers and performers of religious music, the creators of fine works of religious art, and the authors of religious novels or movies may believe themselves to be carrying out a sacred mission glorifying the Lord, and others may agree. But there is little doubt that music, art, books, and movies can be very profitable and serve to fulfill personal agendas. Coincidentally they are also factors in restructuring neural networks of practitioners and audiences, which serve to spread and perpetuate religion.

The vast, pervasive behavioral superstructure of religiosity inexorably creates an indelible stamp on the brain circuitry of the individual practitioner.

Development and Religion

The song that goes "Every time I hear a newborn baby cry, or touch a leaf or see the sky, I know why I believe" is an example of conflating religious notions with other phenomena. Though it is questionable from a scientific point of view, many of those who have grown up as religious utterly believe that the infinitely complex universe could not possibly have come about without the intercession of the supernatural. Another fundamental belief is that there absolutely cannot be any morality without the doctrines and the constraints promulgated by religious belief and monitored by the supernatural. Without God and the prospect of her rewards and punishments, or heaven and the threat of hell, to constrain them, people would blithely perpetrate every manner of wanton and selfish act. They are convinced that it is either God's law or the law of the jungle.

Although there is considerable overlap, moral strictures are invariably the beliefs and doctrines of a particular religion. They are programmed into the neural networks of the brains of adherents. People are assured that their coreligionists, whom they assume all subscribe to the same sense of morality and proper behavior as they do, are good people as compared to those who subscribe to other religions. Their coreligionists are especially virtuous and trustworthy as compared to godless, licentious atheists. It is the "kin instincts" of social animals that are extended to by means of language to include pseudokinship that creates a culture of "our kind." Those who are members of our religious group as opposed to 'those who are not our kind' and who do not subscribe to our religion are not to be trusted. And therefore they can be treated shabbily.

When people are young, their brains have formed fewer and less robust neural networks. As a result they are most vulnerable to religious notions and practices that are inculcated by parents or other trusted individuals. Religious concepts introduced early in life tend to form networks of associated neurons that in many cases affect behavior for life. If neural networks formed early in life are reinforced by mens of later experiences and not challenged by deemed negative outcomes they have a profound influence on behavior.

As religious forms become indelibly superimposed on the culture of a population, they become reified and ultimately provide their adherents with a number of self-fulfilling benefits. There are many examples of these circular, consequent functional benefits of religion. Commitment to a religion supports a sense of certainty, security, and control for individuals, and serves to eliminate self-doubt. In fact, people can often rely on coreligionists to support them against others. Religious strictures preserve order among a population. Of course, these are uses of religion that have been devised by individuals and groups of humans over many years. In that sense the uses of religion, in part, explain religion's persistence (but not its origins).

Secular practices and concepts that are recognized or concocted as beneficial for individuals and for society are co-opted by religion to the point where many consider them to have originated from the belief in religion and the acceptance of those who promote it. The code of Hammurabi early in the second millenium BCE contained many injunctions that were later incorporated into the Pentateuch and still later co-opted by the originators of Christianity and Islam. Other defining precepts of Judaism, Christianity, and Islam are uncredited appropriations from Zoroastrianism. Religion that originated and is perpetuated for some personal benefit may ultimately become woven into many aspects of a culture to the extent that its tenets and practices seem natural and necessary to many of its adherents. Religion, diffused and intertwined with all aspects of culture, becomes integral and its origins obscure. Religious people think religiously. It is not that they are irrational, but that they deal with the world with a religious rationality because their brains are conditioned to operate that way. As Karen Armstrong couches it, they approach reality through the medium of mythos rather than logos.

As goal-directed creatures, it is natural for people to devise methods of gaining maximum leverage in order to increase status in their group. They seek to improve their welfare, by adapting behaviors that may have originated for other purposes. Behavior that is initiated in order to serve a primarily religious function, such as invoking the gods in the hope of more bountiful crops, is adapted and woven into many of life's major events, such as spring or harvest festivals that people enjoy and look forward to.. Eventually the contrived religious behaviors take on a life of their own.

Uses of Religion

It is commonplace for people to use behavior ordinarily undertaken for religious reasons for their own economic advantage or to induce public opinion to coalesce around some religious agenda that they champion. The 2000 and 2004 presidential elections in the United States, when people on the so-called religious right were mobilized to vote for George W. Bush in order to block abortion and gay marriage, are good examples.

It is in this sense that religious behavior can become pragmatic within a modern social context and can result indirectly in an advantage to some group. It is the co-optation of traditional religious behavior with respect to self-interested personal and group benefits rather than as a primary useful phenomenon.

Conventional wisdom indicates that our religious behavior is determined by our beliefs. Conversely imposed and frequently repeated behavior, including religious forms, can have a powerful effect on belief as it is represented in the neural recesses of the brain. Behavior in response to events (i.e., experience) is the most effective method of addressing and altering the brain's neural networks. The effect of experience on neural networks is the established mechanism by which countless generations of animals have learned to survive in the wilds. As John Dewey noted in his famous maxim 'I see, I forget, I hear, I forget, I do and I remember,' behavior is much more potent in altering thought processes than either speech or visual demonstrations.

Language may be a powerful medium for communicating ideas and changing minds, but it is not nearly as potent as real-life experiences. However, when language is combined with experience in the form of repeated ritual, its powers are greatly magnified. Language can also be harnessed by the religious to interpret the experiences of the unsophisticated.

As ritual behavior associated with certain beliefs is repeated habitually, the beliefs associated in the mind with the rituals also become associated with day-to-day activities. In time, although it might be agued that such beliefs are really not functional or even reasonable, they become a part of the individual's core identity and tend to be regarded at an innate neurological level of similar importance to the wildebeest's intuitive desire to keep away from lions.

There are also countervailing experiences, limiting psychological drives, and competing interests that tend to constrain and ameliorate religious influences and compulsions. In extreme cases, however, neurologically embedded religious notions can become so powerful that they induce a need for the pious to truly suffer, to go without food or water for a time, to lash one's own back with a chain until it bleeds, and other forms of deprivation and self-mortification, in the name of a religion. The neural orientation of the religious can induce people, such as Mother Teresa, to live lives of hardship and deprivation in order to help total strangers. And in the extreme, it can allow people to persuade themselves that it is a good thing to martyr themselves and to murder innocent people.

CHAPTER NINE

The Conservation Of Belief

Asymmetry in Belief Acquisition and Extinction

There is an enormous amount of information that is simultaneously and continuously being relayed to the brain from the environment by all of the senses. As capacious as the human brain is, far more sensory input than the brain is capable of processing reaches it. At any given moment, there is a gross overabundance of sensations impinging on the brain to be analyzed and sorted out with regard to the immediate or long-term relevance of its information content..

Not all sensations, nor even most of them, can be given equal attention. Therefore there must be a built-in discriminatory process in the brain that determines which information is critical, which is irrelevant, which should be stored in memory to form beliefs, which should be considered and disregarded, and which sensations should not register at all.

In the precarious times and situations in which predecessor hominid species lived, attending to irrelevant information, misinterpreting information, or acting out of erroneous beliefs could lead to the suddenly death. Too much time taken to analyze incoming information might be fatal. Care had to be observed so that the beliefs that were formed and held in memory were only those that most effectively promoted survival. Misperceptions or unsound sensory information that might lead to counterproductive or disastrous beliefs had to be somehow screened out by cognitive processes. The same principle is true today, although, except for soldiers, motorists driving under hazardous conditions, and those in dangerous occupations, we don't often face life-or-death situations where split-second reactions are critical.

Some method for vetting and screening out incoming sensory information that is either superfluous or misleading with regard to whether a situation at hand is critical. Thus, millions of years ago a process of asymmetrical information flow evolved. For humans, all sensory input to the brain (except smell) connects to individual nuclei of an area of the brain called the thalamus. The thalamus is located in the middle of the brain, between the two cerebral hemispheres. A function of the thalamus is to receive auditory, somatosensory, gustatory, and visual sensory signals from the environment and to relay them to appropriate parts of the brain. The thalamus acts as a relay, for example, in instantaneously relaying sensations that determine fight-or-flight responses to the amygdala, where adrenaline is generated.

The thalamus, acting as a kind of gatekeeper for sensory information, is where all incoming sensory inputs are vetted or screened.[67] Various incoming sensory signals received in the thalamus are then relayed to other parts of the brain, including the hippocampus, which then stores memories in the cerebral cortex. The thalamus also serves as a conduit in the reverse process. Neural information from various parts of the cerebral cortex is funneled through the thalamus and then transmitted as outgoing motor signals with regard to vision, speech, movement, and so forth.

Irrelevant information is simply ignored or blocked at the thalamus. For example, we are often unaware of background noise or conversations as we concentrate on listening to a particular speaker. Information which is inane, unreasonable, or contrary to prior experience and beliefs tends to be disregarded. Only sensory information that is deemed to be pertinent or that can't be ignored is focused upon and passed along to other parts of the brain. The operations of the thalamus may also cause other relevant information to be sought. In this way the ever present potential for information overload is reduced to a much smaller volume of tractable sensations and information.

The flow of information in the other direction, from other areas of the brain, such as long-term memories in the cerebral cortex to the thalamus, however, is not vetted. Since information in cerebral memory was vetted when it was acquired and stored, it is summarily accepted as needed and recalled. Stored information and beliefs that exist in memory are also used in the process of screening new information.

From an evolutionary standpoint, this asymmetric process of information flow appears logical, as long-term memory would not have gotten into the cortex unless it had been evaluated in the thalamus when first received and processed. A second vetting would be inefficient and undoubtedly confusing. In this way memories of past experiences that have been stored in the brain can be used to vet new sensory input in order to determine relevance, decide suitable actions, establish the focus of additional sensory information gathering, and determine the information that is to be transmitted via the hippocampus to long-term memory in the cerebral cortex.

Stored information that is erroneous or does not jibe with situational reality tends to be adjusted as it is retrieved from long-term memory and used in the evaluation of new information. Thus, an important aspect of the sensory information vetting process is that when long-term memories that have been used to evaluate current sensory information are reestablished in long-term memory, they will be combined with the newer information from the latest situation at hand. There is, however, a strong bias to preserve established beliefs.

Cognitive Dissonance and Confirmation Bias

It was Leon Festinger who coined the term "cognitive dissonance" to denote the condition whereby new, externally acquired information that might be questionable is not immediately accepted preconsciously at face value or without qualification. Without realizing it consciously, people tend to engage in search activities for other information that will either corroborate or undermine the new information before it is finally accepted.

With respect to supporting information that is sought, there is what Peter Wasoon termed "confirmation bias." That is, we are not unbiased or neutral in our search for information. Rather, we seek new information that tends to confirm our prior beliefs and justify our prior actions. We are inclined to ignore or reject (if we can) new information that might refute or even undercut our beliefs. Our egos require that we not be receptive to information that might challenge our past choices unless the new information is so blatant and compelling that it cannot be ignored. We tend to straight away accept most confirming evidence and information, while we tend to ignore, rationalize, attach a favorable interpretation to, or reject information that serves to undermine or refute our beliefs.

After purchasing a particular product, people have been observed to continue to shop, that is, they actively continue to compare the price and quality of the product that they have irrevocably committed to with other similar products being sold. It is an attempt to justify the appropriateness of the purchase. In some cases the shopping search activity that goes on after a product is bought and cannot be returned is greater than the original shopping search activity carried on before the purchase was made. The vetting process that occurs in the thalamus after the fact is conditioned by cognitive dissonance. But there is no equivalent of cognitive dissonance with regard to notions or beliefs transferred in the other direction that might be more appropriate. Information transferred from the cerebral cortex's long-term memory to the working memory of the thalamus is summarily accepted.

Alteration of Internalized Beliefs

Because of this asymmetric information flow, internalized beliefs tend to remain in force as determinants of behavior. Established belief can be changed but with difficulty. It takes a fair amount of contrary evidence from believable sources, and it generally occurs slowly over time. Change in fundamental belief can be achieved but only rarely in summary fashion.

Although we are not consciously aware of mental conflict, a great deal of preconscious mental thought with respect to the comparison and evaluation of sensations and notions takes place in the process of arriving at optimal beliefs. Communicated notions and even direct sense information that do not conform to preconceived notions and beliefs tend to be ignored, rejected straight away, subjected to critical analysis in order to discredit them, and mentally restated or reinterpreted so as to reduce the mental discord. Only at last resort are established preconceptions significantly altered or abandoned. Prior beliefs that have proven useful are changed as little and as benignly as possible in order to preserve their utility, our experiences using them, and our commitment to them. In general, for early hominids a precipitous alteration of established beliefs would be most often have been highly dysfunctional, prompting action that would lead to a premature death far more often than it would have been beneficial.

People tend to actively seek new information that will corroborate, generally support, or at least be construed as consistent with their preconceived beliefs. Such support does not have to be objective or scientific or even verbal in nature, as long as it "feels right." It can be anecdotal. Those people who hold particular religious beliefs will tend to regularly experience events and come across various phenomena that are deemed to confirm their beliefs. Others undergoing similar experiences remain unimpressed, as their facility for cognitive dissonance dismisses the purported evidence. Anecdotal evidence is rejected if it conflicts with prior beliefs but accepted if it can be construed as supporting them.

As new information objectively, or even subjectively, is acecpted as supporting or confirming prior beliefs, the beliefs become stronger and harder to change. A supplementary factor with respect to Skinnerian religion, as discussed earlier, is that people do not so much passively associate a proximal event reflexively as being the cause of some adverse condition, so much as they actively and assiduously look for some proximal event, among the many that are always available, which they can plausibly interpret as supporting their own preconceptions or theories. In other words, rather than a serendipitous confusion of proximal and causal events in generating false beliefs, it is traditional beliefs that are used to search for and identify the causal events. Belief is used to manipulate the meaning of experiences.

More Difficulties for Belief Modification

Beliefs are continually being reinforced by means of rationalization and selective interpretation of OACEREs in nature. Thus, although instantaneous and significant transformations to one's core belief systems can be triggered by traumatic events or psychotic episodes, these are rare. The longer an internalized belief has been held, the more associations it is connected with, the more useful it has been in the past, and the more social support there is for it, the more difficult it will be to radically revise it on the basis of new information. Almost every time some new information that invokes a belief occurs, the belief is further experientially validated.

A current widespread internalized belief is that slavery in any form and under any circumstance is immoral, period, without any qualification whatsoever. At the present time, it would be unacceptable if not foolhardy to argue in support of the peripheral benefits of slavery, even under special conditions. The reputations of some of our great heroes of the past and erstwhile paragons of probity such as George Washington or Thomas

Jefferson have been sullied by the knowledge that they were slave owners even though slavery was legal, widely practiced in their time, and accepted by the church and by many otherwise decent God-fearing, churchgoing model citizens of various communities.

A majority of people in those days firmly believed that slavery was normal and necessary. They found much anecdotal evidence in nature to support their belief. The Bible discusses slavery as an acceptable practice. There have even been cases where slaves would rather remain slaves than be freed. Before the U.S. Civil war, many people were prepared to do violence to anyone who opposed slavery.

But we now hold that slavery is unquestionably immoral—bad for the slave owner as well as the slave, and bad for society in general. It is immoral now, and it was certainly immoral in the past as well.

But the institution of slavery itself has not suddenly changed or become worse. (And it has not been eliminated.) There is nothing that we know now that we didn't know then that has forced our beliefs to change. In fact, arguments against slavery go back thousands of years. Slavery is and always has been an abomination, and throughout history there were those who opposed it and who sympathized with the plight of slaves.

The widespread change of basic belief about slavery is not a case of situational ethics or moral relativism. For those who strongly hold the belief that slavery is immoral, the belief is unqualified. For these people the owning of one human being by another is and always has been evil. There can be no situation in which slavery is or ever was acceptable. It is beyond argumentation. Slavery treats human beings as property, corrupts the values of the slave owners and compromises their feelings for their fellow man, and laterally creates a dysfunctional, suboptimal economic system. Spanish conquistadors such as Cortes and Pizzaro are regarded as evil men by many for having oppressed and enslaved South American natives, even though this was the standard operating procedure in their times and they were blessed by the same church that is venerated today.

By the same token, it is also conceivable, even likely, that practices that are universally accepted today, and defended as being reasonable and ethical, may in the future be considered immoral. Obviously it is difficult to come up with a suitable example. As Yogi Berra put it, "Forecasts are very difficult especially forecasts about the future." By definition the practice chosen has to be something that is almost universally accepted at present. But perhaps a hypothetical example will serve to illustrate the point.

If the slaughter of large animals for food becomes regarded as immoral in the future, then, as in the case of slavery, it will have been immoral now and in the past as well. As with the abolition of slavery, such a belief will not be based on any new information that will have been developed in the future that we do not know about right now. It will not be based on situational ethics which argue that it was all right in the past (that is now) because we didn't (don't) know any better but is immoral now (then) and for the future human inhabitants of the earth.

Today, the members of PETA have mounted a campaign for more humane treatment of animals, and the number of young people who are vegetarians based on ethical considerations is growing. Even today the use of "bush meat," that is the slaughter of apes and monkeys for food, is considered by many people to be repugnant. It is not inconceivable that slaughtering cows for food will, like slavery, become an abhorrent practice in the future.

For the vast majority of meat eaters of today, however, there are few, if any, arguments or evidence that might convince them that they are in fact engaging in contemptible, disgusting, immoral behavior by slaughtering animals, which have the right to life, and by eating the flesh of these dead animals—even if they do not engage in the biblically sanctioned practice of boiling a kid in its mother's milk.

Decisions, Reason, and Emotion

According to Joseph LeDoux, modern cognitive science, in its analysis of attention, perception, memory, and other cognitive processes, "has emphasized that emotions are just not part of the cognitive approach to the mind."[68] Perhaps this is because emotions are still regarded as irrational and as such not amenable to rational, scientific analysis. However, most sensations or perceptions are intrinsically bound up with emotional valence. Consider the operations of the brain in acquiring and processing sensations. It is clear that taste or smell can produce disgust or rapture, touch can generate great pleasure or repulsion, sound may be melodious and pleasant or a cacophony that grates on the ears, and sights can be either pleasant or hideous,

Emotion is the most effective mode for memory formation as well as recall and use. Current experience triggers memories of sensations and related emotions from past experiences. These memories are used to analyze and interpret sensations from current experience. There is no practical way to completely strip emotion from cognition, especially where events are likely to affect the welfare of the individual. There is no way to intentionally filter the preconscious data or the emotion conveyed in memory in order to direct or channel the analysis of new information in deterministic ways. Such a recursive process would be confusing and disastrous.

Behavior That Is Determined Preconsciously

The preconscious aspect of the mind is far more active and much more purposeful in determining behavior than has been previously contemplated. Scientists have demonstrated experimentally that having subjects handle either warm or cold cups of coffee on their way to an experiment can influence their attitudes and the results of some experiments.

In playing an investment game, half the subjects performed the task with a leather briefcase sitting on the table in plain view and the other half without it. Although no reference was made to the briefcase, it significantly affected the results of the experiment. In an experiment performed in the Netherlands, subjects were given a questionnaire to complete. A bucket of water with a small amount of citrus-scented cleaning liquid was placed in the room for half of the subjects. After completing their assignment, the subjects were treated to a snack that contained a very crumbly biscuit. Analysis of films of the snack time indicated that those subjects who had subliminally smelled the faint odor of lemon were three times as likely to clean up their crumbs as those who had not.

The brain appears to use the very same neural circuits to execute a preconscious act as it does a conscious one.[69] In the presence of symbols, locations, or persons associated with religion, many individuals will unconsciously act in a manner that is somewhat different than when no subliminal religious cues are present.

As introduced in the section on language, many of the phenomena we observe, and the decisions on which our behavior is based, must deal with complex multidimensional criteria that are beyond the associative capabilities of the human brain. It is a complicated task to sort out which alternative is objectively best versus which is subjectively best for us. As was illustrated by arguments in the recent contretemps in New Haven, Connecticut, with respect to the practice of basing firefighter's promotions on a single pencil and paper test, such matters can be highly complicated. They involve many factors that cannot be measured on a single scale. For example, a point system for sorting our job candidates, mortgage applicants, or potential spouses must necessarily ignore a host of relevant criteria.

When complex, multidimensional, subjective decisions must be made, belief based on preconscious thought and emotion overrides our overwhelmed conscious reasoning abilities. Put in a situation that is perceived to be dangerous, our fear reaction completely swamps our ability to think rationally about our options and unequivocally determines our subsequent response. Unless we have been specially trained in advance to handle the particular situation, our reflexive response will be nonrational and generally suboptimal. In the modern world, this can be very dysfunctional and even disastrous. The sudden shock of discovering that one has been robbed erodes the ability to think calmly and rationally. Such emotional trauma gives thieves a big advantage over their victims.

When in a quandary that is nonreligious in nature, pious believers tend to fall back on emotional religious precepts that seem to apply, if only tangentially, to the situation. Emotion often takes over where the conscious, computational abilities of our minds are inadequate. Much of our behavior depends on, or is shaped by, emotion without our conscious realization.

Our reaction to those we have just met is conditioned by emotion with respect to the person and the context of the situation. Once we have made an initial decision or have acted based mainly on our gut emotions (instincts), we will attempt to rationally justify (rationalize) those decisions and actions. More than just for casual use, we rely on emotional, deep-seated beliefs to guide our behavior. In many cases we seek to verify or rationalize core beliefs or justify actions by selective acceptance or rejection of some of the pertinent information, anecdotal information, or deemed evidence that we can marshal.

Combining and expanding Malcolm Gladwell's "blink" and "outlier" hypotheses, a single snap decision based on intuition can, because of our powers of rationalization, become reinforced as later events are interpreted in light of the snap judgment. At the very extreme, it is conceivable that subsequent experiences will be shaped in order to justify the snap decision. To the extent that some inconsequential arbitrary event leads to a sequence of subsequent decisions and events, it can become life altering. As in Robert Frost's poem "The Road Not Taken," a choice point is often clearly recognized, but there is no indication as to which of two alternatives will be the better path. Yet, as in the poem, on looking back over his life and the arbitrary choice that was made that day, Frost says that it has made all the difference.

Beyond insurmountable difficulties created by the information overload and the multidimensional aspects of even fairly common problems and decision situations, there is another aspect that promotes nonrationality. It involves time. Human beliefs are built up of a synthesis of many discontinuous and disorganized experiences that occur over time. Beliefs are formed from declarative and emotional memories that are initially registered in a haphazard, discontinuous process. These disjointed inputs may not fit any coherent or logical model that is capable of mathematical solution. But somehow the human mind has created subjective coherence or made preconscious sense of the disparate experiences.

Daniel Kahneman and Amos Tversky demonstrated that the results of some experimental decision situations are inconsistent with regard to any model of logical decision criteria. If a subject in a hypothetical K&T experiment preferred to vacation in Rome rather than Paris, and preferred Paris rather than London, by the rule of transitivity, she should logically prefer to vacation in Rome rather than London. However, experimental results showed that a significant number of subjects preferred London to Rome. A decision between two cities for a future vacation may be based simply on the sound of the name of one of the cities or some chance overheard conversation, and all other criteria that might otherwise have been regarded as reasonable and pertinent (but not as decisive) may be disregarded at a given time. Whether or not this is a proper method for making the decision will depend on personal variables and the results of its implementation.

In order to survive, maintain mental health, and not paralyze ourselves with dithering behavior while frittering away vast blocks of time and courting giant headaches, we often accept incomplete information and emotional beliefs that have face validity or are based on anecdotal evidence in making decisions. In some cases, forced decisions are made on emotional considerations even when they are recognized as illogical or problematic. At some level we may realize that some useful beliefs are not based on hard logic. But because of our resolute commitment to rationality, we feel obligated to formulate a rational basis for our cherished emotional beliefs when challenged.

When in doubt we sometimes resort to heuristic methods and solutions even if the situation to which we apply them is appreciably different from situations where such methods have proven satisfactory. In certain cases actions based on heuristics may even be considered successful if they do not prove disastrous.

It is no mystery why faith, conventional wisdom, or unproven and erroneous beliefs arise. These sections of the manuscript seek to explore some of the reasons why they persist tenaciously in the face of well-established disproof and why they tend to be defended with such vigor by believers and advocates.

Temperament and Belief

In laboratory experiments it has been demonstrated that the pups of rat mothers who were anxious, high-strung, and nervous themselves become anxious adults who continue the cycle of anxiety with their pups. This condition was attributed by experimental psychologists to heredity. To test this notion, in the 1950s and '60s, behaviorist experimenters would take a newborn pup from its mother and place it in a nearby box for exactly fifteen minutes before returning it. This procedure was repeated for twenty-one days. When the pups had been weaned, they were tested for a so-called handling effect. Rats that had been handled as pups uniformly released far less cortisol, a stress hormone, when handled as adults than rats that had not been handled in infancy. This was taken as evidence demonstrating a handling effect, and by extension taken to indicate the power of nurture over nature in rats.[70]

In 1989 Michael Meany revisited the handling experiments. Earlier scientists had taken great pains to control the experiments so that the handling of the pups was done in a certain way and so that the handling conditions tested for were the only differences between the experimental and the control groups of rat pups. Meany, however, hypothesized that the mother rat's behavior toward their babies when they were returned, was an important variable that was not controlled for in the experiments.

He and his students replicated the experiments, but this time they observed the licking and grooming behavior of the mother toward the pups when they were returned to their cages. Sure enough, the returned pups got a lot more licking and grooming than the pups that had not been taken from their mothers. The so-called handling effect was in reality due to the rat mother's treatment. In other words it was a mothering effect. Pups that received a lot of TLC from their mothers, whatever the cause or reason, grew to be relatively unstressed adults whether or not they had been handled by humans.

From an evolutionary biology standpoint, this mothering effect makes sense. Mother rats living in difficult conditions of danger and hardship are stressed, so they cannot spend as much time licking and grooming their pups. The pups grow up to be nervous adults whose stress hormones produce fight-or-flight reactions that are pronounced and quickly triggered. Being easily startled is a good survival strategy for rats in adverse, dangerous conditions. On the other hand, a too-quick startle reaction is counterproductive for rats living in relatively safe conditions. The new experiments also demonstrate the effects of nurture, but, importantly, they also demonstrate the significant interaction of the effects of nature (i.e., with respect to mothering impulses) on nurture as well.

As with rats, so it is with humans. John Bowlby, followed by Mary Ainsworth and others, developed what has been termed "attachment theory." Human babies, the researchers determined, become either securely attached or insecurely attached to their mothers. Consistent with the outlier hypothesis, the attachment phenomenon is to an extent self-perpetuating. Babies that tend to be most responsive to their mothers' attentions tend to get more attention. Passive or cranky babies get less affection. Mothers who lavish more attention on their babies tend to induce their babies to be more responsive to attention and affection. Mothers who are absent or who withhold affection tend to have babies that are insecurely attached.

Mothers who are affectionate, comforting, and quick to lavish attention on their babies produce secure babies. Secure children respond to their teachers and classmates in ways that reinforce their secure temperament. In this way secure attachment produced in the first two years of life is continuously reinforced so that it produces secure adults. There are two types of insecure babies: those who are anxious and those who are avoidant. Insecure attachment also tends to produce behavior that is evident in adult temperament. Estimates are that about half of American children are securely attached, while one quarter show avoidant attachment, one fifth anxious attachment, and the rest are indeterminate.

Securely attached babies become adults who are emotionally secure, confident, trusting, and able to form healthy, productive relationships with others. Anxious attachment produces adults who are dependent, with a need for closeness that can never be assuaged, manifesting a constant fretting that he will never have security or will lose whatever interpersonal security he has. Finally the avoidant attachment babies grow up to be loners and compulsively self-reliant people who have little empathy for others and do not form close relationships.

Attachment is only one dimension of temperament, but it is an indicator of how early childhood experience affects how adults relate to others. Temperament, of course, is far from the only shaper of belief, but it is a major element in determining receptivity to, or the tendency to experience cognitive dissonance and the cynical rejection of, beliefs imparted by parents or others. Other things being equal, temperament is a major factor in the intensity of core beliefs, such as those involving religion, that are formed in youth and then either reinforced or challenged in later life.

Criticisms that Strengthen Religious Belief

People are often pressed to defend their religious beliefs, either in an overt confrontation or by implicit social pressure. The devout are inclined to develop rational arguments that support their beliefs and to internalize these arguments. They may recall or reformulate past situations where the beliefs had been useful or valid, and point out how the beliefs were useful and necessary and will likely be useful in the future.

There is a very strong bias for self-fulfilling reinforcement that is obtained by ascribing unexplained occurrences to metaphysical causes. This was true in the Neolithic period, and it remains true among modern sophisticated humans. In regard to religious belief, a single ambiguous experience that is regarded as reinforcing a belief can deflect many significant attempts to disconfirm the belief. For humans, reinforcement of a belief need not necessarily be objectively confirmed, but merely reported, perceived, or rationalized as confirmed, to be effective.

Challenges to religious belief such as those posed by the classical writings of Spinoza, Hume, Locke, Galileo, and Darwin, as well as modern writing of Richard Dawkins, Christopher Hutchins, Sam Harris, and modern paleontologists, all serve to trigger a pushback that strengthens the religious belief of the faithful. Paradoxically the act of having to defend against criticisms tends to toughen the defenses of basic religious beliefs. Belief is defended with sophistry, reinterpreted concepts, rationalizations, and anecdotes. Concepts such as creationism or intelligent design are intended to counter the challenges of evolution, criticism of the divine origins of scripture, and skepticism over the existence of a creator God. The 2005 Pennsylvania trial of the Dover school district as to whether to include creation science as a part of the science curriculum concluded with a complete rout of the creationists. Significantly however, the devastating ruling of the judge seems to have had no discernable dampening effect on the commitment of the beliefs of the proponents of creation science in the district. Some of them continued to send hate mail to the families who had launched the original complaint.

The Achilles' heel of religious belief in particular would seem to be the problem of running afoul of some inconvenient reality that puts the lie to it and can't be ignored. Religions and religious authorities often promise miracle cures and supernatural occurrences that do not come to pass. In U.S. legal system, if a witness is shown to have lied under oath, no other testimony given by that witness will be accepted as legally valid no matter how reasonable it seems. For the religious, however, the reason that prayer, charity, blandishments, or other entreaties fail to deliver is that the supplicant was not devout enough. It is not the fault of religion but the petitioner. As concluded in Festinger's study of failed prophesy, such failure may alter, but it does not weaken, the basic beliefs of the devout. Conversely, it often strengthens it.

The Persistence of Irrational Belief

It is reasonable to assume that rational humans will not persist in a belief that is unrequited, illogical, or proven to be false. Such, however, is far from the case. A core belief, such as that the earth was created by God in seven days a mere seven thousand years ago, has been shown to be erroneous, at least in its literal interpretation. A worldwide flood reaching above the peaks of the earth's mountains in which a single family rescued representatives of all of the animal species on earth (except dinosaurs) in a single ark cries out for a shred of objective and unambiguous corroborating evidence. (Not to mention that it is highly unlikely that every single pair of animals could succeed in perpetuating its species.) One might suppose that even a credible doubt about biblical creation or the flood might lead to doubts, not only of the particular scriptures, but also of all belief in a religious tradition that held such a belief. It does not.

First of all, those people who have faithfully practiced a religion much of their lives and have strong religious convictions that they have made public have their egos invested in the religious belief. As such, they often refuse to acknowledge any contradiction between their beliefs and reality, regardless of the degree of conflict. Such belief is held at the nonverbal preconscious level, where it is shielded from verbal arguments.

Religious people do not generally argue; they simply do not accept a contrary argument. They take comfort in considering themselves to be a part of a venerable tradition shared by a large reference group, all of whom hold similar beliefs. To renounce the shared beliefs would mean social isolation and possibly require a great effort in establishing themselves in some alternative reference group with a different set of beliefs. Preconscious rationality places one's survival and welfare well above the personally meaningless, petty verbal and mental gymnastics of determining whether or not the world was created seven thousand years ago. Such motivated reasoning based on personal benefit easily dominates verbal logic.

Many people have pragmatic reasons for maintaining their religious beliefs in the face of blatant contradictions. Their livelihood may be facilitated by virtue of their beliefs or attachment to a religion. All of their friends and social outlets may involve the religion. And they may believe that, despite any apparent glitches, the lifestyle and family values promoted by the religion are optimal for them, offering safety, security, and a good life. In such cases there is a range of possibilities, from lack of conscious awareness of the contradictions because of a mental block, to sincere rationalization and, at the extreme, cynicism born of self-interest. As Upton Sinclair cynically observed, " It is difficult to get a man to understand something, when his salary depends upon his not understanding it!"

Belief and Survival

In their most basic form, beliefs were critical for the survival of hominids. Thus the processes for forming beliefs, and for altering beliefs, have evolved to support an individual's welfare and survival. Activities that have been successful tend to produce neural associations that represent beliefs about the circumstance in which the activity, if replicated, might be successful in the future under similar circumstances. Neural networks are formed that support the beliefs that have proven useful. The beliefs will be remembered and recalled when they are considered appropriate based on environmental cues. Encountering some cue, in the form of a visual, aural, olfactory, or somatosensory sensation, triggers a cascade of neurotransmitter proteins through the neural network, which results in an action designed to promote the welfare or safety of an individual. The more often the cue is encountered and the activity undertaken successfully, the more adept a creature becomes in dealing with the matter.

Optimally, useful beliefs should be conserved as long as they remain useful. They should be remembered and not be corrupted by intervening experiences that might reduce their usefulness. Things change, and sometimes useful beliefs can become dysfunctional and in need of change. In addition there are times when it becomes advantageous to replace a belief with another that is more effective in more situations. As a result, tension is created between the need to maintain beliefs and the need to improve them.

The human brain does not distinguish between beliefs that have aided survival in the past and belief that has been generated by language. All belief is handled in a similar manner. There is a delightful prologue in the Coen Brothers movie *A Serious Man*, in which a woman who has been told, and believes, that a certain man is dead regards him as a dybbuk when he comes to her house. Believing the man to be an evil spirit who will bring harm to her family, she stabs him in the chest with an ice pick. Her husband, seeing and talking to the man, believes the evidence of his senses and is horrified. The message of the scene is that people act on their beliefs, and that their beliefs may be formed either from direct experience or from synthetic experience—that is, by accepting and believing what they are told.

The rationality of neural processes that evaluate sensations in the light of beliefs that were formed by experience is based on a need to promote the welfare and survival of an organism. What has been construed as emotional behavioral response originates from self-protective thought processes that lie below the level of cognitive awareness. A search for confirmatory information will generally center upon the determination of what is in the primal interest of the searcher rather than what is consistent with synthetic logic of the situation at hand.

In general people tend to seek and more readily accept new information that confirms their prior beliefs, which, by default, have been vetted and determined to be consistent with their own long-term welfare. Prior beliefs established at a neural level are deemed to be beneficial or they would not have been formed. New information tends to be treated with skepticism to the extent that it is not consistent with such established beliefs. People are predisposed by temperament, intelligence, and prior experience to have differences in how they interpret new information received from the environment. This provides for a range of information processing approaches, from tacit or grudging acceptance through skepticism to initiating a search for confirmation, or to outright rejection.

The tenacity and persistence of prior beliefs, which evolved as a function that assists in survival, tends to make it difficult to change or alter established religious belief.

CHAPTER TEN

Predicting And Planning

The Prefrontal Cortex

Whatever the original survival stimulus for the development of the frontal lobes in the *Homo sapiens* brain, these developed to become much larger than any ape or earlier *Homo* species. The prefrontal cortex, also called the neocortex to indicate its comparatively recent development, makes up 30 percent of the human brain. It is larger than that of any other animal of comparable size.[71] The prefrontal lobes of the human brain have been established as the primary area for its executive functions, which include superior ability to anticipate future events so as to facilitate planning, judgment, decision making, proactive behavior, and pattern and relationship discernment with regard to nature. Higher animals with smaller frontal lobes also have been observed to be able to detect patterns in nature and to plan. But the much larger human prefrontal lobes enable a far, far greater capability.

In his book *Stumbling on Happiness,*[72] Daniel Gilbert discusses how the function of the brain's frontal lobes has been discovered as a result of accidents that have disabled this area in various individuals as well as from results of surgery undertaken to remove material from them in attempts to relieve distress in individuals with certain severe mental illnesses or brain tumors.

According to Gilbert, without any ability to sense and make sense of the environment, no animal could survive the continual changes in nature. They could not respond to threats to their existence, mate, or seek opportunities to sustain themselves.

Recent research into animal behavior indicates that some animals have episodic memory to varying extents. They can remember specific past events and plan for the future, and some, arguably, have some form of self-concept.[73] Nature in the wilds operates with, in effect, considerable reinforcement for successful behavior and, as is stunningly apparent, with draconian negative consequences for actions that prove to be unsuccessful or injurious. Even a minor injury may result in death—often a painful, lingering death. Planning increases the chance of success and decreases the possibility of blunders. Humans are so much better at planning that Gilbert suggests the term "nexting" should be used for this function by other animals, as contrasted with human planning. Planning future behavior is a most potent survival function.

Different animals have varying acuities of the senses with which they make their living. Some combination of a keen sense of smell or sight, speed, stealth, strength, thick skin, sharp fangs, and claws are critical for various predators. Some animals, such as hominids, must have relied to a great extent on brainpower and reason to augment the limitations of their other abilities. The increased capabilities that were fostered by the enlargement of hominid's prefrontal cortex were likely a key to the survival of an otherwise inadequate species.

Higher Orders of Motivation

According to Gilbert,[74] human evolution provided for the development of the brainpower that was critically needed for planning. Ancient man planned for survival. Modern human beings plan for what they think will make them happy. Both ancient and modern plans are most effective under conditions of certainty and stability. Therefore one type of planning is to provide for conditions of certainty and stability in order that plans for survival or plans for happiness might succeed.

People project the future benefits of success if their plans should be successfully implemented, and it delights them, even when there is little prospect or intention of actually implementing the plan. According to

Gilbert, people also plan for the sheer enjoyment of the activity itself. Some of this enjoyment comes from delight in imagined success despite the recognition that their planning is merely an exercise, daydreaming, or fantasy.

The survival imperative induces people to long for a benign near and long-term future and to make plans to ensure it. The quest for certainty also leads humans to understand or make sense of the elements of their habitats. For some people assigning an arbitrary meaning to the universe and a purpose for their lives produces a sense of certainty and so leads to a sense of contentment and happiness.

Sensations from experiences produce a sense of happiness by initiating certain neurotransmitter proteins, such as dopamine and seratonin, to course through neurological networks of the brain. In addition, it seems that even without external triggering events, internal brain processes can generate a sense of happiness. For humans, the very act of wishful thinking or imagining success is an enjoyable activity in and of itself. We can become happy when we merely think about achieving happiness even when the prospect of success is acknowledged as unlikely as a result of impracticality of a particular plan. (That's why we buy lottery tickets.)

This phenomenon, which may be termed second-order or autogenerated pleasure, can be illustrated by using as an analogy the example of the sex drive and by postulating discrete categories of reinforcement. *Homo sapiens* are one of the few animals that engage in recreational sex in addition to copulating for the purpose of procreation. Human males are attracted, and their sexual appetites aroused and heightened, not only by seeing females, particular body parts, and especially certain female movements, but also by thinking about them.

Beyond their basic sex drive, humans copulate because it feels good. They have pleasant memories of past couplings and the anticipation of future enjoyment. Humans enjoy recreational sex. At times ego satisfactions and contemplated functional benefits are involved as well. Pleasant past experiences, anticipated future experiences, conquests, and benefits can be construed as second-order motivators that are sometimes more potent than the innate sexual urge itself. Such anticipatory enjoyment is generally not a matter of experience or reason and foreknowledge, as every prostitute knows well.

For modern men stimulation can be artificially created through the printed pictures and movies that, at the margin, have been labeled pornography. Pornography not only initiates thinking about sex but can be pleasurable by itself. It is for the most part an unconditioned response in that it is autoerotic and generally not tied to a possibility of actual copulation. Even some of those males who consciously and publicly acknowledge the decadence of pornography nonetheless enjoy it and are aroused by it. So powerful can pornography be in sexually satisfying some males that it can engender a functional fixation or psychological displacement with respect to their sex drives. Having been exposed to pornography, some aberrant males find that they are more aroused by pornography than by real women, and, in extreme cases, a small percentage of men find that they can only enjoy and be sexually aroused by pornography. Addiction to pornography can be regarded as a third-order effect of the sex drive

Given that males are captives of visual stimulation, from Paleolithic times to the present, females, by means of developing rhythmic dance movements or decorating their bodies with jewelry and fashion, attempt to enhance their natural physical endowments so as to have the widest selection among potential male partners. Even in the modern world, female physical comeliness, dress, and movement are critical elements in attracting Mr. Right—far more than intellectual acumen or accomplishments. As an example of third-order functional fixation for females, the desirability of fashion, which in its Paleolithic roots was devised for purposes of success in mate selection and procreation, has become an end in itself. Many, if not most, modern women who are highly interested in fashion are driven by an asexual esthetic. Married women and lesbians can be consumed with fashion, enjoying it for its own sake, reacting mainly to esthetic visual pleasure and the refined sensibilities of other women while regarding male reactions as merely peripheral.

Compulsion to Seek Patterns in Nature

Humans, like other animals, innately discern and act on patterns of objects and events in their environments as they are driven by survival instincts. The operations of neurological networks evolved to create associations that enable the emergence of patterns of similarity among naturally occurring OACEREs. Establishing patterns in nature is critical for planning. Individuals have a need to know why things happen and especially why things happen to them. Humans have a penchant bordering on compulsion for actively searching for patterns and relationships among objects, events, and conditions in nature whether or not these will be useful for survival in the short run or for ensuring the immediate success of plans. Far more than B. F. Skinner's "mere superstition," in the quest for understanding nature, the mental exercise of trying to discern patterns, speculatively linking effects to causes and the search for meaning, are, in many cases, very functional.

Daniel Gilbert wrote that humans engage in making elaborate plans even when they have no inclination to implement the plans. It is like practicing physical activities so that they become more effective when they are required. Elaborating hypothetical plans seems to provide the practice that improves the process of planning itself. Time spent in planning has also become an activity that yields its own rewards of satisfaction. From a functional point of view, the use of brainpower in practicing planning, though consuming time and energy, in the long run greatly improves prospects for gaining control over aspects of the environment. Planning is very effective in the quest for seeking pleasure and avoiding pain.

For the last few thousands of years, some of those humans who didn't need to spend their time satisfying their basic needs for food, shelter, or mating have spent inordinate amounts of time working out patterns in nature. They have examined cause-effect relationships among many aspects of their natural habitats, even in situations where there could be no near-term functional payoff.

For example, our long ago ancestors spent many hours examining the heavens and the arrangements and movements of the stars at night. In doing so, these ancients, usually the elders, were engaged primarily in what can be regarded as an enjoyable pastime (though they regarded plotting the movements of the heavens as very important). On occasion, there may have been a major payoff (such as with regard to navigation), the self-delusional prospect of one, or the use of arcane knowledge in impressing other tribe members. Most often the delight in determining a pattern was short lived, as new factors tended to ruin the pattern. But the major impetus for continuing to engage in stargazing activity was the pure satisfaction that it gave when stable patterns were determined.

Believing that they had discerned patterns with regard to position and movement in the heavens, the ancients naturally attempted to relate the observed patterns to earthly experiences for their own benefit as well as the benefit of their tribe.

Planning, Urban Myths, and Conspiracies

It is as an indirect effect of the sheer enjoyment of searching for patterns and of planning activities that many humans relish concocting "what if" scenarios and urban myths. People speculate at length and in vivid detail about what might happen if some peculiar but plausible situation should occur and then weaving fabulous stories around the hypothetical events. As with gossip they enjoy developing and sharing such scenarios with others. Because the juicy enjoyment of the story is heightened with the acceptance of its alleged truth, the listeners tend to uncritically accept the storyteller's tenuous declarations of verisimilitude. In addition, such urban myths, like gossip, are often presented within a context of phatic communion,[75] which also deters critical analysis, since critical questioning of the storyteller is regarded as being unfriendly. To convey an air of authenticity, some of the stories include phony testimonials from hypothetical authorities or subplots describing how doubters were subsequently convinced of the tales' veracity.

A survey in 2009 indicated that 6 percent of U.S. residents do not believe that men actually landed on the moon. These people are convinced that the television images were staged at a remote television station. They point to evidence such as the unfurling of the U.S. flag in airless space as proof positive that the public was duped. Despite the fact that the moon landing occurred some forty years earlier, and that there have been a number of subsequent space explorations, including moon landings, the doubters continue to grasp at even the slightest imagined discrepancy or inconsistency in reports of the event as absolute proof that it never happened. In another conspiracy theory, many people have garnered the attention of their fellows by regaling them with "true stories" of why and how President Kennedy was actually killed by men working for Fidel Castro, the Mafia, the KGB, or the CIA.

Many people take delight in listening to and then retelling urban myth stories. When they later retell such fables, they not only enhance the story to appeal to their particular audiences but also repeat and sometimes embellish the claims of authenticity even though they themselves have made no effort to check them out (and even may harbor doubts about details of the story). People consciously and unconsciously add their own flourishes, which they think serve to improve the myth, heighten its appeal for listeners, or make it more believable. That many, if not most, of those who repeat urban myths freely embellish them is an indication that even when the stories are accepted as being loosely based in reality, they are considered to be anecdotes that can be improved upon by adding spurious bolstering details. Therefore the retelling need not be entirely faithful to the version that they heard.

The universal affinity for and enjoyment of myths, urban myths, and fanciful stories can be construed as a third-order effect with respect to the need to plan and to mentally rehearse the planning process. The popularity of such stories is also driven by the value of and the need to gossip, as discussed earlier.

Planning and Religion

Because of the uncertainty of the environment, the vicissitudes of life, and the problematic nature of the planning process itself, we often yearn for some guarantor for our plans. The more desperate we are for our plans to succeed, or the more extravagant our plans are, the more we wish for some means of ensuring a successful outcome. The hoped-for guarantor of plans can be internal, such as a wish for our own super powers or good luck with which we can overcome any and all obstacles. It can be an external guarantor, such as the wish for a patron or the ability to hold influence over another person or persons who have the power to grant our wishes for absolute success. Finally it can be some genie who will grant our wishes or a supernatural power that we can appeal to in the hope that future events will unfold so as to favor our own plans.

A corollary benefit of importuning a god for the successful outcome of future or planned undertakings is that failure can be externalized but without an upsetting apprehension that harm and the causes of failure are due to randomness in nature. We need to know that there are patterns in nature and that all events have logical causes. A supplicant can believe that she did not fail but rather that God had other plans. In addition, she might reassure herself that failure was due to some peripheral cause, such as failure to observe a minor commandment, rather than a personal shortcoming or a problem with the basic plan or its execution. It is less threatening to our egos to blame others or the stars or even our own noncompliance and adverse trade-offs for our own shortcomings with respect to our plans. In addition to benign supernatural forces, there are also malign forces that may be the external causes of our failure or the harm that befalls us. Theologians have been wrestling with the reasons for the existence of evil and misfortune since before Epicurus in the third century BCE.[76]

Religion can be construed as a third-order by-product of evolutionary processes. We plan our behavior so as to maximize our own future welfare and that of our kin, but we can't ensure the success of our plans. As Alexander Pope put it, "Man proposes but God disposes." Those critical phenomena that can't be controlled, comprehended, or anticipated prompt metaphysical explanations in order to satisfy an innate survival urge and the belief that all events have causes. As the seventeenth century philosopher Peter Bayle surmised, such a transference is intended to understand and control that which is vital but cannot be understood or controlled. A cynic might call this a religion of gaps. Such a basis for religion can be characterized as explaining the unexplainable with a nonexplanation, and by doing so, hoping to control the uncontrollable by acceptance.

Why Intelligent People Are Religious

Skeptics will argue that religion only gives a patently flimsy illusion of influence or control over nature that is easy to debunk. Praying for rain doesn't really influence the weather. Praying for a miraculous cure doesn't work reliably. Any valid double-blind, empirical test of the efficacy of religious prayer and entreaties is certain to fail. But, explaining the mysteries of life, such as why we die, by means of invoking an ineffable god who wills it is simply a distinction without a real difference.

Surely even ancient people, being fundamentally as rational and intelligent as we moderns are, should have quickly abandoned religion when they realized how ineffective it was in objectively delivering on its promises and in realizing their plans and their hopes. Only by blatant misdirection and manipulation of anecdotal evidence could religion be construed as objectively improving the people's welfare or their chance of survival by means of appealing to the gods and trying to influence some aspect of nature.

B. F. Skinner and other behaviorists have established that once a behavior has been conditioned, if the conditioning reward is withheld intermittently, the conditioning will persist in effect far longer than if it is simply discontinued once and for all. For example, if a rat is conditioned so that by pressing a lever it will receive a food reward and later the reward is withheld, the rat will continue to press the lever a few times still expecting a reward. After a while, as measured by the number of unrewarded attempts, the rat will give up. However, if the reward is terminated after conditioning in which the rat received rewards sometimes but not others, the rat will continue to try to obtain rewards by pressing the lever many more times and for far longer than in the first case, where the rewards simply began and then stopped.

Of course many people can be convinced that there are some critical benefits from religious belief and practice with respect to understanding nature and the manipulation of fate. If someone is ill and recovers, they can be easily convinced that whatever medication or ceremony was used in the attempt to cure them was successful. Synthetic experience is not as powerful as reality, but it can be effective.

The discovery of an herb or plant that will cure some malady as if by magic lends credibility to many other propositions of faith about other potions and things that are said to have curative powers. The discovery that some killed viruses, when injected into people, can confer immunity from certain diseases led to the practice of homeopathy, where toxic substances are highly diluted and administered or ingested to provide healing relief from various diseases that are linked with the toxic substance. Homeopathy continues to be practiced even though its basic premise has been proven to be false.

From a stimulus response point of view, at some point people, even those people living ten thousand years ago, logically should have begun to doubt the efficacy of the promises of religion that were based on magic when they failed to work on numerous occasions. Reasonably, for intelligent humans, this should be the case, even if the promised benefits work sometimes and under certain special conditions. Most supposed cures in prehistoric times must have failed far more often than they succeeded due to coincidence, luck, or psychosomatic reasons. Humans are pretty fair intuitive statisticians. If their doubts about a cure became unassailable, or even if the doubts were credible, the misgivings should eventually have been spread throughout their communities.

The thought process of the human mind is prone to what is known as the "gambler's fallacy." A fair coin is one that has a 50-50 chance of landing either heads or tails on any given toss. From experience it can be deduced that, when tossed repeatedly, the coin will land heads and tails the same number of time, if the series of tosses is long enough. A gambler's fallacy is when a fair coin has been observed to land heads four or five times in a row. Those who succumb to gambler's fallacy will be convinced that it is very probable, that is, there are much greater than 50-50 odds, that the next toss will result in tails. Similarly, the more often a religious attempt (e.g., using rain dances, herbs, incantations, or other ceremonies to effect a cure, to bring rain, or to bring about some boon to a tribe) fails, the more likely it is that the next attempt will succeed. The trick is to convince people that there is a modicum of validity to the substance or procedure that is used in the religious ceremony. This is often done by relating retrospective anecdotes, that is, creating a synthetic experience, in which the healing system was effective.

All of us, especially as children, accept many propositions told to us by our elders that we don't understand, but since these "seem to obviously work" most or at least a good deal of the time, they are found to be useful. As children and even as adults, we accept ideas and practices that we are told are okay or are good for us by those we depend upon and trust to know the answers. To an extent, the uncritical, if temporary, acceptance of the ideas and practices of others is the path by which human civilization advances over the generations. First, we accept some practice that seems to work, if not for us then for others. We use the practice under conditions where it is supposed to work. If it works we note the conditions, and its benefits and shortcomings, and then we try to improve on it. What works is routinized, and its uses are improved and extended. What doesn't work, but might, is modified before it is abandoned. In this process, both faith and doubt are essential for progress.

It seems that we want to believe. Like Charlie Brown in the old Peanuts cartoons, no matter how many times Lucy removes the football at the last moment before he goes to kick it, we also want to believe that next time a procedure we believe in will work, especially if it has occasionally seemed to produce even a modicum of positive results in the past. There is an element of subjective appraisal to the estimate of success or failure of many endeavors. We rationalize and put a positive spin on events that are not utter disasters. In the 1960s an untested drug called Laetrile was claimed to cure cancer. There were a number of anecdotal proofs and testimonials. Desperate patients lobbied the U.S. Food and Drug Administration to approve it. They rushed to clinics in Mexico in order to obtain expensive treatment with Laetrile. When it was finally tested, Laetrile was found to be completely ineffective.

Albert Einstein defined insanity as retrying something that has failed in the past and nonetheless expecting a different result. With respect to religion, it seems that many of us qualify as insane by his definition. We want to accept, and are eager to accept, the word of others that mysterious potions or metaphysical appeals did work in some fashion, or at least had some positive results, at some undefined time in the past and so therefore may also work in the future. Most people do not diligently look for unequivocal proof or demand operational guarantees in advance. We all have "faith in the system"—we believe in belief. That is in the culture we grew up in, and religion is only one aspect of all of the nonrational beliefs that we accept and hold as important, even if we are somewhat dissatisfied with them and seek to improve them. What is more, when there are occasional cures or favorable outcomes that cannot be otherwise explained, there are many who are quick to attribute them to supernatural religious phenomena.

In our quest for pleasure and the avoidance of pain, at times even when we are aware that the behavior we have adopted or the solution we have accepted is suboptimal and does not maximally satisfy our needs, we are content to accept it, often without a search for a better answer. It is often a case of the devil you know is preferable to uncertainty. At the same time, this does not deter some humans from seeking better or more effective treatments or methods.

Trial and Error Progress

Many of the most significant developments in science, and the many rules of thumb that are effective in daily life, began as unsupported speculative propositions or hypotheses. They were accepted and used as guides for action because they did not seem unreasonable and were in some way useful or at least not harmful. Often an improvement was merely a matter of superior execution of an accepted behavior as a result of practice and improved physical ability. Sometimes minor tinkering with small changes to the original belief or behavior yielded much better results.[77] In the nineteenth century when Ignaz Semmelweiss insisted that physicians wash their hands before providing medical treatment in maternity wards there was an immediate and huge decrease in infections.

As knowledge expands, ineffective practices based on presumptions or incorrect beliefs tend to be abandoned. In the nineteenth century, many devices were contrived that harnessed the supposed healing powers of the newly developed electricity and magnetism. As more was learned about the nature of electricity and magnetism, the devices and electric cures were mostly abandoned (although a few persist and continue to appeal to a fringe element of people).

Over time refinements of many speculative propositions have led to greater understanding and control of nature as they were used. It is argued that many of the original myths, religious strictures, old wives' tales, rules of thumb, conventional wisdom, and traditions were originally thought to be practically useful in some way. Many herbs were actually effective for certain illnesses. Eventually a few of the folk remedies led to an understanding of some process of nature. Thus improved methods and materials promoted the ascent of humans, despite originally having been of questionable value. Unproven or unprovable myths, stories, and old wives' tales persist because they are, or were in the past, seen to be useful in some indirect or peripheral manner, such as their social utility or effectiveness as cautionary tales in teaching and in establishing mores.

In some cases, rules of thumb, cautionary tales, myths, and old wives' tales cannot be rejected out of hand. The burden of proof is on the skeptics to have valid, confirmable reasons for rejection. For example, taking chicken soup for colds does marginally help to hydrate people and ease the symptoms of colds even if it is not a cure. Carrots are good for the eyes, if very slightly, and if not, it is as good a reason as any for parents to encourage their children to eat them. Most importantly, there are no obvious negative consequences to these folk remedies if used in moderation.

Charles Lindblom labeled the common process by which human society advances as the "science of 'muddling through.'"[78] Most advances in human culture, he claims, have been achieved by this method. It operates by means of a process he calls "disjointed incrementalism." In his theory that which seems to work, or is not retrograde, is incrementally improved over time as it continues to be used. Others have suggested that humans naturally tend to use a TOTE—test, operate, test, evaluate—system to refine their strategic behavior in dealing with the environment. In both concepts, humans continue to use, alter, and empirically improve whatever methods seem to work. They use reason and evidence to discard efforts or improvements that seem to be ineffective or counterproductive. I propose that disjointed incrementalism reflects the natural strategy by which the animal brain works to associate seemingly disparate but somehow related elements in order to improve the welfare of the human condition and survival.

The Religion of Gaps[79]

Despite enormous advances in science, there are still many critical but intractable mysteries of life and death. We do not fully understand these existential matters, and neither science nor rationality has been of much help to date. What is the purpose of life? What constitutes consciousness or sentience? How does the brain translate language into neurochemical processes and then neurochemical processes into language? And, beyond an understanding of the physical processes involved, why do we die? These are some of the questions for which there may not be answers or that science cannot satisfactorily answer given human psychological needs. Religion and those promoting it declare that religion holds the answers to such existential questions. Many people, as a matter of satisficing, are content to just accept that some others, whom they trust, seem satisfied with the answers given by religious belief. Religion, Stephen Jay Gould and Karen Armstrong have declared, operates in an essential sphere that is not addressed by science. It is held that to live happily and successfully, we must "believe," and we must develop our spiritual nature. Neurologically supporting this religion of gaps is the need and the penchant to establish patterns of meaning in nature.

Some theorists, I believe going back to Herbert Spencer and more recently including Steven Weinberg, have proposed that religious belief serves to bridge the gaps between what we know and those unknown or unknowable forces and factors that unavoidably affect events in our lives. Our mental processes reflexively attempt to determine the forces and patterns of nature that affect our survival. We have a basic need to control or at least influence our fate, but some important factors seem to be beyond our control. Religious belief posits that there is some mostly benign supernatural force in control of the unfolding of the universe and that we can aspire to influence that force. Because we have an innate need to understand and control our environment, religion offers comfort with respect to these unmet yearnings. We weave patterns that we want to believe, because understanding equates to survival.

Our tendency is to ascribe aspects of nature, which greatly affect us but which we do not understand, to arcane metaphysical or supernatural causes. The earliest pagan religions conjured up gods that controlled various aspects of nature that they themselves could not control, such as good harvests, fertility, and the storms on the seas. By appealing to these gods as intermediaries, they hoped that they might have some influence to ameliorate a potentially malevolent nature and induce it to become benign rather than detrimental to them. Theology may have changed significantly over the millennia, but much of the underlying motivational stimuli have not.

Some of religious beliefs and practices are time tested as having proven pragmatically useful to individuals and to the social order over hundreds, and in some cases thousands, of years. Religious beliefs and practices continue to be incrementally or subtly altered as circumstances change. They are altered if they prove ineffective or if better beliefs or practices are determined. For example, although Christian Science continues to be practiced, its leaders have backed away from their dogmatically held, absolute disapproval of conventional medicine, even while they continue to emphasize the healing power of prayer. Though the first Christians were ascetics and committed to the value of poverty, this is not a theme that is widely preached or practiced today. In fact, a number of present-day preachers actively promote the avid pursuit of wealth as being a Christian value.

Old people who have reached the end of their lives fervently want to accept the proposition that death is not final. The complex patterns in nature that are consciously conceived cannot simply end for an individual. It is unthinkable. By such logic there must be some sort of a continuation of consciousness after death. Even so, the will to survive is strong.

Individuals ill with life-threatening diseases often become so desperate that they accept any arcane prescription or proposition that might help them survive for even a short time. Many modern, highly intelligent people will pay enormous amounts of money, and accept a great deal of inconvenience and suffering, for unproven medicine or invasive medical procedures that someone, who they want to believe, says has even a slim chance of prolonging their lives. These people want to believe, even where prescriptive advice comes from someone who does not have proper credentials or the recommended treatment does not have a track record of successes. In the United States, enormous sums of money are spent by, or on behalf of, people in their eighties and nineties for medicines and treatments of dubious efficacy on the slim chance of prolonging life by a few months or even a few weeks. According to Medicare statistics, 30 percent of its spending is expended for medical treatment in the last year of patients' lives.

There is, and no doubt has always been, a wide variation in the tendency of individuals to believe in supernatural causal forces or to pray and perform arcane ceremonies in the hopes of influencing these forces. There is absolutely no evidence that such beliefs and practices significantly affect survival. There is, however, a very significant evolutionary advantage to the inclination for individuals to cooperate in an attempt to control nature and to overcome its potential for disaster. The evolutionary roots of such a tendency go back many hundreds of thousands of years. Thus the religion of gaps is also a third-order effect of the evolutionary processes. It is an attempt to understand and to control the environment. But it was the enjoyment of planning and complex cooperation enabled by language (aided by a large prefrontal cortex) that fostered human survival, not religion per se.

It should not be dismissed as pure hokum for the naïve and uneducated, or as delusion for the clever and educated, that they can accept a theology based on dealing with the mysteries of nature. In the words of the English poet William Wordsworth, "There is a dark inscrutable force which reconciles discordant elements." Our brains are wired to try to comprehend the incomprehensible.

CHAPTER ELEVEN

Preconscious Control Of Behavior

Behavioral Effects of Psychoactive Drugs

As rational creatures, our actions should be governed by rational conscious processes. We are expected to be able to explain all of our behavior as reasonable. But as Sigmund Freud and many modern researchers in cognition and brain function have determined, a great deal of our behavior is generated and controlled by preconscious neurological processes and not conscious cognitive processes. Even the staid field of economics has come around of late to question the "rational man hypothesis," which has been a fundamental assumption of the discipline.

A patient who is given a psychoactive drug like Prozac may not directly relate the lessening of his anxiety to the effects of the drug despite being aware of having taken the drug for anxiety. Psychoactive drugs work in a subtle, gradual manner, often taking weeks to attain an optimal effect. A problem in the therapy of people with severe mental disturbances, such as paranoid schizophrenia, is that patients tend to believe they are cured, since they do not consciously recognize or link their change in behavior with the medicines they are taking. So they stop taking their medications.

This notion has been addressed recently in the *New York Times* by a thirty-one-year-old woman who had regularly taken antidepressants since childhood and now existentially wonders if it is actually the drugs that have determined her core identity.[80]

Well-meaning friends of severely depressed individuals are quick to offer observations such as that the depressive really has a lot going for him—for example, a loving spouse, great children, a successful career, and so forth. They attribute depression to some life event or condition rather than to brain chemicals. Sometimes the depressives are, by most measures, highly successful, talented, and famous individuals. But counseling them to count their blessings is invariably to no avail. Although the depressive hears the words, these get blocked in the thalamus and do not affect the brain's inner feelings and thoughts of hopelessness and helplessness. We say that the depressive is not operating at a rational level or is at the mercy of some chemical imbalance within his brain. Drugs such as selective serotonin reuptake inhibitors can sometimes alleviate the problem by blocking the production of dysfunctional proteins.

Parasites That Can Control Their Host's Brain

In his book *Breaking the Spell*, Daniel C. Dennett describes the case of an ant whose behavior is controlled by a parasite called a lancet fluke.[81] Dennett's example describes how the tiny lancet fluke penetrates the body of the ant, whereupon it releases a protein that affects the operation of the ant's brain. The protein causes the ant to climb up a nearby blade of grass to its very tip. The ant continues to climb and so falls to the ground, only to repeat its Sisyphean climb and subsequent tumble over and over and over again. This abnormal behavior, while not at all useful for the ant, does benefit the parasite. When ultimately the grass is eaten by a sheep or a cow, the ant and the lancet fluke inside the ant are also ingested thus achieving the fluke's goal. It seems that the parasite needs to get into the intestine of a ruminant in order to reproduce. This species of lancet fluke has evolved a reproductive strategy that, by controlling the brain of its ant host, causes it to behave in a manner that will bring about the host's death in a bizarre manner in order to aid in the parasite's reproductive survival.

Such control of a host by a parasite is not a unique occurrence in nature. Another example is a type of hairworm that spends the first part of its life cycle feeding off the innards of grasshoppers and crickets that it infects.[82] These hairworms, however, can only breed in the water. When the parasite matures, the worm releases a protein into its host's brain that induces the grasshopper to jump into a body of water where it drowns. In order to procreate, the hairworm has evolved the means to induce the grasshopper to commit suicide in its service by carrying it to a place where it can propagate. Even humans are susceptible to the parasite *Toxoplasma gondii*, which can cause significant behavioral changes, although they are not as extreme as in the above cases of the lancet fluke or the hairworm. Dennett's anecdote is intended to be extended indirectly for the human brain, which also operates by means of neuroprotein transmission. We know that psychoactive drugs that are capable of subtly changing thinking and behavior of humans operate beneath the level of their consciousness.

A Little Thought Experiment Apropos of Ants and People

Using Dennett's anecdote as a background, we can conduct a thought experiment. Suppose for the sake of the thought experiment that our ant was intelligent, self-aware, and capable of speech. Further, suppose neither we nor the ant have any knowledge of the action of the lancet flukes or whether our ant has been infected. If we were to inquire about what seemed to us to be the ant's bizarre behavior, how would this hypothetical talking ant likely respond?

It is not likely that the ant would reply, "The lancet fluke made me do it," for the nature of such parasitic invasions is to be surreptitious. They require that their hosts stay alive and do not evolve a defense or take action that would be detrimental to them. The protein produced by the fluke acts in the same manner as neurotransmitter proteins ordinarily produced by the ant. What appears to outside observers as the wacky behavior of the ant would be perceived from the ant's own point of view to have been carried out in a normal manner. The behavior is formulated and implemented by the ant's brain, just as any other normal activity. If asked, the talking ant would say that it climbs the blade of grass because it wants to. Success of the parasite requires that the ant be unaware of its presence and control. Even if an intelligent talking ant happened to know of such parasites, it would have no internal indication that it had been infected and that its behavior was being controlled by proteins released by the fluke rather than those released by its own nerve cells.

If our hypothetical speaking ant were made aware of its self-destructive behavior and asked to explain it, an honest answer by the ant might be, "I have no idea why I'm doing it." The ant is truly unaware that the parasite's protein secretions are controlling its brain and triggering the self-destructive behavior.

Most of us have committed impulsive acts. On later reflection, especially if the result of the action turns out to be awful, we can only scratch our heads and say to ourselves, or to other observers who have called the irrational acts to our attention, "What was I thinking?" Or, "I must have lost control of my senses." But we generally don't say these things to accusers. We attempt to rationalize or excuse our behavior.

Every parent of a small boy is aware of the impulsive, often-destructive behaviors that they are capable of. When asked to explain their actions, the small boy's usual response is, "I don't know why I did it." Even after significant parental badgering, in most cases the best a parent can get from the defensive youngster are a reluctant, often insincere acknowledgement that the behavior was wrong, a hesitant apology, and a half-hearted promise not to repeat the behavior. We expect a rational explanation for all behavior even though there are obvious cases where there is none, at least none that the bad actor himself was consciously aware of in advance of his decision to commit the egregious "thoughtless" act.

It's Crazy, But I Can't Help Myself

If the speaking ant were self-aware, an honest response might be, "I know it is strange behavior, but I just can't help myself."

There are people who compulsively wash their hands over and over again. Such people likely suffer from a condition called obsessive-compulsive disorder (OCD). OCD has been speculatively linked to the production of an excess of the neuroprotein glutamate. Many OCD people, when asked why they act so compulsively, will admit that the behavior is bizarre, or even describe themselves as crazy, but they say that they simply can't help themselves. They are aware, or have been made aware, that they suffer from a compulsion that they can't control, but they are not internally aware of some specific mental mechanism or rationale that causes the problem. If they were, they would stop it.[83]

Further, as some social scientists have noted, all of us have some degree of OCD. The majority of our behavior, perhaps 80 percent or more, though rationally explainable after the fact, is determined and executed at a preconscious level. All incidental habitual behavior, such as hair winding or finger drumming, is not sentient. As long as such nonfunctional behavioral mannerisms are not destructive or dysfunctional, are not publicly embarrassing, or do not negatively impact others, they are generally not seriously questioned.

In another case of compulsive behavior, some people with bipolar disorder or paranoid schizophrenia believe that they hear voices commanding them to perform antisocial, destructive, or self-destructive acts. They feel compelled to obey the voices, often even when they realize that the voices are telling them to do something that they know is wrong and that the voices are only in their heads. Even though many such people accept a diagnosis of mental illness, it is only at a superficial intellectual level. They are not consciously self-aware of their malady and often deny it when told that they are being delusional. Though these people may be aware of their diagnosis of mental illness, for them the voices are real and must be obeyed, and they feel that there must be legitimate reasons for their bizarre or destructive behavior. The behavior is driven at a neurochemical level in their brains, a level which supersedes intellectual parsing and rational analysis.

I Did It for a Very Good Reason

Another approach that the speaking ant might take is to rationalize a reason for the recognized odd behavior. The ant might say, "Well, I need the exercise," or some such excuse, which presumably the ant believes might sound plausible to her interrogators.

Patients with severe epilepsy have been treated by having their corpora callosa[84] (the nerve bundle connecting the two halves of the human brain) severed in an attempt to lessen the severity of their seizures. After the severance, experiments have shown that information learned by one hemisphere of the brain was, in some cases, unknown to the other side and vice versa.

Experimenters could blindfold one eye of a patient/subject who had a severed corpus callosum and then hold up a sign telling the person that at some later signal she was to leave the room and perform an ordinary task, such as buying a drink from a nearby vending machine. On her return, the other eye was blindfolded and the patient was asked in writing why she suddenly left the room (an activity that both brain hemispheres would have been aware of). Invariable the subject, unaware of the original written command but aware of the behavior, would quickly make up a plausible reason, such as, "I was thirsty."

In general, there is a tendency for normal people to concoct socially acceptable explanations of past behavior that has, after the fact, been deemed questionable by others or proven to be embarrassing. This is true to such an extent that it is sometimes difficult not only for an inquirer but also for the person asked to arrive at an unequivocal reason for their behavior and to acknowledge the real underlying reasons. It is both observable and testable that humans have a very great facility not only for after-the-fact rationalizations of their behavior but also for self-deception. (Have you ever watched the T.V. shows *America's Got Talent* or the opening weeks of *American Idol?*) People tend to believe their own excuses.

Sociopaths and psychopaths will explain their perverse, antisocial behavior with whatever excuses they think might justify their actions, even though these reasons may seem to others as patently far-fetched or ridiculous. Reasons such as "The victim was asking for it, even begging for it, by flaunting expensive jewelry on the street" are ludicrous to rational people, but to the sociopath they seem at least credible as excuses for his antisocial behavior. Significantly, it seems that, for the most part, the psychopath or sociopath may actually believe his alibi reasoning (which enables him to be more convincing in his lies), whereas a so-called normal person will realize that he is only desperately trying to excuse or rationalize behavior that is socially sanctioned and is totally unacceptable (and so he will usually betray himself if he had resorted to a far-fetched alibi).

Not Me, I Didn't Do It

Finally, if our ant were behaving in a human manner, it might try to deny what it realized was a strange and indefensible behavior. "It was not me. I didn't do it. Since many ants look alike, you must have mistaken me for some other ant," the ant might say.

Normal people do not want to be in the wrong, and they especially abhor being seen as having been foolish. Psychologists say that the defense of our egos demands that we occupy the rational and moral high grounds in any given situation. In situations where there is doubt about the agent or perpetrator of an action that is seen as bad, wrong, or self-defeating, the perpetrators, if they believe they can get away with it, will often try to deny their culpability or their foolishness. Under some circumstances where the denial is plausible, is repeated, and is not convincingly refuted, the denier may come to actually believe his own fabricated denial, rationalization, or excuse. Along with humans' proclivity and creativity in rationalization and self-deception, it seems that normal human beings tend to come to believe that which has been repeated often and has not been summarily dismissed or refuted by the hearers, even though they may have had their own doubts.

A Further Thought Experiment

The first thought experiment argued that, like our allegorical ant, under some conditions we are not consciously in total control of our own behavior. The psychiatrist Eric Berne, in his 1964 book, *Games People Play*, noted that people are often caught up in repetitive patterns of behavior in their interactions with others. He distinguished three levels of such patterned behavior, which he called games, pastimes, and scripts. The affected people may be aware of the particular types of events that automatically trigger the fixed behavioral patterns, but they are almost powerless to avoid them. Despite an ability to adapt their behavior to the specific triggering event, they are not aware of the nature of their reflexive kabuki-like interactions with others. Once the behavioral patterns are established, the people do not seem to have the ability to break them by significantly altering their responses to events unless they receive external counseling.

Romance is an area of behavior that has long been thought to be affected by brain chemistry. In many cases, romantic attraction between two members of the opposite sex seems to ignore or defy rationality. It is conjectured that differential production of various neurotransmitter proteins in the brain can affect who a person is romantically attracted to. Helen Fisher, an anthropology professor at Rutgers University, has studied the preponderance of various brain chemicals that affect romantic attachment. She maintains that those people with comparatively higher levels of dopamine and norepinephrine fall into a category she calls "explorers." Those with high levels of serotonin are labeled "builders," those with high testosterone are "directors," and those with elevated estrogen and oxytocin are "negotiators."[85] In her model, a person's romantic history is determined as much or more so by differences in the production of such brain chemicals as by reasoned selection or circumstances.

Romance and Neurotransmitter Proteins

Let us now try another, less fanciful thought experiment, which turns on the profound but unrecognized influence of the preconscious on ordinary human behavior. The behavior of both men and women can be activated in this manner without conscious deliberation in advance of the actions taken. Legions of young men, on hearing stirring martial music or watching a military formation marching in their splendid uniforms, rush to enlist in the military and place their lives on the line without due consideration of the ramifications of their action.

This thought experiment involves the physical attraction between young women and young men. Such attraction is very complex and has been endlessly fascinating in its blend of rational functionality and powerful nonrational impulses. It has been the subject of much speculation and scholarship for poets, novelists, philosophers, social scientists, biologists, and many others. The subset of this issue, which is the subject of our thought experiment, is the attraction that some "nice" girls have for so-called bad boys. It has been observed that it is not uncommon for highly accomplished young women from upright, uptight middle- and upper-class families to be attracted to boys who have reputations for high-risk, antisocial behavior and appear to the girls' parents to have few prospects for economic success in a modern society. Males, of course, also are prone to act out of the same preconsious thought processes. Most famously the Duke of Windsor gave up the throne of Great Britain to be with the woman he loved. More recently Mark Sanford, the governor of South Carolina, disgraced himself for the love of an Argentinian woman.

Some evolutionary psychologists have proposed that seemingly irrational behavior in young women originated in Paleolithic times, where more aggressive males were desirable choices as mates for females in terms of their ability to feed and protect them and their offspring. Somehow a residual of this trait is thought to have persisted to this day in the attraction some young females have to males who present themselves as dominant and aggressive but who, in fact, may have few possibilities for being good providers in modern society. Alternatively a clinical psychologist might theorize that the girl's behavior is the attempt to assert her independence from real or perceived, undesired parental overcontrol and demanding expectations. Or it could merely be that the two prurient youngsters had shared positive experiences at a critical or vulnerable time in the girl's life. I suspect that there are other putative explanations for the behavior as well.

Whether explainable through one of the theories of evolutionary or clinical psychologists, or merely a "just so" story,[86] the empirical reality of the phenomenon has long been observed. The strong appeal of inappropriate love has often been used as the background for dramatic tension in many novels and plays. The compelling attraction, assuming other males with better economic and social prospects are available, appears to be contrary to the rational self-interests of the young women, and the normative desires they should have to give themselves and their future children safety, security, stability, and comfort in modern society.

Whatever the explanation, there is little doubt that, in such cases, INP or innate neurological thought processes, of which both the girl and her parents are unaware, tend to dominate LMT or language-mediated conscious thought processes.

Consider the case of seventeen-year-old Amy Fisher, a pretty, middle-class high school girl in Long Island, New York, with no criminal record or history of mental illness. In 1992 she drove to the Buttafuoco residence and knocked on the door, and when Mary Jo Buttafuoco, the lady of the house, came out, Amy shot her in the face. It seems Amy was smitten with Mary Jo's thirty-six-year-old husband, Joey, whom she had met when her car was being repaired in his body shop. I have no special knowledge of the case, but if we don't assume that she was a stark raving lunatic, and there is no indication that this was the case, we have to infer that some sort of primitive, unconscious INP rationality, driven by brain chemistry, played a major causal role in Amy's behavior—behavior which had no overt logically rational explanation from an LMT or conscious perspective.

In 1997 a very conservative thirty-five-year-old teacher, Mary Kay Letourneau, married and the mother of four children, had an affair with a thirteen-year-old student in her class. She became pregnant by him, for which she was sent to jail for statutory rape. On her release from jail on condition that she not have any contact with the boy, she defied the judge's orders and resumed the affair. In 2007 Lisa Nowak, an astronaut and forty-four-year-old married, but separated, mother of three children, drove 585 miles from Huston to Florida and attempted to kidnap her rival for the affections of a fellow astronaut. She later pleaded guilty to felony burglary of a car and misdemeanor battery. Nowak also forfeited her very promising career with the navy by committing an act that could not possibly have had a positive outcome. Such bizarre destructive behaviors, which are so profoundly antithetical to any realistic notion of self-interest, cannot be explained on rational grounds.

More recently Dr. Phil McGraw advised a family that has become known as the Dr. Phil family on his TV show. The daughters in the family, Alexandra and Katherine, two intelligent young women, seem to have unhealthy, irrational attractions to unsuitable men. The family first came to the attention of Dr. Phil when fifteen-year-old Alexandra became pregnant. Six years later she had two children by different fathers and was living with a third man that her mother strongly disapproved of. Katherine was in an abusive relationship with a young man accused of theft, and was in trouble with the law for lying in an attempt to protect him. Despite Dr. Phil's application of conderable resources, his cogent advice and their seeming acceptance of it, the young women persisted in their self-destructive ways.

Psychologists tell us that our behavior is determined by rational self-interest. But the behavior of Amy, Mary Kay, Lisa, Alexandra, and Katherine seem so irrational and so obviously detrimental to their long-term self-interests as to challenge that assertion. The explanation of such irrational conduct is locked within the neural networks of the young women's brains. Dr. Phil's advice, which was so compelling to the members of his audience, and which could not be rebutted at a conscious level by the bright young women, nonetheless did not reach and so alter the preconscious mental processes that drove their behavior.

The Attraction to "Bad Boys"

Let us consider a thought experiment in which we envision a sheltered, "sweet young thing" hopelessly attracted to the boy "from the other side of the tracks" who seems much too sure of himself, just as Sandy Olsson was attracted to Danny Zuko in the movie *Grease*. To raise the stakes even higher, suppose that our hypothetical boy's prospects in later life are severely limited because of his limited education, the bad company he keeps, a spotty job performance record, few other accomplishments, and perhaps even experiences with hard drugs and a criminal record.

When the girl in our scenario, named Ingénue, meets, talks to, and otherwise engages with the "leader of the pack," whose name is, let's say, Rocky, it triggers the production of certain neurotrasmitter proteins in her brain. Visual, auditory, and somatosensory signals received at Ingénue's thalamus are relayed to the ventral tegmental area of the brain, where they result in a dopamine rush that produces a sensation often described as a "high." Dopamine signals are also relayed to the nucleus accumbens area of her brain, where oxytocin and seratonin are released, producing the sensations of thrill and attachment.

In an effect similar to that of the protein introduced by a lancet fluke to the brain of the ant, increases in oxytocin and dopamine in Ingénue's brain promote a strong, hormone-induced attraction for Rocky, which is triggered and reinforced not only by every meeting with Rocky but also simply by thinking about him. The strong attraction is generated preconsciously in her brain, below the level of her verbal consciousness. (We don't have to elaborate on Rocky's very strong INP drives and motives.)

Now if Ingénue's parents or some neutral adviser points out that Rocky might as well have "loser" tattooed in large red letters across his forehead, and that marriage to him will result in a life of hardship and deprivation for her and her future children, how should we expect Ingénue to respond? The stock answer we are all familiar with from plays, novels, and perhaps personal experience is, "But I love him." Or if Ingénue has more insight and perspective on the situation, like some people with OCD, she might say, "I know that he has problems, but I can't help myself. I'm hopelessly in love with him." In many cases, the more strident parents are in their vilifying and cajoling activities, and the higher they raise the emotional and financial stakes, the more Ingénue defends her actions and becomes committed to Rocky.

Even if Ingénue acknowledges that a bleak future with Rocky is probable, since she is unaware of the effects of the seratonin and oxytocin in her brain, a more rebellious Ingénue might lash out by saying, "You don't understand. It's my life, and I will live it as I choose. I know what I'm doing." Or a more defensive Ingénue might try to sell Rocky to her parents by saying, "You don't really know him. He has many wonderful qualities that make me happy. He will do well in life if only you and other people will give him a chance." And the ultimate emotional blackmail, "Don't you want me to be happy?" Ingénue's parents may try to counter with rational arguments and even threats, but to no avail, because Ingénue's behavior is not based on language-mediated rationality.

Ingénue's parents will be baffled and frustrated. How can an intelligent young lady who can master the abstractions of calculus, conquer the complexities of linear algebra, and intuitively grasp the arcane operations of computers be so obtuse when it comes to something as important and long-lasting as committing her future to a patently unsuitable mate? She must know that her parents have her best interests at heart. Why does she reject their rational arguments out of hand without due consideration? Why can't she at least intellectually process the objections so as to mount a cogent defense?

The answer, at least in part, lies with asymmetrical information transfer in Ingénue's brain. The language-mediated rational arguments of Ingénue's parents enter her brain via her ears and are converted to neural protein movement and transmitted to the thalamus. The arguments are vetted in the thalamus against Ingénue's existing unconscious neural beliefs about her self-interest, and they are disregarded. The nonverbal, dopamine/oxytocin/seratonin–inspired desires and beliefs about Rocky that have developed and are internally held as neural associations in Ingénue's neocortex have been established, and they easily overcome all external language-mediated arguments made by her parents regardless of their cognitive logic.

For Ingénue, as well as for others, if there is a conflict between external language input and internal nonverbal input to the thalamus, it is no contest. Though Ingénue will be unaware of any internal conflict, well-established neurologically generated information residing in the brain will easily counter and reject the external information. There is a mismatch of formats, and neurological belief prevails. Since the internal information does not exist in verbal form, in a manner reminiscent of the epileptics who had their corpora callosa severed, Ingénue must concoct de novo a verbal scenario that justifies the intrinsic, nonverbal decision that was preconsciously determined.

The condition is clearest with some abnormal behaviors. Passive-aggressive personality types, for example, are very difficult for psychiatrists. They readily admit their failings, or at least they do not argue or try to defend them. Yet despite their acknowledgments, like those with OCD, they persist in their passive-aggressive behavior. Parents of passive-aggressive children are inclined to mutter in frustration, "Talking to you is like talking to the wall."

Such preconscious neurological effects affect all of us, not just young women or those who are "abnormal." One of my friends, "Luke," a physician, is one of the smartest people I know. He is not particularly religious in his behavior or his declared positions on most subjects. Not only is he brilliant, but he is committed to no-nonsense rationality with regard to the scientific and social positions that he espouses. In some ways Luke reminds me of the character Spock, on the old *Star Trek* TV series, in his commitment to pure, unemotional logic. Luke, however, refuses to accept the evidence for evolution. We have had many lengthy discussions where he trashes the validity of evolution. Although he does not directly argue for creationism, he does argue that because of gaps in the evidence, the acceptance of evolution as fact requires as much of a leap of faith as the acceptance of the divinity of Jesus, or at least the acceptance that there is a supernatural power directing the universe. Luke maintains that the acceptance of the theory of evolution is tantamount to a religious belief.

Luke's father, with whom he was close, was a fundamentalist Baptist minister. Luke received intensive religious indoctrination early in his life, long before he received training in science. My belief is that the root of his skepticism about evolution, although expressed consciously in language, actually originates from preconscious beliefs, which are a product of the arrangement of neural networks formed in his childhood. It is these preconscious beliefs, which exist below the level of Luke's consciousness, that trigger his position on evolution. It is a position that seems, at least to some of his friends, as being at odds with his general stance on most other topics.

Preconscious Beliefs of the Human Mind

Much of human behavior, including verbal defense of, or opposition to, social issues, is initiated preconsciously. But this is not to say that biology and past experience determine absolute, unalterable destiny. Far from it. There is a multitude of intervening factors beyond genetic variation and automatic responses to stimuli, even for other, languageless animals. The degree of gratification or the perception of self-interest that is registered preconsciously in the brain can be changed as a result of other experiences (including priming suggestions, after-the-fact analysis, and lifestyle). The frequency or significance of an experience affects the degree of influence that is registered preconsciously. Social, political, economic, or practical constraints, and external discouragement or encouragement, affect behavior. And there are many more.

Despite many unknowns with regard to the neurological basis of daily behavior, it is clear (to me at any rate) that the influence of INP, preconscious thought as a determinant of ordinary, normal behavior tends to be greatly underappreciated in both cognitive science and normal discourse. Understanding the effects of preconscious processes on behavior is a key to understanding the origins and maintenance of religion.

I trust that these thought experiments have illustrated two major concepts. Like other animals, flows of neurotransmitter proteins in the neural networks of the brain induce people to behave in certain ways and to make decisions that are unconsciously perceived to be in their own survival interest even if they cannot be articulated. In the case of humans, this preconscious influence extends to language as well.

There can also be a disparity between language-mediated input or output and inner neurological thought processes. For various reasons some human decisions or behaviors that seem, to external observers, to be logically inconsistent with regard to the best interests of the decision-maker, and which can have unfortunate results, are regarded by her internal neurological thought processes as beneficial. (Fortunately, these tend to be the exceptions and not the rule.) Second, human beings are inherently unaware of these chemical effects on their brain that can have so great an influence and result in particular beliefs and behaviors. People who become aware of the discrepancy will try to verbally explain or rationalize their overt disparate behavior on language-mediated externally rational grounds.

Called to a person's attention, preconsciously generated inappropriate behavior may be denied, dismissed out of hand, or accepted without explanation. More commonly humans come up with elaborate, often very clever and well-thought-out rationalizations and plausible reasons for their actions, intended actions, or discussion positions. Such excuses are attempts at self-justification and maintenance of social acceptance. Being obliged to mount an ardent public defense of what, to others, is untoward behavior often serves to further entrench the behavior that is being defended and the beliefs that sustain it. As was noted, the defense of religious beliefs and practices often strengthens one's resolve. However, if something should occur, triggering the sudden realization that the underlying beliefs that support such behavior are erroneous, it can cause a precipitous rearrangement of neurotransmitters and neural networks that is highly traumatic. In the extreme it can cause a nervous breakdown. More usually it is merely emotionally painful. And as the old adage goes, "When a woman falls out of love, she suddenly finds that the man she has been dating is a cretin."

As can be inferred from behaviorists' experiments, experience alters the neurological network's distribution of neurotransmitter proteins that support belief, insofar as belief is the basis of future behavior. The implication of this assertion is that there are some general forms, that is, internal physical manifestations, of the beliefs that stimulate future behavior when triggered. These internal beliefs are represented in the arrangement of neural networks of the brain and in the production of neurotransmitter proteins. Although a particular belief may be deeply-held, well-defined, and give rise to specific behavior under particular circumstances, in the labyrinthine recesses of the neural networks of the human brain, its physical manifestation is none-the-less amorphous.

The Resilience of Religion

Religious beliefs and religious urges are often "overlearned." In overlearning an individual has so often used, studied, and discussed some beliefs that they become second nature. The beliefs come to be associated with many events over the years, including various public professions of belief. They become ingrained at the neural level of the human brain by affecting many millions of neurons that are associated with many experiences and activities. Since internal neural networks hold prior religious beliefs that are transmitted to the thalamus and used in vetting new information, established beliefs tend to become resistant to change from casual external signals.

The intellectual, language-mediated arguments of authors such as Richard Dawkins, Sam Harris, and Christopher Hitchens can be read and comprehended by devoutly religious individuals at the level of language. But these authors' arguments do little to affect the belief structures of devout individual readers by changing long-term neural structures. The verbal, logical statements against religious beliefs are countered or rejected in the thalami of religious readers by neural processes. Conversely, counterarguments made by authors, preachers, and people who are known and trusted reinforce the inured beliefs that already exist in a believer's brain. Since the new notions are consonant with prior beliefs, they are therefore not mitigated or blocked unconsciously in the brain's thalamus. They thus become blended with prior long-term associated memories and beliefs so that these become stronger.

The internal screening process, which occurs in the area of the thalamus, was originally developed and remains critical for purposes of animal survival. This makes both proselytization and the negation of established religious belief by means of using external logical, intellectual messages and arguments particularly difficult. What seems to be perfectly clear, momentous, and rational to either the devout missionary promoting religion or to the atheist out to debunk religion, is merely puzzling sophistry to a targeted potential convert. The polemics are easily rejected.

The sociologist Rodney Stark, who has studied the difficulties of converting others in his book *Cities of God*, has concluded that direct approaches by strangers with spiritual and scriptural messages are, for the most part, futile no matter how cogent their polemics or how clever their wiles. In general, people, over time, tend to take on the values of those who are near and dear to them, those who provide social, emotional, and economic support. Proselytization is an organic process that takes a great deal of time, modeling, and social interaction. These are far more critical to success than outright sharing of beliefs.

The acquisition of religious belief by adults with respect to neurological changes in their brains generally comes about slowly over years. It proceeds by means of many activities. Values are gradually changed so as to fit in with some reference group. Prospects tend to want to get close to or please some individual or a desirable group whose members all hold certain common beliefs. In some cases individuals have for a long time attempted to come to grips mentally with unexplainable events, especially those that are traumatic. Those who are impressionable may come around after having significant others interpret current and historical events as supporting religious beliefs. Though there are exceptions, most epiphanies and instant conversions only seem to be precipitous or based on a single event or attributable to the acceptance of a single seminal idea. But , like the straw that broke the camel's back, most epiphanies and conversions that are attributed to some seminal event or experience are rationalizations to explain an apparently sudden change of belief or behavior that has actually built up over a long time, even though the convert may not have been aware of it.

People convert to a new religion because they deem it to be of advantage to them and in the interest of their personal welfare. They convert because of emotional attachments to people they respect, psychological and neurotic needs, or associated economic and social advantages. Although such behavior might seem hypocritical and blatantly self-serving, changes in beliefs are often sincere because they are supported by unconscious mental processes due to gradual changes in arrangements of neural networks. Because of the asymmetrical nature of the process of information transfer to and from the prefrontal cortex of the brain, core beliefs are slow to change. Once core beliefs have been established, they tend to become reinforced through experience. Eliminating or revising long-held beliefs proves to be very difficult. However, at some undefined and subconscious tipping point or points, the information screening process in the thalamus can switch from being skeptical and rejecting with respect to the beliefs of a particular religion to looking for and accepting corroborating sense data for alternative beliefs.

CHAPTER TWELVE

Language, Persuasion, And Proselytization

The Roles of Emotion and Cognition

Beyond the cognitive effects that are elicited by the content of a message, language also produces an emotional effect. The emotional effect, or the "affect" of the language, is semi-independent of a message's overt content. The emotional impact of a message is determined by the mode and style of delivery as well as the context of the situation and the knowledge and experience of the listener.

Storytellers can evoke feelings of great sadness, which bring tears to our eyes, or elation and delight, causing smiles and laughter, by the way they tell a story. In addition to plot lines and straightforward descriptions, a storytellers' tone, enunciation, quality of voice, cadence and prosody, choice of adjectives, adverbs, or other vocabulary, gestures, and facial expressions largely determine the attention paid to the story, the enjoyment of members of the audience, and what they take away from the performance.

Children's stories, such as those about Goldilocks, Hansel and Gretel, and Red Riding Hood, can be told as horror stories, dispassionate cautionary tales, or delightful children's fairy tales, without major alterations to their basic plot lines. Each can evoke a different affect on its audience. I was told that the original voice-over French-language version of the movie *March of the Penguins* was very much a straightforward, reality-based science narrative about the life of penguins. However, when the script was translated and read by Morgan Freeman for the English-language version of the movie, it took on a whole new emotional dimension. The movie was transformed from an interesting science narrative, which appealed to those interested in nature, into movie that tugged at the heartstrings of audiences and became a smash box office hit. To the extent that this anecdote is valid, it illustrates the subliminal emotional power of language.

In addition, as Marshall McLuhan pointed out with his famous dictum, "The medium is the message," the nature of the medium of transmission as well as the situation in which it is heard affects its effect - or rather its affect. Whether reading a message, hearing it in a face-to-face discussion, hearing it over the radio, watching it on TV or in a play or movie, or hearing it in an imam's sermon in a madrassa, all can affect various listeners differently. The neural effects of a message will be different depending on the prior experiences and beliefs of the listeners.

A speculative evolutionary explanation for the discontinuity between the effects of cognition and emotion is based on their separate prehistoric roles in promoting survival. Certain received sensations are so critical that the consequences will be dire if they are not acted upon immediately. For example, sensations interpreted at an emotional level trigger fight-or-flight reactions. On the other hand, survival demands that other received sensations be cognitively analyzed and interpreted in the light of associated sensations and memories so that important opportunities or threats might be determined minutes, hours, or days in advance. It is the tension between the two modes of thought processing as well as a creature's ability to deal with the balance between them that improve its efforts to survive.

Effects of Subliminal Messages

In his book *The Hidden Persuaders*, Vance Packard explored how the advertising industry can manipulate the masses at a subliminal level. People are induced to buy products even though they are not aware of the basis of their motivation. Packard claimed that subliminal messages, for example, text messages that were flashed on movie screens for so short a time that the audience was unaware of reading them, could significantly increase popcorn and soft drink sales at theaters. He also claimed that magazine advertisements, whose images contained implicit sexual cues that were not obvious to the reader, could nonetheless induce people to buy the product advertised.

It is demonstrable that a message conveyed with pleasant music, poetry, catchphrases, or references to impending dangerous or promising future experiences, or delivered by some charismatic personality, tends to be remembered and/or acted upon. The theory of subliminal persuasion goes much further, however. Subliminal persuasion posits that the effects of covert subtext on certain behaviors can be known in advance. Many people, when exposed to such subliminal requests embedded covertly in messages, will have a strong desire to comply with the subliminal requests even though they are not cognizant of the requests.

Although subsequent psychological research has indicated that Packard's claims were vastly overstated, his basic contention, that speech and images can affect the behavior of the hearer or viewer in various ways without their conscious realization, continues to be regarded as valid within limits and under certain circumstances. The presumed validity partly rests on the contention that the causes of the behavior of all animals is based on their beliefs. These beliefs are derived and shaped by inputs from their senses. Such input acts on the neural networks of their brains. In the case of humans many of these inputs are in the form of language. By the same token, some aspect of language, like all other sensory inputs from the environment and experience, also affects the human brain at a noncognitive or a nonverbal level with respect to belief.

Theories about the potency of language that is beyond its cognitive content postulate that subliminal suggestions have an emotional component that allows them to slip under the screening radar of the brain's thalamus. The subliminal notions affect, and so alter, some neurological networks involved in thought processes. These theories are put forth as special cases that override the asymmetric operations of the human mind to preserve established beliefs, thus providing methods by which humans can be manipulated. The argument for the effectiveness of these verbal techniques merely extends the mechanisms by which the normal human brain functions with respect to received messages at a cognitive level.

By bypassing or reducing one's critical evaluative function, the subliminal aspect of a message may alter beliefs more effectively than an overt message that is incompatible with or counter to established beliefs. It has been my personal experience that merely reading self-help books has as great or greater psychological effects as the cognitive effects of absorbing their content. Such books are written with many anecdotes to which one can relate on a personal, emotional level. Merely reading diet, smoking cessation, and financial advice books tends to have a beneficial albeit short-lived effect, even if most of the specific advice in the book is ignored.

The Theory of Memes

A major theory of the noncognitive influence of language on neural processing is the theory of memes. Meme is a term coined by Richard Dawkins to denote language, either spoken or read, which is considered to have a strong and lasting impact on the thought processes of the human brain. According to the online encyclopedia Wikipedia, "the word meme refers to a replicator of cultural information that one mind transmits (verbally or by demonstration) to another mind. Examples include: words, phrases, slogans, god(s), theories, opinions and so forth, which propagate with culture." Of most concern herein is the propagation of beliefs, and in particular, the propagation of religious beliefs.

All sensation, including received language, results in some change with respect to a brain's neural networks. Memes are claimed to have special subliminal characteristics that nonmemetic language does not possess. First of all, memes, as they are defined, have a more profound impact on the neural networks of the brain than ordinary language, which is vetted by the brain's thalamus and generally has a limited tenure in short-term memory. With only a brief exposure, memes can result in long-lasting changes in mental orientation. Memes can induce significant beliefs that are much stronger and more deeply emotionally embedded than ordinary language is capable of, given equivalent exposure. At the cognitive level, memes may be recognized as ordinary language; however, they have a significantly greater subliminal effect. The individual hearer is not explicitly aware of the emotional impact of memes and their role in forming her causal beliefs.

Memes have been characterized metaphorically as viruses of the mind, since different individuals may be more or less susceptible or immune to their "infection" potential. They have dramatic, long-lasting effects on the beliefs and resulting behaviors of the most susceptible individuals that they infect. Like viruses, memes tend to be contagious. They are transmitted and infect others who come in contact with infected individuals, who, depending on their own susceptibility, also become carriers. Even some of those who are themselves immune can be carriers and infect others if they casually repeat the meme. Unlike viruses, however, transmitters often consciously adapt the various memes to fit the particular situation and the nature of the potential target to be infected. Those targeted for infection are often targeted with a replicated form of the meme that is adapted to a particular situation for maximum infection potential.

The concept of memes, that is, their effects, is consistent with the proposed theory concerning the vetting of information by the thalamus and the effects of preconscious neurological processes on behavior and language. The relationship of memes and subliminal persuasion is that overt memetic language serves a dual function in that the explicit message also has an emotional affect. Memetic language has certain characteristics that tend to overcome situational, contextual, or inhibitory constraints so that they resonate with deep-seated beliefs and prejudices. However, if the prejudices are absent, and the memetic notions are inconsistent or in conflict with neural beliefs, the memes will fail to register or will be rejected by the intended target of the meme.

The need to transmit the beliefs and concepts that are reinforced or even implanted by memes is, in part, consistent with the human need for gossip and the ego-driven tendency to want others to share our beliefs. Much of normal human discourse that has a deliberate or even an implicit persuasive intent has some memetic aspect. Its affect will depend on the preconscious mental state of the particular listener. Those that are notionally regarded as memes are the messages that have the greatest emotional impact on the largest number of exposed hearers or viewers.

In the same manner that neural networks can be modified, memetic effects can be neutralized by countermemes, the intellect (if they are found through experience to be wanting), disuse, or other remedies. External vetting and the need for ego reinforcement are reasons why people tend to transmit memes. Memes tend to fade with time, unless they are periodically invoked and either directly reinforced or unsuccessfully challenged, in which case they can grow much stronger and more virulent. Memes that resonate with the inner beliefs of a host, and are used, transmitted, and allowed to have influence over a long period of time without being successfully challenged, become more robust. Needless to say, memes transmitted in language play a vital role in the propagation and perpetuation of religion.

Different people have different degrees of susceptibility or immunity to different memes because of their existing inner belief structures. For example, R. Dawkins, C. Hutchins, and S. Harris all appear to be impervious to religious memes. This condition is consistent with the virus metaphor, where certain people are immune to certain viruses and it does not negate the theory. It is also consistent with the uniqueness of neural networks that are used to vet language. The concepts behind the theory of memes have considerable indirect support with respect to the fields of psychology, neurology, and evolutionary biology. But as yet the specific biological details and the basic processes by which language (or even behavior) affects specific neurological pathways and operations of the brain have yet to be fully understood.

Memes do not take over the human brain in the manner of lancet fluke parasites or the alien creatures in the movie *Invasion of the Body Snatchers*, but their effect is claimed to be robust even if not nearly as extreme. The human host will argue strenuously that he is purely self-motivated and that his beliefs and behavior are determined on purely rational and ethical considerations, based on personal research, logical analysis, or factual and obvious truth. Even where it can be shown that a belief's causal origins were at least in part due to an externally acquired meme, the infected host may argue vehemently that the notions and beliefs are nonetheless self-evident, factually true, or valid so that he would likely have independently developed the belief anyway.

In 2009 a number of people, dubbed "birthers," were infected with the meme that that U.S. president Barak Obama was not born in the United States and therefore not eligible to be president. (We can only speculate about the belief structures and prejudices of those who were susceptible to this particular memetic infection.) Posting his birth certificate on the Internet, and showing both this document and reproductions of the announcement of his birth from two Honolulu newspapers on television, did little to quell the memetic infection. The information only served to generate far-fetched conspiracy theories about the alteration of public records. Attempts to disprove the proposition seemed merely to reinforce the meme.

In the summer of 2009, some people became outraged by a clause in the provisional health care bill before congress that would permit health insurance reimbursement for end-of-life counseling by a physician at the request of a patient even if no other medical procedure was involved. A number of people interpreted the subtext of this clause in the bill as tantamount to a mandate for the denial of medical care to some of the elderly on the basis of excessive cost. This was not merely a matter of gullible people being misled. A number of them who were interviewed on radio and TV insisted that they had come to this conclusion as a result of their own reading and study of the issue. They referred to the clause in the health care bill as proof positive that it would result in elderly people being declared unworthy of keeping alive by means of medical treatment. Pointing out that the relevant clause in the proposed bill said nothing of the sort did not assuage their fears or cool the vehemence of their attacks at political rallies.

Of course, some vectors of memes, such as talk show hosts, were cynical mischief makers who sought higher viewer ratings. Others were sincere opponents of President Obama. They repeated the spurious information, even though they themselves were skeptical of its veracity, because they believed it helped their overall cause. And of course health insurance companies, fearing a loss of revenue, were quick to find fault with the bill and support any who might oppose it for whatever reason. The majority of the infected who became highly emotional and irate, marched in protests, and shouted down speakers at town meetings were sincere in their belief that their beliefs were personally derived and valid. They reacted passionately in their opposition to an act that they feared would impact them and their loved ones negatively.

Framing

A concept of involuntary persuasion that, for our purposes, is similar to memes is the theory of linguistic framing. According to George Lakoff, of UC Berkeley, a frame is the construction via language of "a conceptual structure used in thinking." This neologism is a metaphor for the frame of a picture, which sets the boundaries of some object being considered, as well as for the internal frame of a building or other construction that determines its outward appearance. Analogously, a linguistic frame sets the boundaries and the terms of some proposition under consideration. It both shapes and constrains the discussion about a topic.

The concept of frames connotes surreptitious intellectual constraints that connect to emotions while the concept of memes connotes more of an internal emotional affect of words and phrases. The hearer of a frame is aware of the words but unaware of how they constrain his response and generate an emotional reaction. Although purists may emphasize the differences in the concepts of memes and frames, I have chosen to lump the two together. In both cases, the use of language has a much greater effect on internal belief, including religious belief, as well as consequent behavior than the hearer is aware of. The hearer does not consciously associate his beliefs, behaviors, or arguments with the frame or the meme. The consequent notions and declarations are held to be entirely his own.

Unaware of the constraints imposed by the frame, he considers his position to have been reached by extensive analysis with sound logic, and that his arguments are definitive. Thus frames, like memes, work because of the effects of internal neural thought processes.

Lakoff is most concerned about frames that are used as political catchphrases. For example, he has used the phrase "tax relief" to illustrate a linguistic frame. Taxes have a negative connotation for most people, especially since, beyond a reduction of discretionary income, nonpayment can result in the seizure of property or even jail time. On the other hand, "relief" has a very positive connotation, indicating respite from the imposition of something oppressive or distasteful. Who could oppose something that gives relief for a bad thing? If a TV interviewer asks a Democratic or a Republican politician whether she is in favor of tax relief, she has, a priori, stacked the deck by the very framing of the question. As long as the politician attempts to answer the question within the frame in which it was posed, she is in a no-win position. Frames, in effect, finesse the process of vetting that is performed in the thalamus. (And that is why politicians are trained never to answer a question directly as it was asked.)

Those who oppose a public option for healthcare insurance dismiss it with the label "socialized medicine." In a single short frame, this term collapses the very diverse and highly sophisticated medical systems used in other advanced countries, such as Japan, Britain, Canada, and Taiwan, into a single pejorative category. The term socialized medicine conjures up images of godless communism, government inefficiencies, callous rationing, and lack of choice. It triggers a negative feeling in the minds of most listeners. This is the case even when it is pointed out that statistics indicate that the health care delivery systems of some other countries are as good or better in some aspects than that in the United States. The frame "socialized medicine or run by the government" precludes any rational debate or consideration of adapting various best practices from other health care systems.

If words can be combined metaphorically so that they have strong appeal for a wide segment of the population, they can be very influential in selling products or political agendas. Many linguistic frames, like "death tax" to connote estate taxes, have a strong direct appeal. Paradoxically, the death tax phrase can be used to enlist the vast majority of people to act against their own self-interest because they will never have to pay estate taxes. For most people, who will leave estates of less than a million dollars, protesting the death tax does nothing for them or their heirs.

Some frames are very subtle and appeal to deep-seated prejudices. Frames that overtly relate to: family values, to our kind of people, to patriotism, or to religious morality, may be code words or oblique metaphors to disguise homophobia and racism.[87]

The extent of the power of linguistic frames to subconsciously influence people and their beliefs, even contrary to their own self-interests, is a matter of some dispute. At one extreme, George Lakoff is of the opinion that groups of susceptible people are almost powerless to resist propositions and arguments that are framed to appeal to their internal worldviews and prejudices. Steven Pinker, however, suggests that individuals are continuously checking ideas against their perceptions of reality and self-interest, which serves to limit the longer-term effectiveness of any linguistic frame.

It seems perverse that words and phrases in and of themselves could trigger such strong emotion independent of their overt meanings or the realities of their content. The same sentence that is bland and unmemorable using certain words can become highly charged or disturbing using other words even though the basic meaning of the sentence is unchanged. So-called four letter or "dirty" words carry such emotional baggage that they have repercussions beyond mere discomfort when they are used. Lives have been changed, heavy fines levied, and careers torpedoed because of the use of scatological terms such as the "F" bomb or hot-button words such as the dreaded "N" word.

Entrenching Belief

Nonpragmatic activities that require the sacrifice of time, money, and effort, and "going public" for one's beliefs, entrenches established religious beliefs, including those that have been memetically initiated. The more time spent explaining and defending their religious beliefs to others, the more committed and devout religious people become themselves, as the neurological networks supporting their beliefs expand. Without any support or success, belief tends to weaken as neurological networks change and other, incompatible beliefs are formed. If it happens that potential targets of memetic infection by a devout individual respond with cogent, unanswerable counterarguments, contradictory memes, or stinging ridicule, the memes may dissipate. To avoid such situations, religious organizations put forth great effort to devise methods for continual reinforcement of belief as well as methods for insulating their adherents from countermemes.

The Mormon Church, for an example, trains many young high school graduates to go out as missionaries in foreign lands for two years. At their own significant expense, the youngsters go in groups to most countries of the world. They generally have a "handler" to help them with any problems they might have with regard to either adjustment to being in a strange land or theological quandaries. It is a great adventure. But they are only allowed limited contact with family or friends back home. They learn the language and the customs of the host country. Although success, if any, for these impressionable youngsters is generally hard won, the encouragement of their handlers, the shared adventure and dynamics of framed group discussions away from their familiar haunts, and the activities of ingratiating themselves and confronting those with other religious beliefs tends to intensify their own commitment to the church and its doctrines. In addition, the local members of the church, who are usually a small minority in their respective foreign communities, are heartened by the enthusiasm and energy of the young missionaries.

Some members of the American Amish religion, who lead austere lives on their farms, permit their children, both boys and girls, on reaching the age of eighteen, to go to the "city" and live indulgently on their own for a year or more. It is a practice that they call "rumspringa." After the year of living without religious or parental strictures or supervision, the youth can choose to either return to their communities or stay away and continue to avail themselves of the comforts and diversions of the modern "high life."

Facing the prospect of being cut off from their communities and their families at a tender age, and generally with few marketable skills, the large majority of them more than eighty percent of those who go on rumsringa voluntarily choose to return to their kith and kin.[88] They return to the simple, very demanding religious life on the farms, where they will have few of the modern conveniences or venues for enjoyment that they have seen and partaken of during their rumspringa travels. In many cases, even though it is coerced and loaded, such a conscious choice makes the returnees contemptuous of life in the fleshpots of the city, which they have publicly rejected. It is a defense of their egos to believe that they have made the correct choice. Over the ages, the religious authorities of many religions have used excommunication or social isolation short of excommunication as a powerful weapon for social control.

Conflict in Evident Truths

Another area of much concern, gun control, is an issue that raises extreme passions by defenders and detractors. For gun control advocates, it is a no-brainer that greater restrictions and difficulty in the ability to obtain guns leads to a major reduction in the number and potency of the guns, particularly automatic and semiautomatic weapons, in the hands of the public. Fewer guns, especially assault weapons, must necessarily result in at least some reduction of the carnage caused by weapons, especially massacres such as the killings at Virginia Technical Institute in 2007 or Colorado's Columbine High School the year before.

For gun advocates it is equally obvious that, if it were common for people to carry concealed guns, there would be fewer shootings, since the criminals and the crazies could not be certain that they themselves would not be quickly killed. In cases such as the Virginia Tech massacre, gun ownership defenders maintain that the gunman would have been stopped by someone who had carried a gun to class while most of his thirty-one victims were still alive.

Both sides of the gun issue are absolutely sincere. They both fervently believe their own position and are sincere when they say that they cannot understand their opponents' illogical arguments. They each seek out information and anecdotes that tend to confirm their own preconceptions, or to frame and interpret the information so that it does support their views. It is not so much that they reject contrary arguments after weighing the pros and cons as that they cannot see the validity of them. Contrary arguments are blocked or reformed by their brains' thalami. Both sides often use the same studies and the same data but with different interpretations and conclusions in support of their own positions.

A Speculative Biological Basis for Memes and Frames

The propagation of memes can be rationalized as being logical from an evolutionary biology point of view. Our hominid ancestors learned to react quickly to sensations that had previously proven to be associated as forerunners of either good fortune or great danger. Such shorthand cues could encapsulate complex situations and prospects and invoke emotional memory systems so that they were acted on quickly without analysis or dithering. By the time sensations that triggered danger and fear could be vetted and analyzed, the individual might have become a predator's lunch.

When language became a common means of communication, it was superimposed on native, nonlanguage modes of thought and communication. Eons-old mental processes, which are activated by carriers of sensations to the brain, were extended with respect to the operation of the sensations produced by language as well.

In Paleolithic times a sharp noise might start adrenaline flow, sharpen the senses and bring on a fight-or-flight response. In modern society a sharp command to freeze can elicit a similar mental response. Memes can describe language that similarly is readily accepted and relayed by the brain's thalamus. Just as some sounds or sights trigger instantaneous, reflexive fight-or-flight responses, verbal messages, as well as their metacontent, can be instantaneously transferred so that they affect neural networks that form memory systems in ways that are not perceived by conscious cognitive thought. Memes tend to trigger emotional responses and embed in memory because they resonate with internal, noncognitive beliefs as being somehow critically self-protective or important to a person's individual welfare.

Memes are processed at the preconscious thought level, where they affect beliefs. For example, the deep-seated belief or cultural value that those considered to be "our own kind" are more trustworthy than others plays a large role in the culture of social animals, and was important to tribal loyalty and religious cohesion among humans. The "us versus them" instincts of social animals may be articulated in language by humans, but they are generated and reinforced by noncognitive beliefs.

Such ingrained beliefs go beyond calculated expectations of direct reciprocity. In some cases people appear, irrationally, to extend trust and allow themselves to become vulnerable to family members, religious cohorts, or pseudokin of "their own kind of people" who have clearly demonstrated in the past that they cannot be trusted or that they will not, or cannot, reciprocate favors. Such charity or misplaced trust cannot always be rationalized by arguments of gene survival. In these cases the immediate behavior is determined by the preconscious, which overrides prudence. That is, a strongly held preconscious cultural value can, in some cases, override self-interested, objective rationality of the moment. Of course, impulsive, suboptimal behavior may be tempered on later sober reflection and conscious rational analysis.

The Power of Emotion

The asymmetry of the processes of belief induction and belief retrieval is significant in understanding human behavior. The more ego involvement or emotional commitment a person has to a belief, and the more external or public support it is perceived to have, especially from significant and respected others, the greater will be an individual's struggle to rationalize it. The believer will attempt to find supporting evidence for her belief from almost any and every experience or coincidence that can be construed as being relevant.

Memes operate at an emotional level. This is another way of saying they operate at a preconscious level. Once embedded in cortical memory, belief serves to shape many other related beliefs and actions that are associated with it and so extend the belief. Information and experience that are incompatible with the belief will tend to be ignored or rejected. It is difficult to abandon a strongly rooted belief, even if there is little supporting evidence for it or even contradictory evidence.

Anti-immigrant, anti-Semitic or anti–African American beliefs supported by neural networks that were formed in childhood may lie dormant or unacknowledged for many years in those who do not know or do not associate with any obvious immigrants, Jews or African Americans. People may even hold such latent beliefs while enjoying close friendships with members of the subliminally detested groups. In some cases a dormant, socially objectionable, meme-driven belief can emerge suddenly later in life. This was exemplified a few years back in what has been described as a recorded racist rant by ex-TV show host of *Dog the Bounty Hunter*, Duane "Dog" Chapman, when his son announced his pending engagement to an African American woman. Chapman, of course, professed not to be a racist. He had many African American associates, some of whom vouched for him. Similarly, a justice of the Peace in Louisiana, who protested that he himself is not a racist, recently refused to marry an interracial couple on the grounds that their children might suffer discrimination.

Some people are immune or even oblivious to the effects of particular memes, while others are instantly held in the thrall of memetic language. With respect to most memes, most people fall somewhere in the middle of the range with respect to infection potential. They are affected but not smitten so that many other factors, such as frequent repetition from those who have credibility, are necessary to reinforce the meme-driven belief until it becomes a strong impetus for action and transmission.

It matters little whether an individual acting under the influence of memes can muster arguments that objectively justify or rationalize his or her statements or behavior. Language and internal belief structures are semi-independent. Primarily, those infected think and act "under the influence" of memes, and only secondarily attempt to rationalize and justify their statements or actions when challenged. Justifying beliefs and actions is tantamount to a defense of their egos. The subconscious processes posited by Sigmund Freud were mainly holdovers from childhood trauma, whereas beliefs, though most easily and potently acquired in childhood, can be acquired at any age and can, in general, have a wider range of behavioral manifestations.

Creation of Memes and Frames

Some memes and frames are cooked up de novo by creative ad men, by political advisers such as Frank Luntz, or by religious leaders to serve a particular purpose. In general, though, both memes and frames are not so much created as they are discovered in an organic fashion, in a manner not unlike the way animals can learn from their environment. When a word or phrase or frame, serendipitously used, has a noticeably significant impact on a hearer or on large number of listeners, it tends to be repeated because it seems, to the person using it, to be rhetorically effective. In short order the effective phrase can spread like wildfire across many sympathetic groups. Variations of the attention-getting frames or phrases are used and implicitly tested and refined with various audiences and under various circumstances until language that has a maximum impact has been developed.

From ancient storytellers to modern politicians and standup comics, some people have been exceptionally tuned-in to the reactions of others in response to their uttered words. With replication, a meme becomes polished and is reified. In this way, memes tend to create a reality of their own. It is sort of a double whammy. People who are themselves affected by the meme tend to repeat it because it works. They are initially captivated (infected) by their perception of its effect on their listeners. As a result they are motivated to improve on the catchphrase or frame and to marshal confirmatory anecdotal evidence if they can. The process is partly conscious, involving a desire to influence others. It is also partly unconscious, because the person spreading a meme, its vector, is generally unaware of the nature of the underlying process (except in the cases of ad men and deliberate sloganeers).

Constraints on Memes and Frames

What can we make of all this? That is, what does it mean that real people, like hypothetical ants, are often not in touch with the true neurological roots of their overt behavior or beliefs? Paradoxically, there can be discontinuities between their conscious thought processes, their beliefs, and their behavior. Thus behavior, driven by nonverbal internalized beliefs, does not always seem to others to be rational or truly self-serving. Many beliefs, in fact, are formed under the influence of others who promote agendas that do not necessarily serve the person who is the target of the belief formation. Sometimes the memes and frames are contrary to the self-interest of the infected individual (e.g., death taxes or death panels). Free will does not exist in a vacuum. It is determined by a confluence of many sources and forces.

Fortunately the scariest scenario, of mind control by memes and frames, which conjures up images from *Invasion of the Body Snatchers*, has significant limitations. There is a marketplace of ideas, memes, and frames. We are constantly receiving memes and encountering frames, many of which conflict with others and cancel them out. There is only a certain extent to which memes can rearrange long-standing neural networks. If they are not consistent with the self-interest or the prior internalized beliefs of a certain critical mass of individuals, they do not get traction, and therefore they fade. Beyond that limitation, they are rejected, if not in the short run, certainly after experience has shown them to be counterproductive or inconsistent with self-interest. We tend to reject memes that conflict with well-tested, long-held prior beliefs, including those that would result in harm to ourselves, our egos, or those near and dear to us, as well as those that are inconsistent with the beliefs of our reference group.

The virulent contagion of a meme dissipates over time, as conditions change, if it is ignored or rejected, and unless it is reinforced. We look to new information, as well as old and new experiences, to confirm the validity of acquired beliefs. We continually check our beliefs against logic and experiential reality so that beliefs, whether conscious or unconscious, that are counterproductive, that cannot be supported or rationalized, or that egregiously conflict with the beliefs of our reference group, are eliminated. We also look to other people to share and reinforce our beliefs. If we do not get support or at least some acknowledgment of the validity of our beliefs, we either remain silent or alter our own beliefs. (The danger of the Internet is that people with extreme or radical beliefs, who seldom meet in person because of geographic separation, can nonetheless reinforce each others antisocial beliefs. Normally, radical beliefs would be discouraged or tempered by people they regularly meet face to face, and thus their radical notions would remain quiescent and probably fade. Radical beliefs are bolstered, and people who are outliers in their own community can be incited to act out by communicating with Internet cohorts.)

Developing the analogy of memes to viruses in spreading belief systems, Aaron Lynch has observed that

"... the fate of thought contagion depends on several factors, including how fast it spreads, how much fervor it inspires, how long each host stays infected and how much resistance it encounters in the population. Mainstream ideas can survive a lack of fervor because they meet little resistance. But unorthodox belief systems have to adapt to hostile conditions. One common strategy is to deem the outside world hopelessly corrupt and withdraw from its influence. Another is to declare that heaven is reserved for believers. That a meme not only fosters devotion ... but [also] motivates adherents to spread the word to any that they care about. Doomsday forecasts—complete with such signs as approaching comets or millenniums—provide an added sense of urgency.[89]"

Because preconscious thought is by nature nonverbal, we are not consciously aware of its complexity and sophistication. It can be established, however, that we use such preconscious thought processes many times every day in the determination of important decisions, complex judgments, and actions.

If preconscious thought and belief are so important in determining daily behavior, including opinions and judgments, the question arises as to how they can be reconciled to verbal deliberative thinking. Much of what we state in language as being clearly thought out, rational beliefs, judgments, or positions are, in fact, deliberative, rationalized articulations of our preconscious thinking. When we meet someone we take an instant dislike to, we justify our dislike on some rational or anecdotal basis. When our religious beliefs are challenged, we search for anecdotal and empirical evidence that will logically support our preconscious beliefs. In most cases our verbal expression will be entirely consistent with preconscious thoughts, but such is not always the case.

Preconscious Thought and Religion

Religion has been around for a very long time. The nature of religion is such that the memes and frames that have been devised to support it resonate at a preconscious level and are consistent with many of the basic psychological needs of a wide segment of the population. Religion connects with a need for the reduction of uncertainty, the need for control, and the need for social interaction. It arises from the precariousness of life and the ever present specter of death, especially among older people.

The practice of religion lends itself to attaining comfort from the rote repetition of religious behavior or ritual. The notions of eternal life, heaven, hell, and reincarnation are reassuring. Religious memes condition thinking and behavior. They can spur on and justify proselytizing activity. A belief in a potent fatherlike force that is in control of the vicissitudes of nature and will help us is assuring in times of distress. Our belief in a compassionate and always forgiving mother force who will give us emotional support, whatever the situation, is also most comforting. There is the desire of children to understand the mysterious adult world and to have magical powers that will help them to gain more control within their families. These are notions that appeal powerfully to our primal, preconscious thought processes. These and many other beliefs are fashioned in the service of religion and are powerful core leitmotifs that strongly influence both our conscious and preconscious thoughts.

Most of the early Bible stories and myths that form the core of Western scriptures were time tested and honed for their maximum emotional (preconscious) impact and memorable qualities over many generations of storytellers. Most, were time tested on ancient audiences long before they were committed to writing. Their treatment of universal, deep-seated themes, motifs, and human concerns were polished so as to command the attention of their audiences. The stories purported to explain the mysteries of life and death. They contained prescriptive instructions and commands that are claimed to be of major benefit to the individual and to society at large. In this way the ancient stories virtually begged to be spontaneously passed along to others. In fact, they have been widely disseminated in many forms from ancient days on to the present. Moreover, their lessons, prescriptions, and cautionary tales, whether or not divinely inspired, could, given the mind-set prevailing in earlier times, be readily discerned as being both benign for the individual and beneficent for ancient societies.

When religious frames and memes are repeated from earliest childhood, shared by many, and overtly contradicted by very few, they tend to act as effective influences that shape the brain's neural networks and preconscious thought processes. This sets up a sort of push-pull or circular process. Memes create religious notions. People, acting out of self-interest, repeat, promote, extend, and adapt the memes with regard to new areas and topics, thus developing a religious culture. That in turn generates more religious memes that reinforce and update the old ones, and so on.

Just in case the hearers (targets) of religious stories are too insensitive or immune from spontaneously replicating them and infecting others, the leaders of some religions have urged their followers to initiate the telling of the "good news" to others as a part of their ritual. Some religions advocate strong censure to those who criticize religious beliefs or holy men. One of the most basic tenets of many religions is to inculcate one's own children into its ways and beliefs. Some religions maintain that proselytizing among nonbelievers is the bedrock of what is expected of the devout.

With respect to adults steeped in spirituality, who devoutly believe in God at the preconscious level, hardly a day passes that they do not in some way get anecdotal confirmation of God's existence from events in their lives or in the mysteries, complexities, and vagaries of nature. By mulling over history, unusual or coincidental events that they believe could not possibly have happened except by the intervention of the supernatural, their belief in the supernatural is reinforced.

A return to health of someone who doctors said was certain to die in the near future, some premonition of an occurrence, a narrow escape from death, and so on, are all deemed to be proof positive of divine intervention. This is so even if there was a degree of distortion or a convenient selection among the details of the relevant episode. In this way, prior beliefs are rationalized, and frames and memes are reinforced and become more virulent. By default, for devout people the only explanation for the so-called unexplained is the supernatural—that is, God. It is taken to be proof that God exists. Or could it be merely the natural result of the operation of the mind in ways that constitute spandrels in the evolutionary process? Or are these really the same thing?

Pious people have convinced themselves that it is only through their own systematic gathering of empirical evidence, and rational sifting of information, historical accounts, and experience, that they have formed their religious beliefs. Therefore these beliefs should be as evident to any intelligent person who has followed similar logical investigations of facts. Many of those who reject evolution regard it as simply preposterous that anyone could seriously study the complexities of nature and conclude that they are due to a random process. It is preposterous, they maintain, to contemplate that random processes, such as an infinite number of apes randomly pecking at typewriters, could have created all, or indeed any, of the works of Shakespeare. That notion is regarded as simply silly – which it is. By the same token, it is declared that our wonderful, incredibly complex world could simply not be the product of random processes. For the pious it is not merely on the basis of faith, but also on the basis of their logic and "objective evidence from nature and from personal experience," that they reject evolution and place their belief in God alone.

Chapter Thirteen

Summary And Conclusions

The Need to Explain Religion

Religion has had a pervasive effect on all societies and cultures throughout the ages. It has a powerful influence on individuals, claiming much of their time, money, and energies. It induces people to behave in ways that benefit religious organizations and personnel, but which are often onerous and even at times at odds with their own overt self-interest. Because of religion's perceived importance, many people have sought to understand its origin and to explain the nature of the general phenomenon that is called religion.

There are many theories of religion, and most of them have some validity in a narrow context. One popular group is called "functional theories" of religion. Functional theories are based on psychological, sociological, anthropological, and pragmatic considerations. For the most part, they explain religion on the basis of its use and usefulness by and for individuals, or by groups and classes within groups and societies. Such explanations tend to present a particular use of religion as its source. But this begs the questions: If a phenomenon such as religion can be adapted or shaped so that it is made to be useful for ameliorating an individual's psychological difficulties, or for supporting the cohesion and welfare of a group, should such uses be regarded as its source? Or is this a circular argument?

The Supernatural as the Basis of Religion

Another theory, which I have called the pious theory, is based on theology. The pious theory insists that a creator, God, exists, and that God mandates religious belief and rituals directly, as written in divine scripture and the works of inspired sages; indirectly, through experience and observations of nature; and by logical inferences regarding the nature and purpose of life. The pious explanation purports to answer the major existential questions about the meaning of life that are of major concern to most people. With respect to rational inquiry, however, the use of the pious explanations raises many more questions than it answers. Such explanations rest on and promote propositions that cannot be critically examined or even approached by means of logical analysis of empirical evidence because they rely on the whims of an ineffable power. For the pious, however, God or the supernatural trumps any rational analysis by limited human minds.

Religion as a Product of Brain Functioning.

A more recent kind of explanation of religion is based on scientific studies of the brain and its wiring, or brain architecture. It considers hypotheses about how the animal and human brain has evolved over the eons. Theories contending that it is evolved brain architecture that gives rise to religion can be divided into subtheories. The first subgroup, the adaptationist, or the "main product" group, asserts that religious belief has resulted directly from a series of evolutionary adaptations. It is claimed that religious groups, and the more religious individuals within those groups, had higher survival and procreation rates than individuals in nonreligious groups. The set of genes that somehow gave rise to religion were inherited by their descendants. After many generations, by means of natural selection, all surviving humans had become descendants of individuals possessing the genes that are responsible for producing a religious trait.

The second or "joint product" subgroup suggests that evolutionary adaptations have many consequences, whatever the conditions that engendered their devlopment in the first place.[90] The development of bipedalism, for example, had many other physical and behavioral consequences that affected mating, food gathering, and hunting practices, all of which greatly affected survival. Religion is one of the cultural joint products of evolutionary processes of adaptation for survival. Religion is an inevitable, if secondary, consequence of genotype adaptations that were prompted by survival needs. In the joint product theory, the proclivity for religion is inherited by natural selection, but as a consequence of the operations of a constellation of genes that promoted adaptations for survival, and not the other way around.

The third subgroup, the "by-product" or spandrel group, posits that originally religion had no survival advantage, but once it serendipitously emerged, it was adapted for use in ways that improved survival. Stephen Jay Gould used the metaphor of the staircase of a house that enables access to an upper floor. In constructing a useable staircase, it is necessary to have a hard-to-use triangular space underneath it. This space, in its initial form, is not very useful, but it can be transformed so that it can be used for a coat closet or a useful storage area. The useful space is said to have been created as a by-product of the need for a staircase, and not primarily in order to provide closet or storage space. But the particular use is not an inevitable consequence of the construction of the staircase.

Similarly, religion may be merely an incidental consequence of some neutral evolutionary mutation. The resultant trait due to the mutation was, and is, fashioned by humans to be, in a circular fashion, useful even though by itself it is not fundamentally critical for survival. The by-product theory suggests that although there was no direct survival advantage of religion, it is a neutral trait. The gene or genes that had the secondary effect of producing religion are heritable. By a process called genetic drift, as long as the religious trait does not become detrimental under a prevailing environment, there will be a number of individuals in any given population that have inherited the gene and with it the tendency to be religious.

Religion's Dependence on Language

According to the Gospel of John, in the beginning was the word (the logos). The word gave rise to discrete definitions of OACEREs (objects, agents, conditions, events, relations, and emotions) as well as to abstractions and metaphors. They in turn revealed the glory of God. It was by means of the logos, which gave rise to precise definitions, abstractions, and metaphors, that humans inevitably conceived of religion.

The phenotype that evolved to promote the survival of hominids included the development of the ability for natural language. The evolutionary processes that led to language were driven by a need for sophisticated communication in a vulnerable species that was struggling for survival on the savannas of East Africa. There were a number of consequences to the development of language. One of these was the development of religion.

Whatever the role of either the supernatural or evolved brain architecture, there is little doubt that religion, as we know it, is utterly language dependent. Traditional religious beliefs are transmitted, perpetuated, and harmonized by means of language. Private religiosity involves prayers. Public religiosity is a social phenomenon. Whether it is scripture, prayer, theology, religious indoctrination, or proselytizing, the essentials of religions are all language dependent. But religion arises not in declarative symbolic language per se. Rather it is generated and survives because of the imperfect conversion between conscious, declarative language-mediated thought (LMT) and its transformation to the innate or preconscious nonverbal, neurological thought processes (INP) of the brain, as discussed in chapter five.[91]

Adaptations as Overlays

Evolutionary adaptations are incremental. They occur slowly over eons, and they do not eliminate or change the vast majority of the prior phenotype traits of a species in the short run. Adaptations that enhance a creature's abilities to survive are, in essence, superimposed on preexisting physical, mental, and behavioral traits. Long-established characteristics and functions that are due to a creature's genotype and phenotype continue much as before, with only minor modification to accommodate an incremental adaptation. Such a process provides for a smooth continuum of phenotype changes and slow speciation.

It is because of incrementalism that later adaptations operate almost seamlessly with an accumulation of all of the prior adaptations that have evolved over the eons. Would-be adaptations that are incompatible with significant aspects of existing phenotypes lead to the demise of the individual recipient and, if widespread, the extinction of a species. Despite the smoothness of the process of evolution, it can and does result in some imperfect accommodations or "kludges" with respect to prior functions[92]. However, as long as the kludges due to an adaptation do little to negate the survival advantages of the adaptation, the species can continue to survive and possibly even thrive.

There are often costs as well as benefits to evolutionary adaptations, especially at the outset.[93] Joint products of evolution are not always entirely beneficial. An adaptation that serves to decrease one critical threat may lead to behavior that increases difficulties for individual members of a species in other, noncritical areas. For example, the gene that provides immunity from malaria in African countries also gives rise to sickle cell anemia in temperate countries where there is no threat of malaria.

One of Charles Darwin's greatest insights was that natural selection did not necessarily produce "better" creatures in an absolute sense. An upright stance freed hominid forepaws for carrying food and tending offspring, but it also reduced their facility in climbing trees and increased the likelihood of back problems among later-descended humans. This stance, combined with changes to the throat that enabled speech, also increased problems of choking while eating. It is also hypothesized that the evolution of an ability to speak involved changes to the hominid jaw that greatly weakened it as compared to that of its ape cousins. Under this theory hominids implicitly traded a hard bite, which enabled the use of teeth as effective offensive and defensive weapons, for the ability to speak, which, given their particular needs, was more valuable for their survival.

In the mainly additive process of evolutionary adaptation, the development of natural language by *Homo sapiens* did not eliminate their well-developed, innate neurological thought processes (INP). These nonverbal thought processes evolved over eons in earlier anthropoids and hominids, enabling enhanced powers of both reason and emotion that were advantageous for survival. Despite awesome language ability, however, humans continue to use nonverbal neural or preconscious thinking extensively and in ways similar to precursor species.

Language Mediated vs. Neurological Thought Processes

Cognitive scientists using fMRI machines have found that a great deal of the thinking by which modern humans reason, make decisions, exercise judgment, and lead their lives continues to be carried out by nonverbal neurological thought processes (there are rough estimates of over 80 percent). Despite the development of language-mediated thinking, it is by preconscious, neurological or "animal level" thinking, which does not use deliberative and conscious language, that most of humans' routine daily activities are determined and carried out.

The series of genotype and phenotype changes that enabled language and continue to support language-mediated thought (LMT) have provided humans not only with a much superior ability to communicate explicitly but also with the joint product potential for new modes of thinking. It did not, however, replace neurological thought processes. Language-mediated thinking includes internal self-talk as well as external spoken (and more recently, read) communication.

Language-mediated thinking is largely regarded as *the* mode of human thought, although it is evident that all thinking, at its most basic level in the brain, is a biological (neurological), and not a linguistic, process. At the biological level, the human brain does not process words. But people are not aware of their basic neurological thought processes, so thinking is generally regarded as a linguistic process. Behavior, actions, or reactions that are nondeliberative are regarded as unthinking, emotional, or reflexive. But they are not. They often involve a great deal of lightning fast neurological thought.

Like physical tools, such as pulleys and wrenches that extend physical abilities, language enables modes of thinking that are beyond those available with only innate neurological thought processes. But just as a pulley system enables lifting very heavy objects with minimal force, but only with the hauling of several times the length of rope than the distance an object is lifted, so too does language slow thought process while giving it greater power. The differences that are produced by the two modalities of thought are at the core of this current theory of religion.

Costs and Benefits of Language-Mediated Thought

In addition to enabling much more effective communication, chapter five discusses how language itself has inherent properties that enable the expression and use of abstractions, metaphors, and recursions, as well as the resultant generation and combination of ideas that are beyond the basic functions of the innate neurological thought processes. As Steven Pinker has declared, expository writing "requires language to express far more complex trains of thought than [the brain] was biologically designed to do."[94] By the same token, language-mediated thoughts can manipulate ideas and thoughts in ways that innate neurological thought processes were not naturally evolved or designed for.

Like other biological tools, such as wings or bipedal locomotion, or manufactured tools, such as hand axes, whose fundamental natures or properties must be physically accommodated for optimal usefulness, language has given rise to an important disjunction or "mismatch" with respect to a complete and seamless integration of language-mediated thought processes with innate neurological thought processes. The powerful language "genie," which did so much to advance humanity to dominance by fostering much greater abilities to cooperate and control aspects of nature, also brought with it an inclination to self-doubt and an increased susceptibility to psychological manipulation by others. These were discussed in chapter six.

Development of Language

There is much speculation and disagreement among scientists about the development of language. I believe that the primary impetus for the development of language had to do with a pressing need for effective communication by a relatively weak and vulnerable species living in separate territorial groups on the savannas of Africa.

After being forest dwellers for eons, these species were poorly adapted for the open, treeless savanna. Survival meant a need for close cooperation and coordination. Females lived together and cooperated to protect and raise helpless infants. Hominid infants were born effectively eighteen months prematurely when compared with the development and physical abilities of other newborn animals. Hominid toddlers didn't become self-sufficient for several years.

Onerous child care requirements meant that the females had to rely on their older youngsters, sisters, and menopausal mothers to help them rear their children, and they had to depend almost entirely on males for food. Males had to run a dangerous gauntlet on the savanna, looking for food whose locations were variable and uncertain. Males also had to cooperate to defend their territory against marauding hominids from other troupes. Both of these endeavors required sophisticated communication. Given their lack of natural offensive or defensive faculties, without the development of protolanguage and the beginnings of natural language, hominid species would most likely have become extinct.

Like most physical tools and biological adaptations, language encompassed several joint products or inherent properties that potentially extended its functional uses. Eventually the use of language capabilities was extended far beyond its original use in simple instrumental communication.

Language and Operations of the Brain

The associative processes by which innate neurological thought processes produce and store memories in the brain do not naturally lend themselves to maintaining discrete memories of events, especially not in chronological order. Innate neurological thought processes tend to blend or blur similar experiences that occur at different times and places, in essence subordinating sequential time classification and other boundaries that demarcate discrete events in favor of creating a variety of common threads of association and similarity among past experiences.

Innate neurological thinking maintains only a rough sequence with respect to prominence, based on the primacy and recency of events. By contrast, language-mediated thoughts tend to maintain memories of discrete events and can remember them in chronological sequence. Because discrete language-mediated memories enable the explicit memories of sequences of past occurrences, differentiating them from other similar events by virtue of when they occurred as well as other factors, the assessment of their potential for reoccurrence is enhanced. Discrete recall of memories also provides a vehicle for efficient "time shifting" in recall. The abilities, to sequence memories of past events and consider discrete alternatives and sequeneces of future events that are a functions of language ability is highly advantageous in planning for and about future events.

On the downside, language-mediated thinking is very much slower than neurological thought processes (so much so that chimpanzees have proven to do much better than humans on some tests of working memory; see chapter two). It seems that human reliance on language-mediated thinking has dulled or inhibited some of the overt uses of our innate neurological thinking abilities. It is estimated that the internal operations of a human's innate neurological thinking occur in the order of milliseconds, while, because of the convoluted nature of mentally processing language, language-mediated thought can take seconds to analyze and process. Although it is thousands of times slower, language-mediated thinking has the advantage of enabling abstract thoughts and metaphoric reasoning.

Language, Abstractions, and Metaphors

It takes symbolic language to conceive of and manipulate the abstractions and metaphors that are impossible in the here and now of the associative neurological reality that brain processes evolved to handle. Syllogistic mental logic and metaphors, for example, exist only in declarative language. Preconscious, neurological thought processes do not deal naturally with the logic of syllogisms, discrete categorization, or grammatical recursion. In this sense, metaphors, abstractions, and recursions can be said to be properties of symbolic language rather than native features of human brain architecture that enables neurological thinking.

Preconscious nonverbal thought is geared to quickly select and process actual real-time sense perceptions from a highly complex, multidimensional environment, and to assess their overall effects for an individual's near-term welfare. Immediate responses to external stimuli by innate neurological thought processes are critical to survival in the wilds. Neurological thinking can tap into associated memories in milliseconds, as they operate in parallel fashion across sections of the brain's neural networks.

Pure neurological thought processes are holistic in nature, while language-mediated thought tends to be much more focused, reductionist, and linear in nature. Declarative language enables the discrete mental tagging and cataloging of individual OACEREs (objects, agents, conditions, events, relationships and emotions). Language-mediated thinking enables a powerful deliberative ability that is not possible with respect to the given, associative nature of innate neurological thinking. To paraphrase an old adage, "brain adaptations created language and then language adaptations created the modern mind."

INPs, LMTs, and Religion

It is the inexact transformations between language-mediated thought and innate neurological thought that give rise to and support the spirituality aspects of religion. Neurological memory maintains an adaptable network of associations among the memories of OACEREs. By contrast, to be useful, declarative language must impose precise or at least common definitions onto OACEREs that differentiate them. This imparts to language-mediated thought local consistency, logic, and an ability to communicate unambiguously with others. "Words have stable meanings that are conferred on them by the artificial conventions of current users".[95] This is critical, and it is true even where the definitions are not written down.

Consistent word usage is achieved organically. Individuals converse in groups, and they naturally converge on common meanings for words. Language would not work as a means of communication among individuals or groups unless words could be easily distinguished from each other. In addition there must be common, or at least extensively overlapping, denotations (i.e., informal definitions) of given words that are precise enough to differentiate them and convey similar meanings among the various hearers. This is not a feature of innate neurological thinking, which is unique to the individual and tends to blur distinctions between individual OACEREs at their margins. It is a feature of language. At the margin, language-mediated thinking discriminates among, and emphasizes, the differences between individual OACEREs, while neurological thought focuses on the associations and similarities among them.

Dealing with Reality and Fantasy

Pure neurological thinking readily accepts, and tends to deal ingenuously with, direct experience or perceived environmental phenomena at its face value. Understanding and responding appropriately to irony, for example, is well outside the capabilities of native neurological thought processes of animals. On the other hand, language-mediated thought can conceive of and sustain defined artificial, abstract beliefs, even those conceived to be supernatural, which are impossible in reality. Artificial constructs, plans, daydreams, abstractions, and products of the declarative imagination are contemplated even though they are not real and may not be regarded as bases of action or considered for direct implementation.

The example in chapter five, of the experiment where East Germany and West Germany were regarded by subjects in experiments as the most similar as well as the most dissimilar countries among a group of nations, illustrates that incompatible and even logically impossible beliefs can be sustained at the level of neurological thought as long as they can be mentally compartmentalized. That is, if they are maintained in nonconflicting areas of the memories of life's experiences, and if they will not obviously be injury producing or counterproductive to the self. Many individuals are highly moral and moralistic in church and in other reference groups. But they nonetheless have no pangs of conscience when not declaring dutiable goods as they cross an international border or blithely take advantage of others in their business dealings. As hypnotists can demonstrate, preconscious thinking allows a person to retain and to act on incompatible or even contradictory information.

Human Differences of INP and LMT

All humans have both native neurological thought capability as well as language-mediated thought capabilities, as contemplated by Dijksterhuis and Nordgren (see chapter four) and demonstrated by Myers Briggs and other psychological tests. Human temperaments with regard to these modes of thought differ over a significant range and are stable. Some people tend to readily accept language ambiguity, while others tend to think in terms of precise definitions of OACEREs. If humans had only a conscious declarative language orientation, religion would not likely develop. Paradoxically neurological thought processes, which readily accept mysterious events and strange objects or phenomena that can't be understood or controlled, would also not sustain the trappings of religion.

Religion develops from discontinuities in the nexus between innate neurological thought processes and language-mediated thought. The strange, the mysterious, and the unexplained are simply accepted by neurological thought as aspects of reality to be either dealt with or ignored. They are evaluated by neurological thought processes based on a belief assessment of their consequences for the individual. It is by virtue of language-mediated thinking that mysterious occurrences can be contemplated as patterns originated by an abstract force or the supernatural. It is by virtue of language that the mysterious patterns can be reified and explanatory stories woven around them. It is only with language that definitions and qualities can be assigned to the abstractions and scenarios so that supernatural entities can employ these qualities to interact with nature in determining history and personal experience.

Using language-mediated thought in the game of Dungeons and Dragons, a character or avatar can be assigned specific superhuman or supernatural powers. The avatar can use the assigned supernatural powers to escape danger and defeat enemies. However, during play in hypothetical scenarios where the predefined super powers cannot be used, the avatar is vulnerable and can be captured or killed.

In real life, many actions that must rely on supernatural beliefs are subjected to language-mediated thought or a linguistic mode of logical analysis, and are summarily discredited. Normal people, even those who love to play Dungeons and Dragons, have little difficulty in distinguishing imaginary characters that possess supernatural powers from reality. This is true today, and I believe it was also true in early pagan times. I believe that most ancient people did not literally believe that clay statues of gods possessed supernatural powers themselves any more than the people today who pray to statues of the Virgin Mary or Jesus believe that the statues themselves have magical powers. Idols were merely symbols or placeholders for the supernatural. Significantly, it is younger people whose imaginations are most stimulated by the innovative, fanciful Dungeons and Dragons scenarios. Older people generally respond to more traditional fanciful scenarios.

The Need for Dual Modes of Thinking to Sustain Religion

If language-mediated thought processes were the only mode of thought, humans would summarily discard stories involving supernatural events as both impossible and illogical. Any critical discussions among groups of rational humans using only language-mediated thought would quickly eliminate consideration of the supernatural as unreal and not useful as grounds for rational action in the future. No matter how much a person wished metaphysical forces to be true, they would not be acted upon if declarative thought were the only basis of overt physical actions.

Conversely, if the human species had not developed language, and continued to rely only on unmediated neurological thought processes, as other animals do, religion would also not have emerged. Animals operate, for the most part, in the here and now. Even though some may have some longer-term memory, and may take some near-term future possibilities into consideration in their behavior, they base their actions mainly on working memory and real-time sense perceptions.

I do not believe that animals can contemplate abstractions or act based on metaphors. Long-term neurological memory plays a secondary, minor role in their behavior. Animals' "beliefs" are primarily determined by past experiences. Their actions are based on beliefs and sensations from their immediate environment. Most of their beliefs and actions are dedicated to short-run, local, self-interested, and pragmatic concerns. Animals are fearful of near-term death, but they do not contemplate their ultimate future deaths or even what is likely to occur next year or next week. Despite some genetically programmed, longer-term behavior based on remembering when and where seasonal sources of food are located or used in guiding seasonal migrations, nonhuman animal thinking is far more concerned with the welfare of the moment in their continual struggle to stay alive in the here and now.

Effects of Combining INP and LMT

It is unlikely that even the most altruistic of animals would commit suicide for the sake of some vague, abstract belief. Preconscious neurological thought deals primarily with perceived empirical reality of the moment and uses reality-based associative memory, which is, by and large, fuzzy with regard to the discrete boundaries among OACEREs. Though there are often misperceptions, neurological thought processes, by their nature, simply do not accommodate belief in sophisticated abstractions, metaphors, an eternal supernatural, or higher level concepts derived from them.

The spiritual dimension of religion exists only where both native neurological processes and language-mediated thought processes are present. Unmediated neurological thinking can readily accept the logically impossible, while language-mediated thinking can arbitrarily define and assign characteristics and contemplate hypothetical behavior based on contemplated characteristics of the supernatural.

Using the neurological mode of thought, people can easily believe that a magician truly performs magic. They believe and act on what they see, with only modest interpretation. People oriented to innate neurological thinking could readily accept Superman and his super powers if somehow they were to meet him and see him perform some specific super feat such as flying. But other super activities that were not directly experienced, such as his abilities to leap tall buildings in a single bound, run faster than a speeding bullet, stop speeding locomotives, or his vulnerability to kryptonite, can only be conceived as products of language-mediated thinking. The nonobserved feats are but logical extensions of the basic conception of a Superman. They can exist only in a synthetic reality. Ordinary neurological processes cannot entertain or process these abstract extensions of experience as if they were real. The supernatural, its effects, and its requirements for abstractions and metaphors are conceived and elaborated in language. The existence of a supernatural entity can be regarded as real and acted upon only by adaptively accommodating language-mediated thought to native neurological thought.

A person who is told of the supernatural exploits of Superman (or Santa Claus) by someone who is respected (a parent for example) may initially believe it, but such belief will probably not withstand for very long linguistic logic, empirical comparisons, or a search for confirmatory evidence. Supernatural events and metaphysical concepts introduced by means of declarative language can more easily be accepted and held in long-term memory, if they are said to have occurred in the long ago past or will occur in the distant future. By accepting the far-fetched as having occurred in the past, imaginary constructs of declarative language affect current neurological thinking, and so in turn turn can affect current declarative language thinking.

Spirituality

Spirituality depends upon the personal acceptance of supernatural forces and their influence. A personal, generalized acceptance of spirituality can give rise to specific and elaborate declarative expression with respect to the nature of mystical forces. Nonetheless, it is rooted in nonlanguage, neurological thought processes. Modern surveys indicate that while not all people accept the supernatural, the majority of people do. A 2005 Harris poll indicated that 7 of 10 Americans believe in angels, heaven, miracles, and life after death. An overwhelming majority accepts that supernatural forces can determine their individual fates as well as determine the unfolding of events in the universe.

The sources of spirituality flow from the interpolation and extension of innate neurological thought that is rooted in experience, which is then extended and embellished by means of language-mediated thought. At its most fundamental level, spirituality stems from the use and acceptance of unquestioning innate neurological thinking. The purely neurological versus language-mediated thought disjunction allows humans to ingenuously accept supernatural or spiritual powers, and then using the special powers of language-mediated thought processes, they can concoct, expand on, and articulate hypothetical descriptions of such supernatural powers and their natures.

The neurological beliefs that sustain religion are initially formed either by means of mysterious or unexplained experiences or by stories passed on from others as well as from their language-mediated interpretations of experience. When a disease suddenly ravages a village, many of the villagers can be convinced that it is due to the wrath of the supernatural because they have sinned against it.

Whatever their source, after a while the intense beliefs that sustain spirituality become embedded in neurological memory independent of specific language. Logical argumentation that challenges or refutes propositions that flow from internal spiritual belief will simply bounce off the internal processes of the devout like bullets off Superman's chest.

Appealing to supernatural powers is an attempt to ward off potential harm or improve one's feelings of security and social position where one feels otherwise powerless to change fate. It gives one a greater feeling of certainty. Daydreaming and imagining that one possesses super powers, or controls a genie that possesses super powers, is also an attempt of the imagination to control fate and attain certainty. Children who are subject to the control, and the not-fully-understood whims, of their parents most often escape into such fantasies, but there are adult forms of fantasy as well.

Uncertainty and Religiosity

Humans, like other animals, attempt to discern patterns in order to understand and gain some measure of control over nature. Some patterns are obvious, while others are speculative. Animals, using the associative powers based in their neural networks and memories, often infer connections between events in order to act effectively. Humans, with superior brainpower, can go much further. They can analyze a series of events, looking for corroborating or negating information with regard to potential patterns. In the past this gave rise to effective survival behavior. With the development of language, this same process allows humans to speculate and hypothesize about those forces that significantly impact their lives but which they fail to understand and control. Such suppositions extend to creating scenarios on how we should behave if there is indeed a force that controls the universe and determines our fate and the conditions by which our species can survive.

The development of language gave rise to the joint consequential products of both personal uncertainty and self-doubt, which are a result of the conscious awareness of uncontrollable events. Uncertainty is the natural condition of animals in an uncertain, perilous environment. One way that animals attempt to minimize or avoid uncertainty is to stick to the familiar. Familiar places, objects, events, and agents (people) are generally easier to deal with. Familiar experiences are perceived as less threatening (even when objectively this is not always the case.) For humans, familiar rituals and ceremonies are ostensibly regarded as requirements of a deity. It is a sacred obligation imposed by religious tradition. Ritual also becomes a means of self-soothing, through the performance of familiar repetitive behavior. Because of the nature of neurological thought processes, ritual promotes a subjective feeling of certainty and security regardless of external objective factors. In this way a personal need for the reduction of uncertainty sustains religion.

Self-Doubt

As a result of language, human suppositions of what others are thinking about them can lead to debilitating self-doubt. Individual self-doubt can be devastating for the tribe or clan as well as the individual. Individuals racked with self-doubt may commit upsetting and even injurious acts against others or to themselves in order to deal with it. To remain effective, groups must converge on acceptable standards of conduct that mitigate the negative effects of self-doubt. A group member can feel okay about herself when she observes the accepted code of conduct of the group.

An innate tendency to develop and adhere to acceptable standards of conduct is a joint product in the evolution of some social animals. Frans deWaal, professor of primate behavior at Emory University, has reported a number of instances where groups of monkeys and groups of apes collectively disciplined individual members that had violated the groups' accepted standards of conduct. Among humans the phenomenon is most pronounced among teenage groups and gangs, where the social pressure to conform to group norms is so strong that individuals will defy their parents, engage in clearly self-destructive behavior, and even break the law in order to obey the informal and unspoken norms of their peer group.

The intuitive obligation to conform to group customs and conventions that developed in some social species is a force that ultimately gave rise to religiosity in human groups. Religiosity overtly demonstrates adherence to group mores, and is an indirect indicator of acceptance of group conventions and norms. Conversely the absence of public observance of religious rites and ceremonies by individuals is construed as an overt indicator of the rejection of all group norms. There is strong social, and sometimes coercive, pressure for an individual to publicly and ardently observe religious practices in order to prove his commitment in belonging to the group.

Conforming to norms of behavior and speech that are prescribed by a religion, and scrupulously avoiding speech and behavior that are religiously proscribed, can also moderate self-doubt. The firm belief that one occupies the religious moral high ground can erase self-doubt and impart a sense of moral superiority.

Religiosity and the Role of Gossip

One of the most pervasive uses of religion noted is as a method for sustaining group cohesion. Group cohesion promotes effective cooperation that redounds to the welfare of all group members. It was effective eons ago on the savannas of Africa with regard to competition with other human clans as well as in surviving the challenges of the wilds. It remains effective in modern times in sustaining a coherent group that can successfully compete with outside individuals and other groups. Strong group identity, fostered by cultural/religious cohesion, also tends to promote feelings of personal certainty and self worth.

A language-mediated and effective tool for maintaining cohesion in larger groups is gossip. The practice of gossip has been found to be ubiquitous among all human societies, from the most primitive to the most sophisticated. It is thought that the predilection for gossip goes back tens of thousands of years, well into Paleolithic times. Although the appeal of gossip varies among individuals, the majority of both sexes find it irresistibly fascinating to hear stories about the comings and goings of their fellows, especially if the stories are colorful or "juicy."

Despite its pejorative connotation, gossip serves a vital role in the transmission of culture, the maintenance of group cohesion, and individual feelings of being an accepted part of the group. Even in Paleolithic times, it was a rare instance of cheating or shirking that was not observed or figured out by some other group member who took delight in telling about deeds of the miscreants to his confidants. Gossip is very effective in policing the disruptive, selfish actions of group members.

When a Neolithic couple slipped away into the woods for a forbidden tryst, despite their caution, someone was bound to cotton on to the hanky-panky. The story of their mores-violating behavior would have provided salacious grist for gossip. Today, as then, those who have heard a sensational gossipy story, even if it is third- or fourth-hand, can nonetheless garner recognition and ego gratification by retelling it. If they tell the story particularly well, perhaps by embellishing it, many of those who have heard the story before will enjoy hearing it again. It is the same appeal that entices people to create and retell urban myths, conspiracy theories, and other "human interest" stories.

In a fundamental sense, gossip served as a marketplace of morality in ancient days. Some stories were dismissed as merely ordinary, trivial transgressions or, more rarely, only mildly cautionary and not beneficial. These tended to be passed along to others for a short time but were soon forgotten. Behavior that was widely considered to be beyond the pale, colorful in the sense of being unusual, outrageous, or antisocial, tended to be spread far and wide and had a lengthy half-life. Events that were highly unusual, such as heavenly eclipses, rare weather patterns, escapes from hostile strangers, or health problems, also tended to get included in the stories and to be interwoven with personal narratives for greater impact. Primarily, though, the subtext of gossip was, and is, an implicit evaluation of the doings of familiar people, although these people may not be known personally. The subjects of gossip may be friends of friends, members of some common reference group, or people that we have heard of and relate to in some way. In the modern world, fascination with the lives of famous movie stars and athletes is a manifestation of the ages-old allure of gossip.

The corollary to the enjoyment that people get from hearing gossip about the comings and goings of others is that the tellers of gossip get a great deal of recognition or ego stroking, which encourages them to seek out more gossip to relay. In the distant past, some people found over time that they were naturally better storytellers than others. The ability to tell stories, which long ago captivated listeners and was their primary source of entertainment, could be used in order to earn a living in the barter economies of the times. From later Paleolithic times, storytellers could trade colorful stories for hospitality, including food and various objects of value.

In Neolithic times, itinerant storytellers could go from one clan to another friendly tribe as they plied their profession. Good storytellers could read their audiences. They perfected techniques for keeping listeners engaged. They retained and embellished those elements of a story that held their audience in thrall and eliminated the parts where the audiences became distracted. Stories that were heard as young children and often repeated were naturally incorporated into the themes of stories told by others. Through the intermediation of storytellers, the localized marketplace of morality that had been haphazardly and locally fashioned by means of gossip alone became more definite and stable across more tribes, over a large area, and over generations. Such was the natural development of a "market of morality" by means of gossip.

Although people are mainly fascinated by the adventures and misadventures of other people, ancient storytellers (just as modern movie makers) found that people were most fascinated by extraordinary events, especially if the people of the stories were said to have some unusual or supernatural powers. (As modern fan magazines and sports magazines clearly illustrate, we want stories that feature extraordinary humans.) The performances of itinerant storytellers and preachers also spread cautionary tales and practical lore, thus shaping a common morality that determined the lines between what was acceptable and unacceptable conduct.

Belief and Asymmetric Information Processing

Using the medium of language for intraspecies communication, humans not only learn from their own direct experience but also from hearing and reading about the experiences and ideas of others. Like direct experience, language information that is heard or read must be interpreted. Nonexperiential information tends to have less impact than direct experience.

The brain screens the enourmous amounts of auditory, visual and somatosensory information constantly being received via the senses in an area of the brain called the thalamus. Confusion as a result of information overload is prevented. The thalamus is neurologically looped to the cerebral cortex as well as another organ called the amygdala. Information that presents a critical danger is transmitted to the amygdala for immediate response without deliberation. Irrelevant, wrong, counterintuitive information, or information that might get a person to act against her self-interest, is blocked or rejected in the thalamus. The neurotransmitter protein dopamine plays a critical role in the process.

Information that is not screened out in the thalamus may be acted upon directly or shuttled to long-term memory in the cerebral cortex to be used at a later time. Prior vetted and interpreted sense information that has been stored in memory circuits of the cerebral cortex is used to vet subsequent sense information received from the environment that is transmitted to the thalamus.

Information flow in the brain is asymmetric. Much of the new sense information from the environment is blocked or altered in the thalamus as being irrelevant, misleading, or misperceived by virtue of information from memory in the cortex. But the stored information that is retrieved from memory in the cerebral cortex and transmitted to the thalamus for use in vetting new sense information is accepted straight away without being vetted a second time. The nonverbal, internal neurological information flow easily trumps language-mediated information flow received from the environment. Where new language-mediated information conflicts or is inconsistent with prior vetted and stored information or belief, it is rejected or altered so it can be integrated with past experience. In this way established beliefs and values tend to be preserved. Because of asymmety, except for special circumstances, changing established belief can be a slow process.

To paraphrase what psychiatrist Eric Berne noted in his book *Games People Play*, the longer a preconscious belief has been held, the more often it has been invoked, the more useful it is subconsciously perceived to have proven, the more activities and concepts it is associated with, the greater will be the preconscious mental effort to preserve or conserve it. As the belief survives over time, and is invoked many times and in diverse situations, the neural networks of association grow. If it were to be accepted, new, contradictory, or undermining information that challenges well-established beliefs would require extensive restructuring changes to the comprehensive neural networks that had previously been established. Such radical change might occur in special traumatic circumstances but tends to be resisted. New information that challenges firmly held beliefs tends to be ignored as a result of the process of vetting by the brain's thalamus. If it can't be ignored, it is reshaped or construed so that it does not clash with cherished beliefs or the contradiction is at least minimized. People whose core beliefs are challenged often do not directly address or respond to the challenge. They ignore it if they can, or they respond to their own interpretation of the challenge.

Confirmation Bias and Cognitive Dissonance

Information asymmerty supports confirmation bias effects and cognitive dissonance effects in regard to belief. People actively look for and accept new evidence or interpretations of their experiences that are deemed to confirm their previous neurologically stored beliefs and values. They tend to ignore, reject, or twist any contrary language-mediated information that is received. Well-developed neurologically held personal beliefs are compared prejudicially with other belief information so as to convince oneself of the wisdom of one's own beliefs and prejudices.

People seek out others who share their beliefs so that they can all reinforce each other's beliefs and values. Those who don't share a person's beliefs are kept at a distance physically, socially, or emotionally. People tend to associate primarily with other like-minded people to the point where it tends to seem to them that a majority of right-thinking people in the general population share their beliefs and prejudices, even if this is actually far from the case. Such people seldom hear contrary beliefs or opinions from their friends. They easily dismiss infrequently heard contrary notions as the opinions of a small minority of wrong-headed individuals. It is very rare that a comment made by an outsider that points out the fallacy, logical inconsistency, or even ridiculousness of a long-held core belief will change a person's belief system in any substantive way. In fact, as noted by Leon Festinger, it is the opposite effect that most often occurs.

The more often a core, neurologically based belief is unsuccessfully challenged (as perceived in the mind of the believer), the stronger and more resistant to change the belief becomes, as the neural networks related to the belief expand. Thus, as individuals hold, promulgate, and defend the beliefs that form the core of their spirituality, and they continue to practice the ritualistic behavior that reinforces religiosity, their belief system tends to become entrenched, self-perpetuating, and resistant to change. Core beliefs, for the most part, are altered only incrementally as it becomes obvious that a belief is wrong-headed, personally damaging, or not shared by respected others. Precipitous alteration of long-term core beliefs, and hence major restructuring of neural networks, can cause psychological trauma.

Beliefs, including religious beliefs, though they tend to be preserved, are not rigid so that they remain unchanged forever. As environment changes, the effect of unchanging belief may progressively fall in a range from inconsequential through detrimental to catastrophic. Beliefs can be changed both overtly and surreptitiously. Beliefs that are obviously counterproductive are either revised or they truncate gene survival. Beliefs, such as religious belief, that are intrinsically neither benign nor harmful can also be changed. Because of the subtle nature of changes in belief structures, when they occur, a person is not always aware of the change. People tend to claim that they have always held the same beliefs and that differences pointed out by others are merely situational variations of the same basic belief.

If an individual befriends and lives among significant others who hold different religious beliefs, or if he is socially or economically dependent upon those who hold different religious beliefs and values, he will gradually come to take on their beliefs. If the values of his reference group and their beliefs are in his economic and social self-interest, his own beliefs will converge on those of the majority. At its fundamental core, this is an ingrained process of a social animal that goes far back in evolutionary time and well before natural language developed. Its ancient effect was to reduce conflicts among members of anthropoid groups and then hominid clans so that they might cohere and cooperated effectively in order to survive and thrive.

Social Manipulation

Language is capable of conveying multiple levels of meaning that can alter beliefs in a manner that is not evident from its overt content. Gossip, entertaining stories, or tropes that contain a moral are examples of where there can be conflicting ideas that are embedded as subtext in narratives. On their face, the stories are so appealing that they may get past the vetting processes of the thalamus. The stories are accepted even though the raw implications of their subtext might otherwise have been rejected. As discussed in chapter twelve, some of the techniques for manipulating other's beliefs have been variously labeled memes, framing, priming, and psycholinguistics. Characteristics of such linguistic psychologically manipulative techniques are as follows:

- They are surreptitious in that the receiver does not realize that they lead to a subtle shift in his beliefs. Changes may occur in small increments per exposure. If a shift of attitude does occur, the receiver does not attribute it to the particular source. There is a subtle tipping point where the new belief begins to supersede the old.
- Once the tipping point has been passed, because of confirmation bias and to reduce cognitive dissonance, the receiver will tend to seek confirmatory evidence and reject contradictory evidence. (This magnifies the problem of attribution.)
- The receiver will staunchly defend the new or altered beliefs as being his own ideas, which were logically and empirically derived and should be obvious to any other clear-thinking individual. Thus the belief becomes more entrenched.
- The nature of manipulative language, such as memes or frames, is such that many of its receivers are inclined to pass the concepts along to others in a replicated form that is tailored to the situation and the receiver for the maximum chance of acceptance.
- This inclination to spread beliefs and notions is helped by the primitive enjoyment of gossip, a confirmation bias, and an ego need to determine that friends and associates hold compatible beliefs.

Beliefs held in neurological networks greatly influence behavior. A great deal of daily behavior is determined preconsciously. It has been said that a man will apply more conscious deliberation to picking out his tie than he gives to selecting a wife. When challenged, or if some inconsistent experience or contrary information is encountered, the person holding certain beliefs tends to attempt to logically justify them, rationalize them verbally, and look for confirmation of her beliefs in anecdotes and the corroboration of others. It is internal neurological processes that determine public statements, even though this source is often not fully appreciated.

Conclusion

Many critics, some in the field of religious scholarship, have become skeptical of divine revelation received by means of dreams, voices, visions, or insights of holy men. They question the divine origins and the divine inspiration of all holy scriptures, including the Pentateuch, the New Testament, and the Koran.[96] Scientific advances continue apace to produce results that are often construed as being incompatible with religious dogma and teaching, scriptural narratives, or the notion that dreams, visions, and voices are capable of transmitting paranormal information from the spirit world. In the face of such criticism, many religious leaders have chosen what I believe to be a high-risk strategy of denying the validity of widely accepted scientific propositions, such as evolution, rather than seeking compromise or synthesis with religious belief.

Although traditional religions deal with creation, the basic and personal need for religion does not derive from a need to understand creation or other scientific conundrums. For ancient as well as modern people, myths are not a search for truth or a way of knowing. Rather, the need for religion is as a means of offering a narrative that resonates with the human condition. Religious stories supply the tropes that can provide meaning and purpose to life as well as a framework for social relationships with family and larger groups. Even though myths may superficially deal with explanations of creation, floods, and other natural phenomena, they are not, nor were they, intended as quasi-scientific explanations of nature. Instead, they exist to address human psychological needs in dealing with uncertainty as well as for gaining a sense of belonging and acceptance.

In another context, for example, some patients who present with generalized symptoms of widespread unfocused pain, painful response to pressure on diverse parts of their bodies, debilitating fatigue, sleep disturbances, and joint stiffness may be beside themselves with worry and desperately seek relief by going from doctor to doctor. In some cases, when they are given a diagnosis of such as neurasthenia, idiopathic fibromyalgia or other medically unexplained syndromes, they are greatly relieved even though neither the cause nor the cure of the malady is known. This is not merely sophistry or a distinction without a difference. It seems that our brains are wired in such a way that merely having a name for something that differentiates it from other things is comforting and reduces anxiety. We assume at some level of our thought processes that phenomena which can be named can be controlled—if not now then eventually.

Similarly the need for survival has wired our brains to seek explanations and meanings for all natural phenomena that have the potential to impact us. Science has provided an understanding of many of the mysteries of nature that have perplexed humans from time immemorial. But as yet science has not succeeded in explaining all of the matters that are of deep-seated, existential concern to most people. Many, but not all, people seem to be satisfied when they receive explanations of the unexplainable with nonexplanations, especially from influential people.

Those who are preoccupied with a fear of death or disease, a need to understand the meaning or purpose of life, the existence of unrequited evil, or the unhappy state of their life are often content to ascribe the answer to all of these quandaries to the existence and operation of a supernatural power, God—even though God, by universal definition, is ineffable and they acknowledge that fact. Regardless, such an explanation gives many people a sense of certainty and security that our animal natures crave. It reduces their anxiety. Whether such a nomenclature phenomenon is accepted as indisputable ontological proof of the existence and operation of a creator, or as, instead, a joint product consequence of evolutionary processes on the human brain (or both or neither), seems to me to be moot. With regard to understanding existential mysteries such as the meaning of life, answers that rely on an ineffable power (God) are equally as cogent, or as inane, as those that are based on any other unknown process.

It has been said that if by some strange happenstance there were no such thing as religion today, it would not be very long before some new form of religion would emerge because of the human need for religion. Of course, new religions are being created all the time, but they are invariably confected from one or more of the older established religions in order to command a devoted following that is familiar with the general nature of the newly modified precepts and rituals. The frames, memes, and tropes of venerable religions are powerful. They are egregiously imprinted even on the minds of the apostates of the old religions. Therefore, prospective members of the new religions, despite their unhappiness with the old religion, have a need to preserve many of its aspects. Those who search for new answers from a different religion often require some of the notions of their old familiar, comfortable religions. This makes it all but impossible to start over with a blank slate and create a completely new religion that is totally free of the tropes and forms of established religions.

It is an accident of history that some of the ancient religious concepts and stories that were prevalent at the time when writing became widespread became fixed in scripture. Thus these religious notions have endured ever since, with some variation and reinterpretations, both large and small, to fit the changing times. But, if writing had not been developed at that time, and none of the familiar concepts and stories of venerable scriptural religions with their tropes or memes existed, new forms of religion would doubtlessly still have been created in short order.

The disjunction between preconscious thinking and declarative language thinking would soon result in attempts to elaborately explain unexplainable phenomena so as to produce a first attempt to gain control over them. New concepts and tropes, even if they were acknowledged as being tenuous and only raising an illusion of control and personal certainty, would be created and accepted. In time, by the circular processes discussed earlier, tropes, beliefs, and rituals would come to grant a sense of certainty, control, security, belonging and social utility to believers.

Language is needed in order to conceptualize, in discrete terms, the mysteries of the environment. It requires the use of abstractions and tropes that affect the brain at a preconscious level but can only be communicated in language. As with established religions, the expression of the new religion would clothe the requisite mysterious or supernatural concepts with intricate detail fashioned in language, and it would clothe the normal activities of life with new holy rituals. Once created, the emergent religion would be internalized, and then it would surface in diverse ways to be used by individuals to gain acceptance and status, manipulate others, coordinate groups, maintain communities, and assuage self-doubt. The new forms would likely also provide a structure for those who wish to help their fellows.

If there were no stories, symbols, and concepts from the venerable old religions, the new religion would have to invent new ones. With regard to Western revealed religions, if Bible stories of creation, the patriarchs, and the life of Jesus, or the stories and teaching of the Koran, were unknown, they surely would not be recreated in a similar form today. It is hardly likely that the foundational myths of a brand-new twenty-first century religion would center on a holy man who was executed and his grave found empty after three days, or a prophet who heard voices while he sat alone on a mountain. It is unlikely that the beloved stories of creation, such as a talking snake, a gigantic flood, a man being swallowed by a whale and living to tell the tale, or a seminal exodus from Egypt by six hundred thousand male cousins and their families that involved the parting of a sea, would or could form the basis of a wholly new twenty-first century religion.

As it was with ancient religions, the concepts of the new religion, with their supporting beliefs and tropes, would arise from our current culture and states of knowledge. They might involve some elegant mathematical model or an extrapolation from physics, like string theory, quantum mechanics, relativity, the big bang, or some other modern leitmotif. The new religion might, in part, take a form similar to present-day science fiction and fantasy literature that appeals so much to youngsters. The new tropes might be illustrated in print and video formats, with computer-generated graphics and special effects.

Nonetheless, any new multimedia scripture would continue to be rich in profound mystery and layered meanings. It will be as rife for situational interpretation as the old religious dogmas. The new religion would address many of the same age-old questions and problems as the old religions: the meaning of life or ultimate reality, the existence of unrequited evil, the implications of death, and the promotion of certainty in an uncertain world or the means to accept uncertainty. The new religion would still include elements of pseudokinship. This would unite followers into cohesive groups and engender a sense of security, belonging, specialness, and well-being.

Twenty-first century religious dogma would differ from ancient established religions in that it would not accord different status or treatment among men and women, either heterosexual or homosexual, of various races. To survive and become widespread, the new form of religion would involve and promote a spate of ritualistic behavior that would be connected with most of modern life's events, such as sports event, shopping, and the Internet. There would be extensive use of multimedia presentations. Like established religions, though, the new religion would have to develop forms and events with which to support a cadre of people who benefit or earn a living from it, and who would, as a result, actively promote its rituals and beliefs.

Concepts and fanciful stories with regard to life after death, heaven, and hell will be problematic for completely new twenty-first century religions. Such concepts are potent and very useful for manipulating others. But it is hard for many to believe that such unsupportable concepts should morally be, or could be, effectively wielded for manipulation given the state of science and level of knowledge in the twenty-first century. At most, notions of life after death might be reworked as peripheral and tenuous propositions. Life after death, or the promises of heaven and hell, would not likely be regarded as the powerful core beliefs that are central to a twenty-first century religion. Although the abandonment of the primacy of the concept of life after death as a cornerstone of religious belief will be difficult to achieve, I maintain that it is not only ethically necessary but critical for rational acceptance of a twenty first century religion.

As long as discontinuities exist between neurological and declarative thinking, some type of spirituality will continue to be generated by the human mind. As long as people have a need to talk others into accepting and subscribing to their worldview and various other propositions, new religions will form. As long as people have self-doubt, fear death and sickness, wish to ally themselves with a like-minded group, long for a guarantor to reduce all forms of personal and physical uncertainty, and ensure the success of their plans, spirituality and religiosity will survive and thrive. But humanity must get past the notion that support of one religion must necessarily mean the trashing of all other religions.

Alas, the roots of present day religions go deep into the preconscious neural networks of many people. They hark back twenty-five hundred years, to the axial age and the popularization of writing. Religious beliefs are inculcated in children from their earliest most vulnerable ages and have become entwined with most of life's major events.. Religious rituals and forms provide employment and incomes to a large number of people as well as conveying a sense of belonging and acceptance to the many.

The genie is out of the bottle and can't be forced back in. But sensible people can work to reconcile ancient rituals, beliefs, and rules with modern civilization and a world in which human population is exploding, some critical resources are becoming scarce, and the natural environment is being fouled. The future of humanity depends on it.

NOTES

(Endnotes)

1. See, for example, *Misquoting Jesus*, by Bart Ehrman.
2. See Taliaferro, Charles, '*Contemporary Philosophy of Religion*' Chapter One, for a discussion of the difficulties of defining religion.
3. Peter Berger, *The Sacred Canopy* (1967). ISBN 0-385-07305-4
4. See Steven Pinker, "My Genomic Self," *New York Times Magazine* (January 11, 2009), p. 31.
5. Lewis Wolpert, *Six Impossible Things Before Breakfast: The Evolutionary Origins of Belief* (2006) ISBN 978-0-571-231-23168-3, p. 123.
6. Because I regard the concept of God as neither male nor female but definitely not as an "it," I have alternated the descriptors Him and Her when referring to God.
7. Contemporary scientists and academics who defend God, to name a few, are physicist Gerald Schroeder, philosopher John Haldane, Gary Habermas, mathematician John Barrow, physicists Paul Davies and John.Polkinghorne, chemist Paul Arthur Peacock, and biologist Michael Behe. Wikipedia

has a long list of famous scientists of the past who were creationists.

8. *New York Times June 24, 2007*
9. *New York Times* June 24, 2007)
10. 10 Adrew Newberg, *Why We Believe What We Believe* (2006).
11. Zoe Elizabeth Buck, *Detroit Free Press*, July 31, 2008, p. 6A.
12. John Noble Wilford, *New York Times*, April 17, 2007, p. D1.
13. Science Times, *New York Times Science Times*, October 9, 2007, p. 4.
14. Malcolm Gladwell makes this exact case in his book *Blink*.
15. Steven Pinker, *The Blank Slate: The Modern Denial of Human Nature* (2002).
16. Monty Roberts, *The Horse Whisperer*.
17. In the experiment, outlines of nine squares, numbered 1 through 9, were scattered randomly on a computer screen. When the chimpanzee touched the square with the number 1 on it, all of the numbers were instantly erased and only blank squares remained on the screen. The chimpanzee had to touch the eight remaining boxes in the order that they had been numbered. Chimpanzees could do it without any error in less than two seconds. Few humans were able to complete the task without error, and none could come close to completion in under two seconds. (Source: National Geographic Magazine)
18. Henry Fountain, "The Observatory," *New York Times*, August 14, 2007, p. D3.
19. George Lakoff, Book Review, Letters, *New York Times*, July 6, 2008, p. 4.
20. Based on human and animal studies, emotions such as fear responses occur before there is evidence of overt brain processing.
21. Benedict Carey, "Blind, Yet Seeing," Science Times, *New York Times*, December 23, 2008, pp. D5 and D7. A video of the blindsight walk is available at www.beatricedegelder.com/books.html.

22. This portion of the manuscript is based on the memory of a lecture given by Herbert Simon at McMaster University in Ontario sometime in the 1980s.

23. See Christine Kenneally, *The First Word: The Search for the Origin of Language* (Viking, 2007).

24. Michael Porter, in connection with SWOT analysis, has postulated that overcoming weakness is a greater spur to development than is the exploitation of strengths. Although his pronouncements were made in the context of economic development, they seem to have relevance to biological evolution as well. The historian Arnold Toynbee too has noted that adversity can be a spur to development of a nation.

25. *Skeptical Inquirer* (Sept/Oct 2006), 35–38.

26. Italics are mine.

27. "Taxes Pleasure? Check the Brain Scan," *New York Times*, June 19, 2007, pp. D1 and D4

28. Scientists do classify neurons on the basis of dendrite configuration and other features, but at a gross level their construction and functions are similar in nature.

29. Michael Craig Miller, "Sad Brain, Happy Brain," *Newsweek*, September 22, 2008, pp. 51, 52, 56.

30. Wikipedia

31. Andrew Newberg and Mark Robert Waldman, *Why we Believe What We Believe* (2006).

32. Sharon Begley, , April 14, 2008, p. 41.

33. Even Gould's theory of punctuated equilibrium in evolution postulated long periods of no adaptation punctuated by periods of rapid adaptation rather than any radical transformation.

34. Unlike computers that cease to function at all if minor hardware or software problems occur, the brain is highly fault tolerant and will continue to function, if imperfectly, even after severe trauma or physical damage.

35. It has been established that there is a separate area in the human brain that is responsible for recognizing human faces.

36. What Dijksterhuis and Nordgren label as unconscious thought may be termed subconscious or preconscious thought in this manuscript. Unfortunately, the term subconscious, which would ordinarily be my preferred term, was preempted by Freud, whose use of the subconscious involves repressed memories—very different than my notion of subconscious, which connotes implicit memory.

37. Ap Dijksterhuis and Loran F. Nordgren, "A Theory of Unconscious Thought," *Perspectives on Psychological Science* 1, no. 2 (June 2006): pp. 95–109.

38. See "Who's Minding the Mind," by Benedict Carey, *New York Times*, July 31, 2007.

39. Satisficing is a term coined by Herbert Simon to connote choosing or taking action that is good enough to end a search even though it may not be optimal or maximal.

40. I am indebted to Gary Marcus for these examples.

41. Daniel Gilbert, *Stumbling on Happiness*, p. 100.

42. The experiment was performed before German unification.

43. Jeffrey N. Rouder and Roger Ratcliff, "Comparing Exemplar and Rule-Based Theories of Categorization," *Current Directions in Psychological Science* 15, no. 1 (February 2006): pp. 9–13.

44. Steven Pinker, *The Language Instinct*.

45. Sharon Begley, *Newsweek*, May 07, 2001.

46. Satisficing is the acceptance of a threshold or minimally "good enough" solution or alternative rather than pursuing an optimal alternative that might require additional time or money.

47. "Mysteries of Science," *U.S. News and World Report*, special ed., 2009, pp. 59–61

48. *Mirrors in the Brain: How Our Minds Share Actions, Emotions, and Experience*, by Giacomo Rizzolatti, and *Mirroring People: The New Science of How We Connect with Others*, by Marco Iacoboni.

49. People for the Ethical Treatment of Animals is an organization dedicated to alleviating all animal suffering at the hands of humans.

50. A gorilla, given a simple puzzle box with food in it, will perform many trials until it is successful in opening the box and obtaining the food. Given the same puzzle box a little later, the gorilla will open it easily, having learned how to do the task during the first iteration of the experiment. However, if a second gorilla is put into the room during the first trial, it will not ordinarily observe the operation closely. If that second gorilla is later given the same puzzle box, it will go through a struggle of many trials to open the box. By contrast, in the same situation a human would ordinarily be curious about the activities of the other and would focus on her fellow human as she attempted to open the box. Later on, given the same simple puzzle box, she would immediately know how to open it quickly, most likely on the first try.

51. Marie-Helen Grosbras et al. "Neural Mechanisms of Resistance to Peer Influence in Early adolescence," *The Journal of Neuroscience*, July 25, 2007, pp. 8040–8045.

52. *The Economist*, December 23, 2006–January 5, 2007, p. 10.

53. An incident was reported by Franz deWaal where juveniles who were playing delayed the feeding of an entire group. The next day the juveniles were punished by the adults.

54. John Tierney, "Psst: Facts Prove No Match for Gossip," *New York Times*, October 16, 2007, p. D1.

55. A term coined by Bronislaw Malinowski.

56. Sociologists have noticed that people behave, and behave toward others, based on the stereotype of a uniform. For example, a first-year medical student puts on a white coat and a stethoscope and at once is sought out for medical advice, which he unhesitatingly dispenses.

57. For a discussion of the recognition of songs by means of hearing one or two notes and the origin of this ability for survival, see "Music of the Hemispheres," *New York Times*, December 31, 2006, sect. 2, p. 1.

58. John Dewey said, "I see, I forget, I hear, I forget, I do, I remember."

59. An example of this method involves memorizing ten common objects identified with the numbers one through ten and then associating a series of new items with each of the common objects in their sequence. Another memory trick is to visualize the new item along with some familiar item.

60. The McMartin preschool trial was a day care sexual abuse case of the 1980s. Members of the McMartin family, who operated a preschool in California, were charged with numerous acts of sexual abuse of children in their care. Accusations were made in 1983. Arrests and the pretrial investigation ran from 1984 to 1987, and the trial ran from 1987 to 1990. After six years of criminal trials, no convictions were obtained, and all charges were dropped in 1990. It was the longest and most expensive criminal trial of its time, and is believed to have contributed to the satanic ritual abuse panic of the 1980s and '90s.

61. Lewis Wolpert, *Six Impossible Things Before Breakfast* (Norton, 2006).

62. I don't know of any experiments to confirm this proposition with regard to people, but it doesn't seem far-fetched in light of the animal experiments and from casual observation of human behavior.

63. Leon Festinger, *When Prophesy Fails.*

64. Alfred North Whitehead, *Introduction to Mathematics* (1911). English mathematician and philosopher (1861–1947).

65. E. O. Wilson, *On Human Nature*, p. 159.

66. Charles Lindblom has characterized this as "the science of 'muddling through.'"

67. A verbal description of the details of nonlinguistic evaluation of information will be left to others to explore. We are content with scientific observations that not all information passes the thalamus.

68. Joe Ledoux, *The Emotional Brain* (1996), p. 35.

69. Benedict Carey, "Who's Minding the Mind?" *New York Times*, July 31, 2007, p. D1.

70. This example was taken from the book *Train Your Mind, Change Your Brain*, by Sharon Begley.

71. Although the neocortex of the echidna comprises 50 percent of a smaller brain.

72. Daniel Gilbert, *Stumbling on Happiness* (2006).

73. Carl Zimmer in the *New York Times*, April 3, 2007, pp. D1 and D6.

74. Daniel Gilbert, *Stumbling on Happiness* (2006).

75. A term coined by Bronislaw Malinowski to denote conversation and other interaction designed to build personal relationships rather than transfer functional information.

76. Epicurus's paradox can be stated as, "If a beneficent, omnipotent god allows evil to exist, he is not a beneficent god; and if he cannot prevent evil from existing, he is not an omnipotent god."

77. Although the example hardly ranks as a major achievement, it changed the world of high jumping. Approaching the bar running at an angle to it and throwing one's leading leg over the bar, followed by the prone body trailed by the second leg, was believed to be the natural method for optimal success. But in the 1968 Olympics, Dick Fosbury revolutionized high-jump technique by turning at the last moment so that he approached the bar with his back to it, backflipping over the bar headfirst with body supine as it crossed and with both legs trailing. This new revolutionary technique was made possible as an unintended consequence of raising a foam pad on the back side of the bar to within a few feet of the height of the bar.

78. Charles Lindblom, "The Science of 'Muddling Through,'" *Public Administration Review* 19, 1959, pp. 59–79.

79. The use of this term is not to be confused with the theory that there was a gap in time after the dinosaurs and that the world was then re-created as per the genesis story. The current usage

relates to those theories suggesting that religion provides a bridge to the inescapable unknown.

80. Richard Friedman, "Who Are We?" Science Times, *New York Times*, 15April 15, 2008, p. D5.

81. Daniel C. Dennett, *Breaking the Spell: Religion as a Natural Phenomenon* (Viking Press, 2006), p. 3.

82. *New York Times*

83. Recently there has been some success with cognitive behavioral therapy in curing or ameliorating OCD behavior.

84. Or should it be corpi callosum

85. Alina Tugend, "Blinded by Science in the Online Dating Game," *New York Times*, July 18, 2009.

86. *Just So Stories* was a collection of fanciful stories written by Rudyard Kipling to explain nature in an entertaining way (for example, he gives a far-fetched explanation of how the tiger got its stripes).

87. Paul Krugman, *New York Times*, September 24, 2007 p. A27. "Southern white exceptionalism is about race much more than it is about moral values, religion, support for the military or other explanations sometimes offered. There is a large statistical literature on the subject. Whose conclusion is summed up by the political scientist Thomas F. Schaller in his book *Whistling Past Dixie* "Despite the best efforts of the Republican spinmeisters to depict American conservatism as a non racial phenomenon, the partisan impact of racial attitudes in the South is stronger than ever."

88. *Rumspringa: To Be of Not to BeAmish,* **by Tom Shachtman**

89. Aaron Lynch, *Thought Contagion*, Published by Basic Books As Referenced in *Newsweek article*, April 14, 2002, p. 14.

90. The literature only considers by-products, as conceived by Stephen Jay Gould. Main products are inferred because, by definition, there cannot be a by-product unless there is a main product. It seems to me, however, that the metaphor naturally extends to joint products as well.

91. "Subconscious," the more common word, has come to be associated with Freudian processes involving the ego, id, and superego. It was Freud himself, I believe, who first coined the term preconscious with respect to thoughts just below the level of consciousness that nonetheless are the basis of deliberate actions.

92. A kluge is a jury rigged work around. For further explanation see Kluge by Gary Marcus ISBN 978-0-618-87964-9

93. These can be differentiated from Stephen J. Gould's spandrels, which are defined as merely incidental to instrumental evolutionary adaptation and without function of their own that can be explained. The conception herein envisions a more dynamic process where many coincidental evolutionary developments (or spandrels) eventually find or are given functional uses and ultimately become factors in future evolution as the environment changes.

94. Pinker, *The Language Instinct*, p. 415.

95. Pinker, *The Language Instinct*, Harper Perennial Modern Classics ISBN 978-0-06-133646-1 p. 238.

96. Some examples are Bart Ehrman, in his book *Misquoting the Gospels*, or the Jesus Seminar, a group of committed Christians who have scrutinized the Gospels for events that may have been embellished.